RavenDB 2.x Beginner's Guide

Build high performance NoSQL .NET-based applications
quickly and efficiently

Khaled Tannir

BIRMINGHAM - MUMBAI

RavenDB 2.x Beginner's Guide

First published: September 2013

Production Reference: 1280813

Published by Packt Publishing Ltd.
Livery Place
35 Livery Street
Birmingham B3 2PB, UK.

ISBN 978-1-78328-379-8

www.packtpub.com

Cover Image by Khaled Tannir (khaled.tannir@orange.fr)

Credits

Author
Khaled Tannir

Reviewer
Alonso Robles

Oren Eini

Acquisition Editor
Anthony Albuquerque

Lead Technical Editor
Sweny Sukumaran

Technical Editors
Sampreshita Maheshwari

Chandni Maishery

Project Coordinator
Shiksha Chaturvedi

Proofreader
Mario Cecere

Paul Hindle

Indexer
Tejal Soni

Graphics
Ronak Dhruv

Abhinash Sahu

Production Coordinator
Pooja Chiplunkar

Cover Work
Pooja Chiplunkar

About the Author

Khaled Tannir has been working with computers since 1980. He began programming with the legendary Sinclair Zx81 and with Commodore home computer products (Vic 20, Commodore 64, Commodore 128D, and Amiga 500).

He has a Bachelor's degree in Electronics, a Master's degree in System Information Architectures, in which he graduated with a professional thesis, and completed his education with a Research Master's degree.

He is a Microsoft Certified Application Developer (MCAD) and has more than twenty years of technical experience leading the development and implementation of software solutions and giving technical presentations. He now works as an independent IT consultant and has worked as an infrastructure engineer, senior developer, and enterprise/solution architect for many companies in France and Canada. With very significant experience in Microsoft .NET and Microsoft Servers Systems, he has extensive skills in online/offline applications design, system conversions, and multilanguage applications.

He is always researching new technologies, learning about them, and looking for new adventures between France, Canada, and the Middle-east. He owns an IT and electronics laboratory with many servers, monitors, open electronics boards such as Arduino, Netduino, RaspBerry, and .NET Gadgeteer, and some smartphone devices based on Windows Phone, Android, and iOS operating systems.

In 2012, he contributed to the EGC 2012 (International Complex Data Mining forum at Bordeaux University, France) and presented, in a workshop session, his work about "how to optimize data distribution in a cloud computing environment". This work aims to define an approach to optimize the of Data Mining algorithms such as k-means and Apriori in a cloud computing environment.

He aims to get a PhD in Cloud Computing and Big Data and wants to learn more and more about these technologies.

He enjoys taking landscape and night photos, traveling, playing video games, creating funny electronic gadgets with Arduino/.NET Gadgeteer, and, of course, spending time with his wife and family.

You can reach him at contact@khaledtannir.net

Acknowledgments

All praise is due to Allah, the Lord of the Worlds. First, I must thank Allah for giving me the ability to think and write.

Next, I would like to thank my wife, Laila, for her big support and patience throughout this project. Also, I would like to thank my brother Khalil for his support during this project.

I would like to thank everyone at Packt Publishing for their help and guidance, and for giving me the opportunity to share my experience and my knowledge in technology with others in the .NET NoSQL community.

Thank you as well to the technical reviewers, who provided great feedback to ensure that every tiny technical detail was accurate and rich in content.

About the Reviewers

Alonso Robles is a husband, a father, and is currently a Principal Consultant at Headspring, a leading software development company. He has developed numerous software solutions over the last decade, solving real business problems for companies in many industries including, but not limited to, finance, insurance, biotech, entertainment, manufacturing, education, technology, and even local government. He is a passionate advocate for emerging technologies who believes in using the right tool for the right job. Most recently, his time has been focused on software projects that leverage various NoSQL technologies. Alonso can usually be found delivering technical presentations at various community events, leading multiday training curriculums, and even authoring blog posts and white papers.

Oren Eini has over 15 years of experience in the development world with a strong focus on the Microsoft and .NET ecosystem, and has been awarded Microsoft's Most Valuable Professional since 2007.

An internationally known presenter, Oren has spoken at conferences such as DevTeach, JAOO, QCon, Oredev, NDC, Yow! and Progressive.NET.

Oren is the author of the book *DSLs in Boo: Domain Specific Languages in .NET*, published by *Manning* (http://manning.com/rahien/).

Oren's main focus is on architecture and best practices that promote quality software and zero-friction development.

Oren, using his pseudonym as Ayende Rahien, is a frequent blogger at http://www.ayende.com/Blog/.

Oren Eini is the founder of Hibernating Rhinos LTD, an Israel-based company, offering:

- Consulting and mentoring services
- Code reviews
- Architectural reviews and system design
- Developer productivity tools for OLTP applications such as:
- NHibernate Profiler (nhprof.com)
- Linq to SQL Profiler (l2sprof.com)
- Entity Framework Profiler (efprof.com)
- LLBLGen Profiler (llblgenprof.com)
- No SQL solutions
- RavenDB - a native .NET second generation document database (ravendb.net)
- RavenMD - a native .NET distributed queuing and messaging system (soon to be released)

Oren is the author of Rhino Mocks, one of the most popular mocking frameworks on the .NET platform, and is also a leading figure in other well known open source projects including:

- NHibernate
- RavenDB
- Rhino Tools Suite
    - Rhino Mocks - mocking framework
    - Rhino Commons - infrastructure framework
    - Rhino Igloo - MVC framework for WebForms
    - Rhino Security - security infrastructure for NHibernate
    - Rhino DSL - Domain Specific Language building toolkit
    - Rhino ESB - Distributed Service Bus framework
    - Rhino Licensing - licensing infrastructure
    - Rhino ETL - Extract/Transform/Load framework
    - Rhino PHT - Persistent Hash Table for .NET
    - Rhino DHT - Distributed Hash Table for .NET
    - Rhino Queues - Distributed queuing infrastructure
- Castle project

His hobbies include reading fantasy novels, reviewing code, and writing about himself in the third person.

www.PacktPub.com

Support files, eBooks, discount offers and more

You might want to visit www.PacktPub.com for support files and downloads related to your book.

Did you know that Packt offers eBook versions of every book published, with PDF and ePub files available? You can upgrade to the eBook version at www.PacktPub.com and as a print book customer, you are entitled to a discount on the eBook copy. Get in touch with us at service@packtpub.com for more details.

At www.PacktPub.com, you can also read a collection of free technical articles, sign up for a range of free newsletters and receive exclusive discounts and offers on Packt books and eBooks.

http://PacktLib.PacktPub.com

Do you need instant solutions to your IT questions? PacktLib is Packt's online digital book library. Here, you can access, read and search across Packt's entire library of books.

Why Subscribe?

- ◆ Fully searchable across every book published by Packt
- ◆ Copy and paste, print and bookmark content
- ◆ On demand and accessible via web browser

Free Access for Packt account holders

If you have an account with Packt at www.PacktPub.com, you can use this to access PacktLib today and view nine entirely free books. Simply use your login credentials for immediate access.

Table of Contents

Preface

RavenDB is an open source second generation NoSQL document database written in .NET. With its schema-less and flexible data model, it is designed to meet the real-world applications and allow you to build high-performance applications quickly and efficiently.

RavenDB 2.x Beginner's Guide introduces RavenDB concepts to the .NET developer who has some background in building desktop and web applications.

This book teaches you everything, right from installing RavenDB to creating documents and querying indexes using the .NET Client API through a series of clear and practical exercises. It starts off with an introduction to RavenDB and its Management Studio before moving on to cover dynamic and static indexes that use Map/Reduce to process datasets. With the help of detailed examples, you will learn how to create, manage, and query these indexes. Also, you will learn how to manage document attachments and patching documents using JavaScript.

With this book, you will learn how to deploy RavenDB in a production environment and how to profile and optimize it to boost performance. You will also learn how to create shards and implement replication to improve data availability and how to interact with RavenDB using the HTTP API.

Finally, you will learn to create an ASP.NET MVC application that uses RavenDB as a baking store to put all learned concepts together.

What this book covers

Chapter 1, Getting Started with RavenDB, introduces the underlying concepts of RavenDB and provides a step-by-step guide on how to install and run a RavenDB server on a computer to create your first RavenDB database.

Chapter 2, RavenDB Management Studio, introduces the RavenDB Silverlight client to let you easily manage documents in RavenDB. You will learn to view, create, edit, or delete documents, as well as how to manage indexes, issue queries, view the errors log, import/export, and so on.

Chapter 3, RavenDB .NET Client API, covers all aspects to interact with RavenDB using the Microsoft .NET framework. You will learn to connect to RavenDB, create, update, and delete documents, and how to query a document collection.

Chapter 4, RavenDB Indexes and Queries, covers RavenDB dynamic, static, and stales indexes. You will learn to create and query RavenDB Map/Reduce indexes and learn to manage temporary indexes.

Chapter 5, Advanced RavenDB Indexes and Queries, introduces the AbstractIndexCreationTask class and shows you how to use it to create the Map/Reduce indexes. Also, you will learn how to create multi-map indexes, use the TransformResults function, search over documents, and page query results.

Chapter 6, Advanced RavenDB Document Capabilities, explores the RavenDB document attachments and shows you how to handle document relationships using the Include statement and how to patch a document or a document collection using JavaScript.

Chapter 7, RavenDB Administration, shows you how to configure, backup, restore, import, and export RavenDB databases. Also, this chapter explores RavenDB bundles and you will learn to implement the SQL replication bundle to replicate data to Microsoft SQL Server.

Chapter 8, Deploying RavenDB, explores the different ways to deploy RavenDB in order to be used in a production or testing environment.

Chapter 9, Scaling-out RavenDB, introduces RavenDB sharding with its two modes: the blind and smart modes. Also, you will learn to mix sharding and replication to shard with dedicated or internal failover nodes.

Chapter 10, RavenDB Profiling, shows you how you can profile RavenDB server in real-time and use this information to optimize and improve the server performance.

Chapter 11, RavenDB HTTP API, shows you how to interact with RavenDB using the RavenDB HTTP API, which follows commonly understood RESTful principles.

Chapter 12, Putting It All Together, uses ASP.NET MVC to build a web application that uses RavenDB as a baking store. This application shows you how to implement a basic RavenDB controller, paging query results, create Master/Detail and Search views, and some other features.

What you need for this book

The following are the prerequisites that you need for this book:

- RavenDB 2.x distribution package, which includes RavenDB Server and Client (`http://ravendb.net/download`)

- A web browser that supports Microsoft Silverlight 5.0

- Microsoft Visual Studio 2012 (any version) to create, build, and run C# .NET projects (`http://www.microsoft.com/en-us/download/details.aspx?id=34673`)

- The NuGet Package Manager, included in Visual Studio 2012 (`http://visualstudiogallery.msdn.microsoft.com/27077b70-9dad-4c64-adcf-c7cf6bc9970c`)

- *Chapter 7, RavenDB Administration*, requires Microsoft SQL Server Express (included in Visual Studio 2012) to be installed on your machine (`http://www.microsoft.com/en-us/download/details.aspx?id=29062`)

- *Chapter 11, RavenDB HTTP API*, requires RESTClient 3.1 or newer (`http://www.wiztools.org/`)

Who this book is for

This book is great for experienced .NET developers new to document-oriented databases, and who are looking to get a good grounding in how to build applications that take advantage of such NoSQL databases. Having a working knowledge of relational database systems is not needed but will help in grasping some of the concepts quicker.

Conventions

In this book, you will find a number of styles of text that distinguish between different kinds of information. Here are some examples of these styles, and an explanation of their meaning.

Code words in text, database table names, folder names, filenames, file extensions, pathnames, dummy URLs, user input, and Twitter handles are shown as follows: "A `Collection` is a logical way of thinking of document groups."

A block of code is set as follows:

```
{
"CustomerId":"A54309",
"Item":"Paper Set",
"OrderDate":"11/17/2011",
"UnitCost":25.99,
"Units":5
}
```

Any command-line input or output is written as follows:

```
wbadmin start backup -backupTarget:e: -include:C:\RavenDB-Build-
    2261\Server\Database\Databases\World
```

New terms and **important words** are shown in bold. Words that you see on the screen, in menus or dialog boxes for example, appear in the text like this: "We will open Start.cmd in the **Notepad** application to learn how RavenDB will be launched".

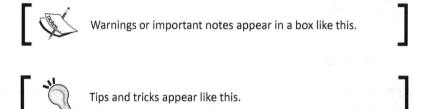

Warnings or important notes appear in a box like this.

Tips and tricks appear like this.

Reader feedback

Feedback from our readers is always welcome. Let us know what you think about this book—what you liked or may have disliked. Reader feedback is important for us to develop titles that you really get the most out of.

To send us general feedback, simply send an e-mail to feedback@packtpub.com, and mention the book title via the subject of your message.

If there is a topic that you have expertise in and you are interested in either writing or contributing to a book, see our author guide on www.packtpub.com/authors.

Customer support

Now that you are the proud owner of a Packt book, we have a number of things to help you to get the most from your purchase.

Downloading the example code

You can download the example code files for all Packt books you have purchased from your account at `http://www.packtpub.com`. If you purchased this book elsewhere, you can visit `http://www.packtpub.com/support` and register to have the files e-mailed directly to you.

Errata

Although we have taken every care to ensure the accuracy of our content, mistakes do happen. If you find a mistake in one of our books—maybe a mistake in the text or the code—we would be grateful if you would report this to us. By doing so, you can save other readers from frustration and help us improve subsequent versions of this book. If you find any errata, please report them by visiting `http://www.packtpub.com/submit-errata`, selecting your book, clicking on the **errata submission form** link, and entering the details of your errata. Once your errata are verified, your submission will be accepted and the errata will be uploaded on our website, or added to any list of existing errata, under the Errata section of that title. Any existing errata can be viewed by selecting your title from `http://www.packtpub.com/support`.

Piracy

Piracy of copyright material on the Internet is an ongoing problem across all media. At Packt, we take the protection of our copyright and licenses very seriously. If you come across any illegal copies of our works, in any form, on the Internet, please provide us with the location address or website name immediately so that we can pursue a remedy.

Please contact us at `copyright@packtpub.com` with a link to the suspected pirated material.

We appreciate your help in protecting our authors, and our ability to bring you valuable content.

Questions

You can contact us at `questions@packtpub.com` if you are having a problem with any aspect of the book, and we will do our best to address it.

1

Getting Started with RavenDB

In this chapter, you will learn about RavenDB database server which is a document-oriented database and belongs to the NoSQL database family. RavenDB is an open source software and it does not use SQL language to manipulate data, but it stores what we call "Documents".

You will start by learning briefly the basics of NoSQL databases, to be familiar with its concepts, and then you will learn about document-oriented databases and the JSON format (JavaScript Object Notation). Before you can start working with RavenDB, we have to set up an environment with system requirements, where you can test and play around with, to get familiar with RavenDB. Then you will go forward by learning how to launch RavenDB and its embedded management tool the RavenDB Management Studio and understanding the basic configuration file application key settings.

Once RavenDB is installed and running, you will learn to open the Management Studio to access the database and create some sample data. Then we will move forward and learn how to shut down the RavenDB server in the Console mode.

In this chapter we will cover:

- Basics of NoSQL databases
- What is RavenDB and how it works
- RavenDB documents and JSON format
- Downloading and installing RavenDB
- Configuring RavenDB
- Running RavenDB in the Console mode

Understanding the basics of NoSQL Databases

What is NoSQL? What makes NoSQL different from a relational database and why do we need it? These are some questions that we attempt to answer in a few lines.

NoSQL is a term used when talking about non-traditional databases. It is a very wild term. It basically defines a database that uses other Data Manipulation Language (DML) than SQL. This is why NoSQL is literally a combination of two words: *No* and *SQL* and it means "Not only SQL".

We use SQL when we want to manipulate data and access relational database servers such as Oracle, MySQL, Microsoft SQL Server, and all other relational databases. **NoSQL Databases** are not relational and they don't use the Codd's model.

> E.F. Codd was a famous mathematician who introduced 12 rules for the relational model for databases commonly known as Codd's rules. The rules mainly define what is required for a DBMS for it to be considered relational. For more information about Codd's model follow this link: `http://fr.wikipedia.org/wiki/Edgar_Frank_Codd`.

In a relational database, we can have a table and in this table an ID column which is used as a foreign key in another table. NoSQL Database does not have relational enforcement and it does not use SQL language to interact with stored data.

A **NoSQL System** aims to be easy to scale out. Scalability is the ability of a system to change its size while maintaining proportions and this usually means to increase throughput with addition of resources to address load increases. The problem with **Relational Database Management System** (**RDBMS**) isn't that they don't scale, it's that it becomes cost prohibitive to scale *vertically*, versus scaling *horizontally*. **Vertical scaling** means that you scale by adding more power (CPU, RAM, Hard disk space) to your existing machine, while **horizontal scaling** means that you scale by adding more machines into your pool of resources.

A good example for horizontal scaling is Cassandra, MongoDB, and **RavenDB**. A good example for vertical scaling is MySQL – Amazon RDS (the cloud version of MySQL) which provides an easy way to scale vertically by switching from smaller to bigger machines, but this process often involves downtime.

Typical RDBMS makes strong guaranties about consistency. This requires to some extended communication between nodes for every transaction. This limits the ability to scale out because more nodes mean more communication.

 In general, NoSQL Systems are open source, freely available on the Internet, and their use is increasingly gaining momentum in consumer and enterprise applications.

Types of NoSQL Databases

NoSQL itself is a very large concept and it involves a large number of technologies. In this section, we will introduce the different types of NoSQL but we will focus only on the RavenDB NoSQL Database type, the **document-oriented** database. The concepts we are introducing here apply on RavenDB and some other NoSQL Databases but not all NoSQL Database types.

Currently, the NoSQL databases types can be categorized in more than ten types. But we will only focus on the four major different types:

- **key-value databases**: A key-value database has a key and a corresponding value together as dataset. In key-value models, the key has to be unique and the value is associated with that key. Values can be of different types such as strings, integers, floats, or byte arrays. Some databases do not even care about the data type of the value, they just store what you feed. These inputs are called blobs, meaning an arbitrary binary object, which the database does not need to interpret. It is a very simple kind of database; it is operating as a dictionary. Examples of key-value NoSQL Databases are Amazon Dynamo, Redis.

- **column-oriented databases**: The basic idea behind column-oriented databases is that the data is not a dataset with its attributes stored in one unit as in SQL databases (row oriented) but one attribute of a set of datasets is stored in one unit (column oriented). From the simplicity of the columnar approach may accrue many benefits, especially for those seeking a high-performance environment to meet the growing needs of extremely large analytic databases. Google's BigTable, Cassandra, HBase, Hypertable are examples of column-oriented NoSQL Databases.

◆ **graph-oriented databases**: The graph-oriented databases originated from the graph theory, where you have vertices (singular: vertex) and edges connecting the vertices. In databases, vertices are entities like persons and edges are relations between entities. These relations are similar to the relations in Relational Database Management Systems. Twitter uses FlockDB the graph-oriented database, Facebook and LinkedIn use also a graph-oriented NoSQL database.

◆ **document-oriented databases**: The document-oriented databases use entire documents of different types as datasets. The document types are structured human readable data format such as XML or JSON. Document-oriented databases can be interpreted as particular cases of a key-value database. The database knows the format of document and it interprets it. This is the biggest difference to key-value storage. Therefore, in a document database, it is also the server itself that can operate with the document and not just the client. Ergo, it is also possible to directly work with the data in the document on the server side. Document store databases are schema free. In a schema free database you do not have to predefine what your documents looks like. For the storage this does not seem to be a problem, because the documents do not depend on each other. When the documents have some kind of structure or schema it is called semi-structured. Other examples of document-oriented databases are CouchDB, MongoDB, and obviously RavenDB.

RavenDB is a NoSQL document store database. In the context of RavenDB or a document-oriented database, you can think of a document as a web page with a hierarchical nested structure and all this data can be retrieved and fetched in one time. A document store can have a key and then it will have a document associated with that key.

The NoSQL Databases website (http://www.nosql-database.org/) currently lists more than 150 databases.

What is RavenDB?

RavenDB is an open source document-oriented NoSQL designed especially for the .NET/Windows platform. It requires commercial licensing (with a special pricing available for BizSpark startup organizations). A free edition is available for open source projects, but it must be applied for.

RavenDB supports multiple databases and, as other database servers, a database acts as a container of data. RavenDB can easily handle hundreds or thousands of databases on the same instance and was explicitly designed with multi-tenancy (or multi-instances) in mind. This allows RavenDB to manage large numbers of databases, but at any given time, only one database is active and taking resources.

Each RavenDB database contains a set of documents which can be divided into collections. A `Collection` is a logical way of thinking of document groups. Within a `Collection`, documents share the same entity name.

 RavenDB's collections are very similar to MongoDB's collections which is another document-oriented NoSQL database.

A `Document` is a unit of data and it contains a set of fields or key-value pairs. It is important to note that values can be arrays, complex types, or even arrays of complex types. The keys are strings; the values can be of various types such as strings, integers, and so on. You can even store a document as the value of a field.

RavenDB database contains `Indexes` which works differently than RDBMS indexes. RavenDB uses indexes to satisfy queries. You may index the whole query's field or specify the fields you want to index in a document. RavenDB takes the query, analyses it and extracts an index which can answer the query. Also, it has the ability to auto generate indexes from your queries.

RavenDB uses **JSON (JavaScript Object Notation)** to store documents. JSON is a way to serialize data and is a lightweight data-interchange format. On the client side, this is used primarily by RavenDB and then data is serialized to .NET objects. But on the server side that data is all JSON, all the time.

RavenDB does not have a schema (schema-less) and documents do not have to have a specific field or column. Also, there are no explicit relations among the documents that exist in RavenDB. We might have some `Document` when we build a store `Document` and maybe we want to use a `Document` to lookup in other `Document`, this relation is only in data and not enforced by the database.

 RavenDB is a document-oriented database and is not relational. That means it doesn't maintain foreign key constraints.

RavenDB is fully transactional. That means, it fully supports both implicit and explicit transactions and we can take full advantage of this feature. Unlike most NoSQL databases that adhere to the **BASE** properties, RavenDB supports the **ACID** properties for write operations. ACID, as we all know, stands for Atomicity, Consistency, Isolation, and Durability, and support for ACID is what makes us so comfortable using RDBMS systems with respect to data integrity. BASE, on the other hand, stands for Basically Available, Soft state, Eventual consistency.

RavenDB stores `Indexes` data and allows storing large data files through using attachments. Attachments are a large chunk of data (**BLOBs – Binary Large OBjects**) that are used to store images, music files, videos, and other kind of binary data. Attachments in RavenDB can have metadata and can be replicated between nodes. Also, it can be cascade deleted on document deletions (which requires the `CascadeDelete` bundle called `Raven.Bundles.CascadeDelete` to be activated) and are HTTP cacheable.

 RavenDB `Indexes` look like a LINQ query, but they aren't. They are used to build an `Index` that you can then use just such as in RDBMS.

From relational databases to RavenDB

Developers and database administrators with a background on working with relational database systems will quickly recognize the similarities between the logical abstractions of the relational data model and the RavenDB data model. The next figure gives a quick view of a relational data model and their equivalent with those of the RavenDB data model:

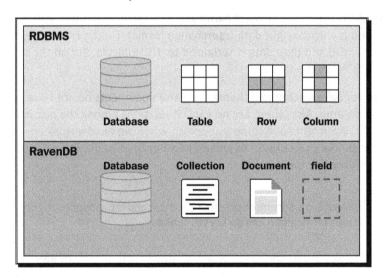

 A `Document` in RavenDB will typically contain data from multiple tables in a Relational Database Management System (RDBMS).

When you work with RavenDB, you need to consider that RavenDB is non-relational. The reason is that RavenDB treats each document as an independent entity. There are no foreign keys in a collection and as a result, there are no JOIN queries. Constraint management is typically handled in the application layer. Also, because of its flexible schema property, there is no need for the expensive `ALTER TABLE` statement in RavenDB and you can have user defined content much more easily.

RavenDB is able to store large amounts of data and also is able to optimize the way documents are stored and managed. It supports Horizontal scaling and each document can be stored on any node of the horizontal resource pool (this is called sharding).

Why RavenDB?

Let's move forward and take a look at the basics of RavenDB, why it is different, and why the new approach has made everybody excited about using RavenDB. Looking back at the NoSQL databases history, most of them have started as ways to address problems that people have with the relational databases. RavenDB was produced out of the needs and necessities of a better environment. Developers are becoming more savvy every year, with better environments, better tools, and simpler and more straightforward methods for achieving a range of goals.

The benefits of NoSQL solutions depend on use cases. When considering a NoSQL solution, users must choose the appropriate database management system that best suits their applications. An appropriate choice brings best performance or decrease a costs.

Why does RavenDB make managing document-oriented data easier? Here are the main advantages of adopting RavenDB:

- RavenDB is written in C#, .NET, and it is easy to learn how to use it. This is a real advantage. Data can be queried efficiently using LINQ queries from .NET code or using **RESTful (REpresentational State Transfer)** APIs.

- In RavenDB, the database schema is no longer fixed, data is stored schema-less as the JSON documents, so the documents can have arbitrary structures and attributes associated with them. Internally, RavenDB makes use of **Indexes** which are automatically created based on your usage, or were created explicitly by the consumer.

- RavenDB is highly scalable and is built for web-scale. It offers replication and sharding support out-of-the-box.

- RavenDB is fully transactional with the **ACID** support.

You can use RavenDB in many cases and it is the perfect choice. For example, RavenDB can be used to archive a huge number of documents, it can be used as a content management database, to store orders, inventory, and suppliers in an e-commerce solution. For some reason, there are a lot of real estate/rental people using RavenDB.

But the case that we don't recommend using RavenDB for is reporting. This is because in many cases, reporting requires dynamic data aggregation over large dataset, and that isn't an **OLTP (Online Transaction Processing)** task, which is what RavenDB was designed for. For reporting, we recommend just throwing that data into a reporting warehouse database (either star schema or a cube) and doing the reporting directly from there.

With the RavenDB SQL Replication bundle, you can replicate to an Microsoft SQL Server and do the reporting from there very easily.

How RavenDB works?

When you are using RavenDB, basically you have a client application that communicates with a database server. The client application will communicate with RavenDB database server over HTTP. It will look like any web service and **REST (REpresentational State Transfer)** based web service. REST is an architecture that uses the strengths of the web to build services. It proposes a set of constraints that simplifies development and encourages more scalable designs. In REST, resources are identified by a unique **URI (Unique Resource Identifier)**.Client applications interact with resources using four main HTTP verbs.

The following figure illustrates basics of RavenDB client/server application architecture:

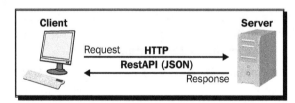

In the RavenDB architecture model, the data is communicated across the network in JSON format from the server to the client.

RavenDB can be launched in different modes. It can be launched in:

- ◆ **Console mode**: This mode is good for learning and testing.
- ◆ **Hosted by IIS (Internet Information Server)**: This is probably the most common scenario to run RavenDB in a production environment.
- ◆ **As a Windows Service**: RavenDB will create its own HTTP server and process all requests internally.
- ◆ **Embedded mode**: In this mode, RavenDB will be embedded in your application and may run completely in memory.

Also, RavenDB comes with built-in authentication functionality and it supports two types of authentication:

- ◆ **Windows authentication**: This authentication method is chosen when a request needs to be authenticated and no other authentication method is detected.
- ◆ **OAuth authentication**: OAuth is an open authorization framework that enables application to obtain limited access to an HTTP service, either on behalf of a resource owner by orchestrating an approval interaction between the resource owner and the HTTP service, or by allowing the application to obtain access on its own behalf.

As stated, the RavenDB databases were designed with multi-databases support. In order to do that, RavenDB will only keep one database open, the active database. When accessing a database for the first time, that database will be opened and started, so the next request to that database wouldn't have to be opened again, which is good for performances. But if a database hasn't been accessed for a while, RavenDB will clean up all resources associated with the database and close it.

Anatomy of a Document

In RavenDB, data is stored as `Documents` and must be serialized from the native .NET objects to the JSON format before being sent to RavenDB database engine, they are later deserialized from JSON, and then to native .NET objects.

The flexible document-based structure reduces the need to worry about the structure of the data, either before or during the application development. You do still have to think about the structure of data in terms of identifying natural transactional boundaries (which in this case is the `Document`).

This helps in mapping the data and allow querying, combining, and filtering the information. Replication is also easy-to-use so you can copy, share, and synchronize your data between databases, machines, and even continents.

In a typical database, we store different related pieces of data. We might have an object and we might model this object using multiple objects. Take the example of a desktop computer in a company with different softwares installed by a user. We want to keep track of all these installed softwares. By modeling the **Computer** entity and its related **Inventory**, we will have a tree of related objects. Usually, in traditional RDBMS, we will store each one object as a part of the data tree in a table in the database and relate them together.

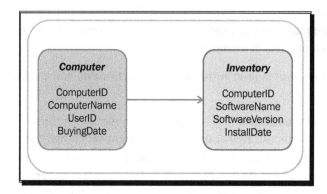

In a `Document` type database we skip the task of splitting the model in smaller entities and the entire structure will remain as a one single object. This object is stored in the database using a single REST verb (POST or PUT) and there is no need to split the object, or separate its data into primary entities. When we want to retrieve the object, we retrieve it entirely and we do not care where the data went or how to join it from different entities or documents.

Document-oriented databases are not limited to just storing keys and values. Instead, you can store complex object graphs as a single document. In a relational database, a row can only contain simple values and more complex data structures need to be stored as relations. In RavenDB, a `Document` can handle complex structure and we can store all the data that we need to work with as a single document.

 To enhance the overall performance of your system, it is a good practice to include all of the information you need in a single document when using RavenDB and you are encouraged to do so.

At a collection level, this allows for putting together a diverse set of documents into a single collection. `Document` databases allow indexing of documents on the basis of not only its primary identifier but also its properties.

 Do not confuse "`Document-oriented` databases" and "Document Management Systems". The `Document-oriented` databases connotes loosely structured sets of key-value pairs in documents and a Document Management System is a computer system used to track and store documents.

Each RavenDB document contains data (other than yours) that describes other data (metadata), which aren't a direct part of the document. Metadata provides information about the CLR-type, the entity-name, the last-modified date, and so on. These metadata are attached to the document and are being used internally; but they can be exposed to your code.

The JSON format

JSON, short for JavaScript Object Notation, is a generic text format easy for humans to read and write and it's easy for machines to parse it and generate it. This format is used by RavenDB to store data and databases' metadata. RavenDB can write the JSON document directly, simplifying the writing/updating process. It is important to know that the JSON format may "denormalize" data. We might be storing the same class object multiple times in the database but that is not a problem because we are storing the entire document and we retrieve it as a document and not as a piece of data.

The JSON format is built on two structures:

- A collection of name/value pairs. Programming languages support this data structure in different names such as `object`, `record`, `struct`, `dictionary`, `hash table`, `keyed list`, or `associative array`.

- An ordered list of values. In various programming languages, this is realized as an `array`, `vector`, `list`, or `sequence`.

The following screenshot illustrates a `Document` entity as it will be stored in RavenDB using JSON format:

```json
{
    "ComputerID": "1234",
    "ComputerName": "KTAWIN8",
    "UserId": "963258",
    "Buying": "2010-03-06T20:35:08.8068415Z",
    "Inventory": [
        {
            "SoftwareName": "Adobe Reader",
            "SoftwareVersion": "10",
            "InstallDate": "2012-10-25T12:55:18.8058315Z"
        },
        {
            "SoftwareName": "Microsoft Office",
            "SoftwareVersion": "2010",
            "InstallDate": "2011-05-02T09:15:10.4068815Z"
        }
    ]
}
```

In this JSON example which describes the `Computer` entity, the object begins with { (left brace) and ends with } (right brace). Each name is followed by : (colon) and the name/value pairs are separated by , (comma). So, the `"CompuerID"` entity represents the key name and `"12345"` represents the value assigned to that key name.

The `"Inventory"` key name is an array and is an ordered collection of values. In JSON, an array begins with [(left bracket) and ends with] (right bracket). Values are separated by , (comma). In this example, the `"Inventory"` array contains two object instances where each one is composed of three name/value pairs `"SoftawareName"`, `"SoftwareVersion"`, and `"InstallDate"`.

 You can learn more about JSON structures at: `http://www.json.org/`.

Downloading and installing RavenDB

We are done with the theoretical part, at least for now. It is important to get familiar with all these concepts to take advantage of using RavenDB. It is time for us to download, install, and start using RavenDB on the computer.

What do you need to run RavenDB?

Basically, the primary installation target of RavenDB is Microsoft Windows. The Microsoft's .NET Framework should also be installed on the computer where RavenDB will run and where the application client will run. The RavenDB package comes with different client versions. To run the lightweight RavenDB client on your computer, Microsoft's .NET 4.0 Framework Client Profile is required.

 We recommend that the latest Microsoft's .NET Framework should be installed on the computer where RavenDB will run.

The RavenDB Management Studio is a Silverlight application and it needs Microsoft's Silverlight plugin to be installed on the web browser. The minimum Microsoft Silverlight version required to run Management Studio is Silverlight version 5.0 (the current version).

 If your computer does not run Microsoft Windows operating system, you can still use some RavenDB features (at the time of writing) on a Linux or a Mac OS environment by installing the Mono framework which is a free open source implementation of Microsoft's .NET Framework. For more information about the Mono framework go to `http://www.mono-project.com/Main_Page`.

To run RavenDB server or RavenDB embedded, you need at least Microsoft's .NET Framework v 4.0 to be installed on a computer running on Microsoft Windows operating system. To run RavenDB server as a Microsoft Windows service or to host RavenDB by **IIS** (**Internet Information Server**), a Microsoft Windows operating system is required.

Time for action – downloading and installing RavenDB

We are going to learn how to download and install RavenDB on a computer running on Microsoft Windows, using the following steps:

1. To download RavenDB, head to the download page on the RavenDB official website, `http://ravendb.net/download`.

> On the official website download page, we will find a couple of selections and different versions that can be downloaded. We can download the latest official release, the latest unstable release which is not recommended for use in a production environment.

2. Click on the download link for the latest stable release under RavenDB's latest official release. This will start downloading a ZIP archive.

> At the time of writing, RavenDB v2.0.0 Build 2375 was the latest version. If a newer stable release is available, you should download that version instead.

3. Once the download is finished, open this file up, and extract everything to `C:\RavenDB-Build-2375` (which is the name of ZIP archive file at the time of writing).

4. Open `C:\RavenDB-Build-2375` and explore it. It should look like this:

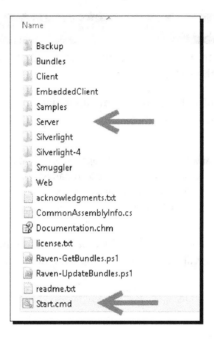

What just happened?

In steps 1 and 2, we downloaded the ZIP archive containing the .NET assembly files for the RavenDB server.

As an alternative to the official RavenDB website, RavenDB is also available for download via the NuGet package manager: `http://nuget.org/packages/RavenDB.Client`.

The NuGet package manager is a Visual Studio extension that makes it easy to add, remove, and update libraries and tools in Visual Studio projects that use the .NET Framework.

You can also download the source code of RavenDB and some other bundles, which are additions to RavenDB to extend its features and functionalities.

In step 3, we extracted files from the ZIP archive file to `C:\RavenDB-Build-2375`.

In step 4, we explored the different files and folders of RavenDB.

We do not have to be concerned about all the folders extracted, there are different versions of a RavenDB client. You have the lightweight client compatible with the Microsoft's .NET 4.0 Framework Client Profile and the Embedded RavenDB Client that you can use if you want to embed RavenDB in your application. The extracted files folder contains some samples that can be useful to learn how to do different things in RavenDB especially more complex things such as Sharding.

The important directory that we will really worry about here is the Server directory. The Server directory contains the Raven.Server.exe file which is our main executable file that we will run to launch our database server.

Raven.Server.exe can be run directly from the Server directory or by using the Start.cmd file located at the root of our folder C:\RavenDB-Build-2375.

> The latest RavenDB installation package includes these directories:
>
> - Client: A lightweight client for use with .NET 4.0
> - Silverlight: Silverlight 5.0 client
> - Silverlight-4: Silverlight 4.0 client
> - EmbeddedClient: The files necessary for using RavenDB in embedded mode
> - Server: The files required to use RavenDB in server mode
> - Web: The files required to use RavenDB under IIS
> - Bundles: The files for extending RavenDB in various ways
> - Samples: The sample RavenDB applications to get you started

Running RavenDB server in the Console mode

Running RavenDB in the Console mode is pretty good for learning and testing purposes and it is not suitable in a production environment. In production environment, RavenDB must be run as a Windows service or be hosted by IIS as a web application. This assumes that RavenDB will be more secure and will run faster.

Exploring the Start.cmd file

The RavenDB distribution package provides a command file, named Start.cmd, which you can use to launch RavenDB server in the Console mode. This file is located on the root of the package.

Time for action – exploring the Start.cmd file

We will open `Start.cmd` in the **Notepad** application to learn how RavenDB would be launched.

1. In Windows Explorer, go to `C:\RavenDB-Build-2375`.

2. Select the `Start.cmd` file and open it in the **Notepad** application. It should look like this:

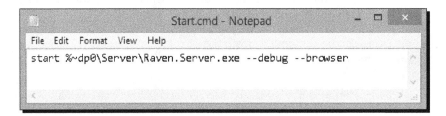

What just happened?

In steps 1 and 2, we opened the `Start.cmd` file and took a look at its command line parameters.

The `Raven.Server.exe` file is launched with two parameters `--debug` and `--browser`. The `debug` parameter is used by developers for applications debugging purposes and the `browser` parameter is used to open the Management Studio in the web browser automatically.

Configuring the RavenDB server

Before launching the RavenDB server, you might need to configure it. We can do configuration by editing the `Raven.server.exe.config` file located in the `Server` directory. This is a text file and can be edited and modified with the Notepad application.

There are three key-values in the **appSettings** section. These keys settings that you can modify to meet your needs are:

◆ **Raven/Port**: This setting represents the TCP/IP listening port

◆ **Raven/DataDir**: This setting lets you define the directory where the data will be stored

◆ **Raven/AnonymousAccess**: This setting defines the security level access which you can use to define which user can do which action on the server

`Raven.Server.exe` runs by default on port 8080. The `Start.cmd` file will run the `Raven.Server.exe` file with the command-line parameter `-browser`. This will automatically open the Management Studio in the web browser and point to this location: `http://hostname:port/raven/studio.html`.

```
Raven.Server.exe.config
 1    <?xml version="1.0" encoding="utf-8" ?>
 2    <configuration>
 3      <appSettings>
 4        <add key="Raven/Port" value="*"/>
 5        <add key="Raven/DataDir" value="~\Database\System"/>
 6        <add key="Raven/AnonymousAccess" value="Get"/>
 7      </appSettings>
 8      <runtime>
 9        <loadFromRemoteSources enabled="true"/>
10        <assemblyBinding xmlns="urn:schemas-microsoft-com:asm.v1">
11          <probing privatePath="Analyzers"/>
12        </assemblyBinding>
13      </runtime>
14    </configuration>
```

A few points to be noted about default values:

- The * value assigned to the `Raven/Port` indicates that RavenDB will find the first available port from 8080 and upward. By default, RavenDB server selects the 8080 TCP/IP port if it is not already in use. And once this is done that port is fixed.

- The path for the database directory is defined by the `Raven/DataDir` key. The use of `~\` indicates to start from the RavenDB root directory, in which case the path will start from the server-based directory. The default value is: `~\Database\System`.

- The `Raven/AnonymousAccess` key by default is set to `Get` and it determines what actions an anonymous user can do. You can control the access level by setting this key to one of these values; `Get` for read only, `All` for read/write, and `None` allows access to authenticated users only.

Launching the RavenDB server in the Console mode

When RavenDB is launched in the console mode it will open a CMD prompt window which will stay open until the user has entered one of the four available commands:

- `cls`: This command is used to clear the screen
- `reset`: This command is used to reset the RavenDB server
- `gc`: This command is used to initiate the garbage collection
- `q`: This command is used to shut down the RavenDB server and terminate the CMD prompt window

Time for action – launching RavenDB in the Console mode

You have already downloaded the RavenDB package and extracted it to a local folder on your computer. Now you are ready to launch RavenDB in the Console mode. You will run the database server using the Start.cmd command file:

1. In the Windows Explorer, select file C:\RavenDB-Build-2375\Start.cmd and press *Enter* or double-click on it to launch the RavenDB database server in the Console mode.

```
C:\RavenDB-Build-2375\Server\Raven.Server.exe                    -  □  ×
Raven is ready to process requests. Build 2375, Version 2.0.3 / 5a4b7ea
Server started in 3,676 ms
Data directory: C:\RavenDB-Build-2375\Server\Database\System
HostName: <any> Port: 8080, Storage: Esent
Server Url: http://ktawin8:8080/
Available commands: cls, reset, gc, q
_
```

 While the Raven.Server.exe application is running, it logs any activity on the RavenDB server. In the Console mode, the log activity is displayed within the command prompt window.

2. Click on the command prompt window to activate it and take a look at the RavenDB activity log.

What just happened?

We learned how to launch the RavenDB server.

In step 1, we launched the RavenDB server using the command file C:\RavenDB-Build-2261\Start.cmd.

In step 2, we activated the command prompt window and analyzed the RavenDB activity log.

Let's have a closer look at the activity log displayed within the launching process of RavenDB and analyze it.

The first log line indicates that the RavenDB server has been launched and it is ready to process requests. We can also see the RavenDB server's Build version, in our case it is Version 2.0.3 with 2375 as the Build number. If you have downloaded a newer version of RavenDB, you might have another version number and/or another Build version number.

The second line of the server activity log displays the time indicated in milliseconds that was needed by RavenDB to be launched and ready to process requests. This launching time will be different from one computer to another, based on the computer hardware configuration, the CPU activity, and the available memory resources.

Other configuration parameters are also logged and displayed such as the `Data Directory`, which indicates the directory where your data will be saved, the `machine hostname`, and the TCP/IP listening `port number` which is a part of the Server URL.

Creating your first RavenDB database

We are going to explore another great feature of the Management Studio by creating a new database and add some sample data that we can use to learn more about the Management Studio and RavenDB.

Many times, when you start building an application, you want to see what the data will look like in the user interface well before the database (or the web service) is actually ready. RavenDB makes it easier to see that data, compared to other systems. To do this, we can use the Management Studio.

Time for action – creating a new database and adding sample data

Currently, the server is empty and we have an empty default database named `system`. In order to see what the data will look like in the `Document` database, we are going to use the Management Studio features to create a new database and create some sample data to populate the database with these data.

 We assume that the RavenDB server is running and the Management Studio is open in the web browser. If not, you can refer to the previous section to launch the RavenDB server in the Console mode.

1. Click on your web browser to activate it. The RavenDB Management Studio is open.

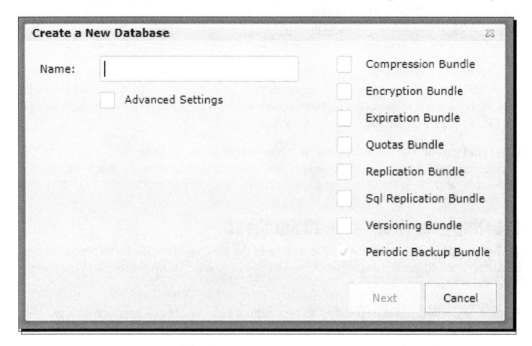

On the right side of the wizard form, you can choose to activate features provided by some available bundles (the RavenDB extensions). You can choose to activate data compression or data encryption and so on. These choices are inclusive and you can activate more than one bundle.

2. Create a new database using the wizard form and name it `Sales`.

3. Click on the **Tasks** tab to display the tasks screen.

4. Click on the **Create Sample Data** button to create the sample data.

5. Click on the **Documents** tab to display the **Documents** screen and verify that the sample data has been added to the current database.

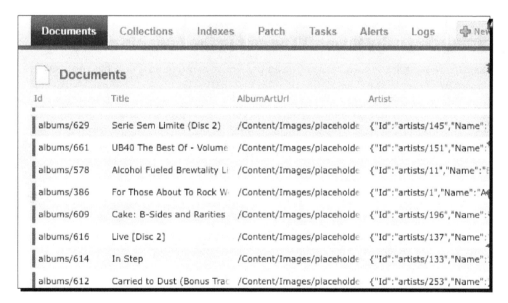

What just happened?

We just created a new database and populated it with sample data.

In steps 1 and 2, we created a new database named `Sales` using the Management Studio's **Create new database** wizard.

By default, RavenDB allows anonymous access only for read requests (`HTTP GET`), and since we are creating data, we need to specify a `username` and a `password` to generate the data. You can control this by changing the `AnonymousAccess` setting in the server configuration file, which requires the server restart to apply changes.

In steps 3 and 4, we generated sample data using the Management Studio features.

When we create sample data using the **Create Sample Data** feature of the Management Studio, the current database must be empty and there shouldn't be any documents in the database, otherwise, the data generation action will fail.

While inserting the sample data into the `Sales` database, the Management Studio displays the progress log. When the process is done, there are about 250 documents and four new indexes in the database.

In step 5, we opened the **Documents** screen and verified that the sample data has been added to the `Sales` database.

Shutting down the RavenDB server in the Console mode

As easy it is to launch the RavenDB server in the Console mode, it is also easy to shutdown the RavenDB server in the Console mode.

Once the `Start.cmd` file is executed, a new command prompt window is opened and it shows the server activity log. This RavenDB server instance would still be running until you press the *q* key command which will shutdown the RavenDB server and close the command prompt window.

Time for action – shutting down RavenDB

We assume that RavenDB is running in the Console mode, otherwise, please refer to the previous sections to launch the RavenDB server in the Console mode.

In the command prompt window, enter the `q` command and press *Enter* to shutdown the RavenDB server. This will also close the command prompt window.

What just happened?

In this one step, we learned how to shutdown the RavenDB server using the q command in the command prompt window.

When Raven.Server.exe is launched with the -browser parameter, it will automatically open the Management Studio in the web browser. But when the RavenDB instance is shutdown, it will not close the Management Studio and it should be closed manually.

Have a go hero – connecting to a RavenDB server on a networked computer

Suppose your computer is connected to a local area network. There is another computer in the network where RavenDB was installed and is currently running on the IP address 192.168.1.26 and listening on port 8080. You can access the Management Studio from your computer simply by typing the complete URL in your web browser that points to the Management Studio, providing the IP address, and the listening port where RavenDB is running. The URL should look like: http://192.168.1.26:8080/raven/studio.html.

Downloading the example code:

You can download the example code files for all Packt books you have purchased from your

account at http://www.packtpub.com. If you purchased this book elsewhere, you can visit http://www.packtpub.com/support and register to have the files e-mailed directly to you.

Summary

We learned a lot in this chapter about the RavenDB server and NoSQL and their concepts.

Specifically, we covered the document anatomy in a NoSQL document-oriented database and how it is represented in the JSON format. We learned the RavenDB concepts and how they work. Also, we looked at how to download and install RavenDB on the local machine. We covered how to launch and shutdown RavenDB in the Console mode and took a look at its activity log and its basic configuration file parameters. Finally, we created a new database in RavenDB and populated it with sample data using the RavenDB Management Studio wizards.

Now that we've learned about the RavenDB server, we're ready to start using the Management Studio, which is the topic of the next chapter.

2
RavenDB Management Studio

The RavenDB Management Studio is a graphical integrated environment for accessing, configuring, managing, and administering the RavenDB server. It embeds a group of rich editors and viewers which are easy to use and very helpful to developers and administrators of all skill levels.

In this chapter, you will learn to use the RavenDB Management Studio to create or edit Documents and Collections, to create Indexes, or to view logs and other useful features of the Management Studio.

In this chapter we will cover:

◆ The Management Studio's main interface

◆ Viewing and managing Documents, Collections, and Indexes

◆ Patching documents using the Management Studio

◆ Importing/exporting data using the Management Studio

Introducing the RavenDB Management Studio

The RavenDB Management Studio that comes with RavenDB is a Silverlight based application which is used to manage the RavenDB server. It is a very useful tool to look at the server databases and the activity logs to understand what's going on at the server-side. With the Management Studio, we can create new databases and new documents; we can modify data directly if we need to. Also, when using RavenDB, this will be very handy in debugging and application development.

The main Management Studio user interface has a few different tabs on the top: **Documents**, **Collections**, **Indexes**, **Patch**, **Alerts**, and **Logs**. We can use these tabs to access the different screens and manage different parts of the database server. There is a **New** button list; by clicking on the arrow of the **New** button, there are several options shown such as: create a **new Document**, create a **new Index**, or create a **new Dynamic Query**. On selecting and clicking on one of these options, the respective screen page for each option is shown.

The Management Studio provides a search box feature which lets you go directly to a document stored in a collection and display it in the edit mode. It also provides the **Export** feature which can be used to export all the documents/queries for a given database to a CSV format. Also, it is possible to export all documents and indexes in a JSON format to be able to import them to another database or as backup.

The **Export** feature is available in the **Documents**, **Collections**, and **Index Query Results** views and it is context sensitive:

◆ In the **Documents** view, it will export all documents in the database

◆ In the **Collections** view, it will only export the documents found in that collection

◆ In the **Index Query Results** view, it will export the documents matching the query

At the top-right corner of the Management Studio graphical interface, we have a colored dot that represents the status of the RavenDB sever. The red color indicates that the server is offline and the green one indicates that the server is online.

The status-bar at the bottom of the Management Studio displays the RavenDB server statistics such as how many documents are stored, how many indexes, triggers, errors, and tasks. Also, in status-bar we have the information about the RavenDB server Build number and the client Build number.

The Management Studio is opened automatically when RavenDB server is launched using the `Start.cmd` file. To open it manually after the server is running, you can browse the URL that RavenDB is listed to. By default RavenDB is listening on port `8080`. So, it can be opened with you Internet browser using this URL: `http://localhost:8080/raven/studio.html`.

Management Studio's multi-databases feature

RavenDB supports multi-databases, the Management Studio provides an easy way to create and manage new and multiple databases from the same user interface. On the left-side of the Management Studio, the toolbar shows a hyperlink button with the name of the current database we are working with. This hyperlink button is used to display the **Databases** screen and show the list of all the other available databases. You can shift the current database by selecting a new one from the list of available databases.

Also, we have the **Settings** button (the cogwheel button) which allows us to set common options for all databases and specific bundle (which is the RavenDB extensions) options.

Creating a new database

When the Management Studio is started up, it shows the **Databases** screen and displays the list of all hosted databases. Each database in the list is displayed in a rectangle with the number of documents that this database has. On selecting a database from the list, the Management Studio status bar displays more statistics information about the selected database.

The **Databases** screen allows you to create a new database using the **Create a New Database** wizard form which also allows you to add some functionality to your database, such as database replication, data compression, data encryption, and so on.

Time for action – creating a new database

To begin using the Management Studio, we need to create a new database and populate it with the sample data. In this section, you will learn to create a new database using the Management Studio wizard form.

1. Launch the RavenDB server using the `Start.cmd` command file.

2. In the Management Studio, click on the **Databases** link.

3. Click on the **New Database** button to open the **Create a New Database** wizard form.

4. Enter Orders for the **Name** of new database and click on the **Next** button to create the new database.

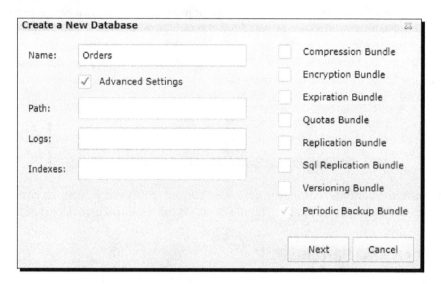

What just happened?

We just created a new database named Orders using the **Create a New Database** wizard of the Management Studio.

In steps 1 to 3, we launched the RavenDB server and opened the **Create a New Database** wizard to create the new database.

After clicking on the **Next** button, the Orders database is created. It will become the current database and will be added to the hosted databases list.

If the server has no hosted database, yet the **Create a New Database** wizard form will open automatically, otherwise, you have to click on the **New Database** button in order to open the wizard.

Management Studio's Documents screen

The **Documents** screen shows a list of all documents from different collections in the RavenDB server instance. Documents from different collections are striped with different colors. Within the **Documents** screen, you can display documents in different view modes; there are six different view modes which you can switch between. Each view mode defines the size of the document preview in the listing:

◆ **Details**: This view will display document's data in rows and document's fields in columns.

◆ **ID Only**: This view will display only the document ID. This view mode is useful for low bandwidth connections.

◆ **Small Card, Medium Card, Large Card**: Each of these modes will display documents as cards in a different size. You can choose the size of the card to display in order to show more or less cards on a single page.

◆ **Extra Large Card**: This view will show the whole data of the document as a JSON string.

The default view mode, when the Management Studio starts up, is the **Details** view mode.

Time for action – creating your first document

You will learn to create some new documents using the Management Studio and add them to the `Orders` database.

1. If it is not running, launch the RavenDB server.

 To open the Management Studio manually in your browser, go to this URL: `http://localhost:8080/raven/studio.html`.

2. Ensure that the current database is `Orders`, otherwise, click on the **Databases** hyperlink button to display the **Databases** screen and select the `Orders` database.

3. In the Management Studio toolbar, click on the arrow near the **New** button and select **New Document**.

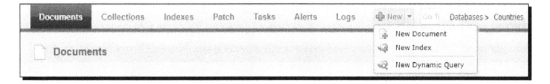

4. Enter the document ID `Orders/A179854` and enter the following document data values:

```
{
"CustomerId":"A54309",
"Item":"Paper Set",
"OrderDate":"11/17/2011",
"UnitCost":25.99,
"Units":5
}
```

5. After that, click on the **Save** button to insert the document into the
Orders database.

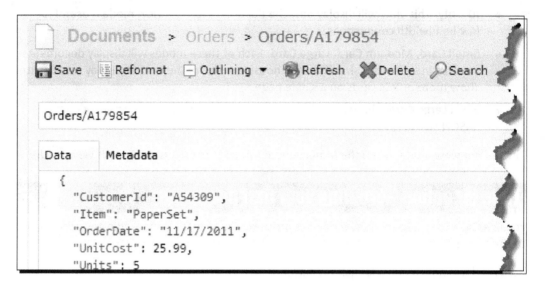

```
Documents  >  Orders  >  Orders/A179854

  Save      Reformat    Outlining  ▾    Refresh   Delete   Search


  Orders/A179854


  Data      Metadata

    {
        "CustomerId": "A54309",
        "Item": "PaperSet",
        "OrderDate": "11/17/2011",
        "UnitCost": 25.99,
        "Units": 5
```

6. Repeat the steps 3 and 4 to add new documents to the Orders database using the
following data:

Id	CustomerId	Item	OrderDate	UnitCost	Units
Orders/A655302	A54309	Pen	10/31/2011	15.99	35
Orders/A154230	A54309	Pencil	4/18/2010	1.99	75
Orders/B768920	F843098	Rubber	5/12/2011	0.99	10
Orders/B765760	F843098	Pen	5/12/2011	15.99	10

What just happened?

You just populated the Orders database directly by using the Management Studio editors
with five new documents.

In steps 1 to 3, we created the Orders databases and in steps 4 to 6, we added five new
documents to the database.

If you save a document without providing the document ID, RavenDB will create a new `Guid` and assign it to the document as its unique ID.

Time for action – loading a document

You will use the Management Studio to load a document from the `Orders` database to view it and modify some values.

1. Select the `Orders` database from the **Databases** screen to activate it and make it the current database.

2. Select the **Documents** tab screen to display the documents list.

3. Click on the **Switch between views** button and select the **ID Only** view mode.

4. Select the document with the `ID = Orders/B765760` and click on the pencil icon in the bottom-right corner to open the document in the edit screen.

 In the **Details** view mode, you might double-click on the row that represents the document to open it in the edit screen mode.

5. Change the `Units` field value to be `20`.

6. Click on the **Save** button to make the changes permanent.

Documents > Orders > Orders/B765760

Save   Reformat   Outlining ▼   Refresh   Del   ❮❮ ❮ Document 1 of 5 ❯ ❯❯

Orders/B765760|

Data   Metadata

```
{
    "CustomerId": "F843098",
    "Item": "Pen",
    "OrderDate": "5/12/2011",
    "UnitCost": 15.99,
    "Units": 20
}
```

❯ 0 Errors

What just happened?

We learned how to load the document with the ID `Orders/B765760` from the `Orders` database in the edit screen mode and change its `Units` value directly in the Management Studio.

In steps 1 to 3, we used the pencil icon to open the document in the edit mode, then in steps 5 and 6, we change the `Units` field value and save the changes.

Time for action – searching for a document

You will use the Management Studio to search the document with the ID `Orders/A154230` in the `Orders` database to view it or to edit it.

1. In the Management Studio, click on the **Go To Document** search box.
2. Search for the document with the ID `Orders/A154230` (which belongs to the `Orders` database).

3. Press *Enter* to validate your typing and then the whole document data is loaded in the edit screen.

What just happened?

We used the Management Studio's **Go To Document** search box to load the document with the ID= `Orders/A154230` in the edit mode.

In case that the document you are looking for does not exist in the database, you will be redirected to the **Documents** tab, otherwise, the **Document** edit page will load with the requested document.

Note that while typing suggestions will appear for you.

Exporting a database to a CSV file

In order to use your documents outside RavenDB, you can convert a RavenDB database document to a comma-separated values (CSV) text file by using the **Export to CSV** button. Exported data is saved in a text file using the Unicode UTF8 format.

Time for action – exporting documents to a CSV file

You will use the Management Studio to export the Orders database documents to a CSV file.

1. In the Management Studio, select the **Document** tab screen.

2. Click on the **Switch between views** button and select the **Details** view mode.

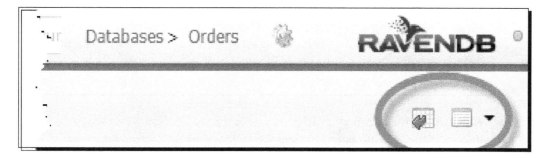

3. Click on the **Export to CSV** button to export the database documents to a CSV text file format.

4. Click on the **OK** button of the security warning dialog box to confirm the database documents export.

5. Choose a filename and folder and click on the **Save** button to save the exported file.

What just happened?

We learned how to export all documents of the Orders database to a CSV file.

In steps 1 and 2, we opened the Management Studio and displayed the **Documents** screen. Then switched to the **Details** view mode to show the **Export to CSV** button.

 The **Export to CSV** button will only appear if you are in the **Details** view mode.

In steps 3 to 5, we exported all documents of the Orders database to a CSV text file format and saved it on the computer.

RavenDB documents metadata

There are other data stored in RavenDB. These data are called metadata and are usually used to store additional information about entities. The first type of data you might store in addition to the document might be its owner or the one who last modified the document.

Each RavenDB document has metadata properties attached to it, which are being used internally but can be exposed to your code. Here is a list of some properties RavenDB stores as metadata for its documents:

- **Raven-Clr-Type**: This metadata is used to record the CLR type which is the type that defines the class object for the data. It is set and used by the JSON serialization/deserialization process in the Client API.

- **Raven-Entity-Name**: This metadata records the entity name and determines the name of the RavenDB collection this entity belongs to.

- **Non-Authoritive-Information**: This metadata is a boolean value and is used to indicate if the data has been changed. Its value will be set to true if the data received by the client has been modified by an uncommitted transaction.

- **Temp-Index-Score**: When querying RavenDB, this value is used to store a mathematical result value calculated by RavenDB to determine how relevant a given document is to a user's query.

- **Raven-Read-Only**: This metadata indicates that a document should be considered read-only and RavenDB must not allow the document to be modified.

- **Last-Modified**: This metadata value is a time-stamp and indicates the last time the entity has been modified.

- **@etag**: Every document in RavenDB has a corresponding **ETag** (entity tag) stored as a sequential **GUID (Globally Unique Identifier)** which is a unique sequence. This e-tag is updated by RavenDB every time the document is changed.

- **@id**: This metadata value is the entity identifier, as extracted from the entity itself.

More metadata keys are used for storing replication information, concurrency, bookkeeping, and **ACL (Access Control List)** which is used for securing entities. A consumer application may choose to use those properties for indexing or adding key-value pairs of its own, if required. It is also possible to add your own data to the RavenDB metadata.

Time for action – adding a custom metadata key

You will open a document from the Orders database in the Management Studio, add a new metadata key, and set its value.

1. In the Management Studio, open the **Document** screen.

2. Double-click on the document with the ID = `Orders/B765760` (chosen arbitrary) to open it in the edit mode.

3. Click on the **Metadata** tab to display metadata related to the document.

4. Add a new custom metadata key-value, `Developer-Name`, and set its value to `Khaled`.

5. Click on the `Save` button to make the changes permanent.

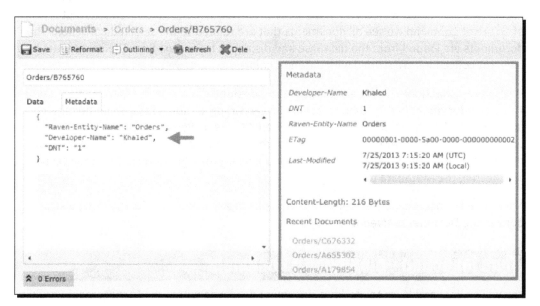

What just happened

You just loaded a document and added a new custom metadata key.

Metadata are key-value pairs and are stored using the JSON format. Each document may have more than one metadata. The metadata document begins with { (left brace) and ends with } (right brace).

Each key is followed by : (colon) and the key-value pairs are separated by , (comma).

So the `Developer-Name` represents the key name and `Khaled` represents the value assigned to that key name.

Note that some of the current metadata are displayed on the right-side of the edit screen.

Management Studio's Collections screen

In RavenDB documents are stored in `Collections`. A `Collection` is a simple logical way to group related documents together and should not be considered as a "database table". Usually, `Collections` are used to group together documents that have a similar structure, but this is not a compulsion. From the database standpoint, a `Collection` is just a group of documents that share the same entity name.

The **Collections** screen shows a list of all available collections in the database and the documents associated with them. In the **Collections** tab screen, we can see different types of `Collections` and we see all documents that are related to the selected collection. The documents are loaded from the database and displayed by newest first. The documents from different collections are striped with different colors.

Within the **Collections** screen, a document can be edited directly in the Management Studio. To get the document in the editing screen, you can simply double-click on that document in the list or click on the pencil icon on it. In the **Edit** screen, you can view and modify the whole document data. Also, you can view and modify some of the metadata related to the document being edited. The metadata are displayed on the right of the edit screen section on selecting the **Metadata** tab.

Navigating the documents section within the **Collections** screen is done the same way as it is done in the **Documents** screen.

Time for action – modifying a document

You will explore and learn to modify a document displayed within the Management Studio's **Collections** screen.

1. In the Management Studio, select the **Collections** tab to display the **Collections** screen.

In the **Collections** screen section, we can see that we have one collection named Orders which contains five documents.

Under the **Documents** screen section, we see all documents related to the Orders collection which is the active selection in the **Collections** section.

2. Choose the **ID Only** view mode to display only the ID of each document in the **Documents** screen section. (The **Switch between views** button is located on the top-right corner of the **Documents** screen section).

There are six different view modes we can switch between: **Details**, **ID Only**, **Small Card**, **Medium Card**, **Large Card**, and **Extra Large Card**.

3. Select the document with the ID = Orders/B768920 from the **Documents** screen section and click on the pencil icon on the bottom-right corner to open it in the edit mode.

```
Documents  >  Orders  >  Orders/B768920

 Save    Reformat    Outlining ▼    Refresh   Delete   s      Document 4 of 5

Orders/B768920

  Data    Metadata
  {
     "CustomerId": "F843098",
     "Item": "Rubber",
     "OrderDate": "5/12/2011",
     "UnitCost": 1.99,
     "Units": 10
  }

 ☆  0 Errors
```

4. Modify the selected document directly by changing the value of the UnitCost field to 1.99 and then click on the **Save** button to save the modified document.

What just happened?

We used the **Collections** screen to load the document with the ID = Orders/B768920 in the edit mode screen and modified its UnitCost field value.

When modifying a document be sure that the JSON structure is still valid otherwise you will get an error which will be displayed in the **Errors** screen section.

Management Studio's Indexes screen

The Management Studio's **Indexes** screen displays a list of all the available indexes in the database.

An `Index` in RavenDB is a map or map and/or reduce/transform query written in LINQ. The **Mapping** expression gathers the set of data to query. The **Reduction** function (which is optional) will "reduce" the map by a set of criteria or transformations. Think of map simply as the selector for all the data that your query cares about. The reduce expression is then performed on the map data to group or summarize it.

In RavenDB, `Indexes` might have one or more map function; the `Reduce` function is not required but an `Index` might have only one `Reduce` function. When using the RavenDB 2.0, only one `Transform` function is permitted and more than one in RavenDB 2.5.

> RavenDB Indexes, `Map/Reduce/Transform`, will be discussed in detail in *Chapter 5, Advanced RavenDB Indexes and Queries*.

The general idea is that we create a LINQ query that returns the data elements that should be indexed. RavenDB then does the rest. When a query is performed often enough and you did not explicitly specify the index, RavenDB creates automatically a temporary index. This can be handy and requires no work on our part. We can also define indexes manually. This is typically what can be done in the editing mode of the **Indexes** tab screen.

> The recommended way to create the RavenDB Indexes is to use the .NET API. Which is discussed in detail in *Chapter 5, Advanced RavenDB Indexes and Queries*.

By default, the Management Studio creates an `Index` named `Raven/DocumentsByEntityName` for its own use which will not be deleted when the **Delete All Indexes** button is used to delete all indexes in a database.

> Raven is self-healing. If the `Raven/DocumentsByEntityName` index is deleted, Raven will recreate it when the server is restarted.

Creating your first index

The **Indexes** screen displays the list of all the available indexes for the current database. Each index is displayed in a rectangle where appears the name of the index and a pencil icon which you can use to edit the related `Map/Reduce` query to that index.

The toolbar for the **Indexes** screen contains a button which allows you to create a **New Index** or a **Dynamic Query**. Also, you can list the **Recent Queries** or **Delete All Indexes**.

You will learn to create an Index directly in the Management Studio using the **New** button and choosing to create a **new Index** in the dropdown list. When you click on the index name in the **Indexes** screen, a query page will load with the ability to query the result of the index.

When creating an index it must have both: a unique `Name` and at least one `Map` function.

Time for action – creating an Index

You will create your first Index using the Management Studio's **Indexes** screen.

1. In the Management Studio, select the **Indexes** tab and click on it to display the **Indexes** screen.

2. Click on the **New Index** button in the toolbar to open the **Edit Index** screen.

3. Name the new index `TotalOrdersPerCustomer`.

4. In the **Maps** section, enter the following code snippet:

```
from order in docs.Orders
select new {CustomerId = order.CustomerId, TotalCost = order.Units
* order.UnitCost}
```

5. Click on the **Save Index** button to save the index which will appear in the available indexes list.

 The Management Studio will not save the index if it detects an error in the LINQ query.

6. Click on the **Indexes** link to return to the **Indexes** screen.

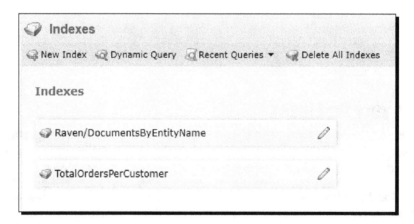

What just happened?

We created our first index named `TotalOrdersPerCustomer` using the Management Studio. This index contains, for now, a single `Map` function which is a LINQ query that returns a two-column dataset, one of which is a calculated column.

The first column named `CustomerId` will contain the `CustomerId` field value. The second column is a calculated field named `TotalCost` and will contain the operation result of the `Units * UnitCost`.

Executing a query against an Index

To query the index, RavenDB executes the `Map/Reduce` implementation in the background and returns the query execution result which is displayed by the Management Studio. The indexing operation is triggered when new indexes are created/updated or when documents are created/updated. Internally, the implementation for this background operation makes heavy use of `Etags` to allow for incremental index building.

Clicking on the index name from the indexes list in the **Indexes** screen will query that index and the query result is displayed on the **Query Index** screen. By default, the **Query Index** screen displays result matching documents, but this can be changed using the **Query Options** button in the **Query Index** screen toolbar.

Time for action – querying an Index

We will learn to query the `TotalOrdersPerCustomer` index we have created in the previous section and visualize the query result.

1. In the Management Studio, select the **Indexes** tab and click on it to display the **Indexes** screen.

2. Click on the **TotalOrdersPerCustomer** index from the indexes list in order to execute the index and display its result in the **Query Index** screen.

3. In the **Query Index** screen, click on the **Query Options** button and check the **Index Entries** to show the index entries instead of the matching documents.

What just happened?

We just queried the `TotalOrdersPerCustomer` index and modified queries display options to customize the result display. We did this in order to show the index entries instead of the matching documents.

At the bottom of the **Results** section, there are displayed some statistics and metadata about the query that just has been executed.

Editing an Index

Editing an index in the Management Studio means to bring up the C# code of the `Map/ Reduce` LINQ functions and edit them. The **Edit Index** screen allows you to add or remove the `Maps` and/or `Reduce` functions, Transformation functions, and fields.

To open an index in the **Edit** mode, you can click on the pencil icon next to the index name in the available indexes list.

Time for action – editing an Index

We want to enhance the `TotalOrdersPerCustomer` index by adding a `Reduce` function. For that, we will open the index in the **Edit Index** screen and modify its related LINQ functions.

1. In the Management Studio, display the **Indexes** screen.

2. Click on the pencil at the right of the name of the `TotalOrdersPerCustomer` index.

3. In the **Edit Index** screen, click on the **Add Reduce** button to add a new `Reduce` function

4. In the **Reduce** section, enter the following code snippet:

```
from result in results
group result by result.CustomerId into g
select new {CustomerId = g.Key, TotalCost = g.Sum(x=>x.TotalCost)}
```

5. Click on the **Save Index** button to save changes.

6. Click on the **Indexes** links to show the `Indexes` list.

7. Click on the `TotalOrdersPerCustomer` index to query it and display results in the **Query Index** Screen.

What just happened?

We enhanced the `TotalOrdersPerCustomer` index and added a `Reduce` function.

This `Reduce` LINQ function aggregates the result of the `Map` function (written in the previous section) and returns a two-column dataset: `CustomerId` and `TotalCost` for each `CustomerId`.

The `Map` function result is grouped on the `CustomerId` key and the `TotalCost` field is aggregated in each group.

The Query Index screen

The Management Studio's **Query Index** screen allows you to query an index result dynamically. For that, you can use the query designer area to write a query expression.

The **Query Index** screen has a toolbar with an **Execute** button which lets you run the query and will show the results. We have the **Add Sort By** button which you can use to display the query result in a specific order. Also, you can display the index statistics by clicking on the **Index Statistics** button or by deleting all the documents resulting from the query.

To write a query expression, you will use the `Lucene` syntax which is a custom query syntax for querying the indexes. In the query area, you can use *Ctrl + Space* for hints on the field names.

Technically, Raven makes use of the `Lucene.NET` library, which was ported from the Java based `Lucene` library. Lucene is a fully-featured text search engine library written entirely in Java.

To get more details about `Lucene.NET`, you may browse this link: `http://lucenenet.apache.org/`.

Time for action – querying an Index

We will query the `TotalOrdersPerCustomer` index and will apply a query expression to filter the index result using the `Lucene` syntax query.

1. In the Management Studio, select the **Indexes** tab to display the **Indexes** screen.

2. Click on the `TotalOrdersPerCustomer` index to query it and display results in the **Query Index** Screen.

3. In the **Query** area, enter the following code snippet:

   ```
   CustomerId: A54309
   ```

In the **Query** area, press *Ctrl + Space* to show the index fields list and select the `CustomerId` field.

4. Click on the **Execute** button to show the results of the query.

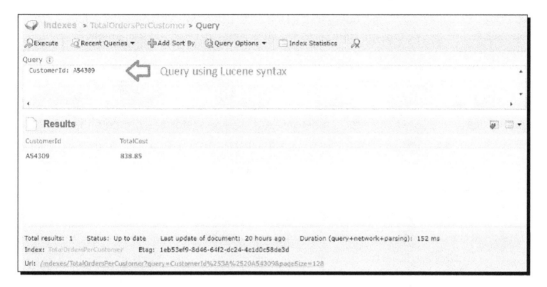

What just happened?

We queried the `TotalOrdersPerCustomer` index and filtered the query result.

Once the result was displayed, we wrote a `Lucene` query expression to filter that result and display all documents which matched the `CustomerID = A54309`.

The query engine will search index result documents collection in the `CustomerId` field matching the value we have specified. Think of it as the "where" clause parameter.

Creating a Dynamic Query

Dynamic queries refer to queries that don't specify which index they use. The **Dynamic Query** and **Query Index** screens have similarities and layouts the same. The only difference between the two screens is that instead of saying what index to use, you say what collection to query.

You can use the generic query designer to write a dynamic query expression using the `Lucene` syntax. In the **Dynamic Query** screen, you can choose to query all documents or only a specific collection.

When creating a new dynamic query, RavenDB will create a temporary index and give it a name that starts with `Temp/`. When a temporary index gets a significant usage, RavenDB may decide to promote it permanently. When this happens the name of the index will change from `Temp/` to `Auto/`. These indexes are really easy to spot in the Management Studio's **Indexes** screen. Also, you can promote a temporary index manually to permanent.

You can create a new dynamic query by clicking on the **Dynamic Query** button on the **Indexes** screen or by using the **New Dynamic Query** button on the Management Studio's main interface.

Time for action – creating a Dynamic Query

You will learn to create a dynamic query using the `Lucene` syntax and promote the related temporary index to permanent.

1. In the Management Studio, select the **Indexes** tab to display the **Indexes** screen.

2. Click on the **Dynamic Query** button to display the **Query Index** screen.

3. Click on the **Dynamic/** list and select the `Orders` collection.

4. In the **Query** area, enter the following code snippet:

   ```
   UnitCost: [1 TO 20]
   ```

> In the **Query** area, press *Ctrl + Space* to show the index fields list and select the `UnitCost` field.
>
> To do search on the data, instead of a lexical search you can use `Unitcost: [Dx1 TO Dx20]`.

5. Click on the **Execute** button to show the results of the query.

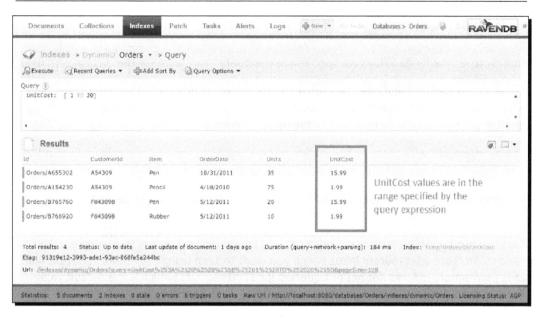

6. Click on the **Indexes** link to show the **Indexes** screen.

7. Right-click on the `Auto/Orders/ByUnitCost` index to show the contextual menu and click on the **Promote to auto index** button.

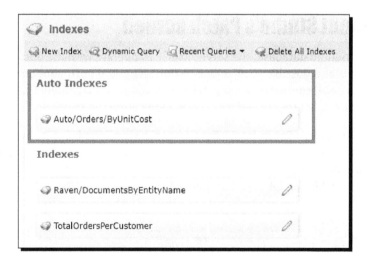

What just happened?

We created a dynamic query which will retrieve all the documents in the `Orders` collection that matches the range values we specified in the query expression for the `UnitsCost` field.

In this `Lucene` expression, we use a range query which allows us to match documents whose field(s) values are between the lower and upper bounds specified by the range query. Range queries can be inclusive or exclusive of the upper and lower bounds.

The query engine will search all the documents belonging to the `Orders` collection that the `UnitCost` field value will match with the value range we have specified `1 TO 20`.

By executing the dynamic query, RavenDB will create a temporary index named `Temp/Orders/ByUnitCost` which will be found in the available indexes list.

Then we promoted the temporary index created by the dynamic query to permanent. You need to promote a temporary index only if you want to keep using that index. RavenDB will purge temporary indexes if it has not queried for 1200 seconds (which is the default value fixed by the `Raven/TempIndexCleanupThreshold` configuration key).

Managing temporary indexes is discussed in detail in *Chapter 4, RavenDB Indexes and Queries*.

Management Studio's Patch screen

In a document oriented database, the server itself can operate with the document and not just the client. It is also possible to directly edit the data in the document on the server-side. This action in RavenDB context is called **patching**. With the Management Studio, you can choose to patch a Document, a Collection, or an Index using the JavaScript.

The Management Studio's **Patch** screen has two main areas. The first area is reserved to the **Patch Script** and **Parameters** and the second area is used to visualizing the state of a document before patching and how it will looks like after patching. This is useful because you can validate the patching script before applying it.

RavenDB's patching will be discussed with more detail in *Chapter 6, Advanced RavenDB Documents Capabilities*.

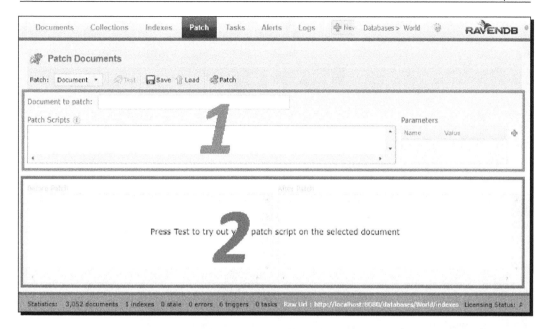

Time for action – patching a document

You will learn how to patch the document with the ID `Orders/A655302` using a patching script that combines the JavaScript and parameters.

1. In the Management Studio, select the `Orders` database to be the current database and click on the **Patch** tab to show the **Patch** screen.

2. In the **Patch type** list, select the **Document** type.

3. In the **Document to patch** textbox, enter `Orders/A655302`, which is the ID of the document we want to patch, and press *Enter*.

4. Click on the **Add new Parameter** button (the green plus sign to the right of the **Parameters** section) to add a new parameter.

5. Enter `ItemName` for the **Name** and `Ink Pen` for the **Value**.

6. In the **Patch Scripts** zone, enter the following JavaScript code snippet:

   ```
   this.UnitCost = this.UnitCost * 1.15
   this.Item = ItemName
   ```

7. Click on the **Test** button to test the patch script on the selected document.

8. Observe the changes in the **After Patch** section and verify that the document has new fields value.

9. Click on the **Patch** button to execute the patch scripts to make the changes permanent.

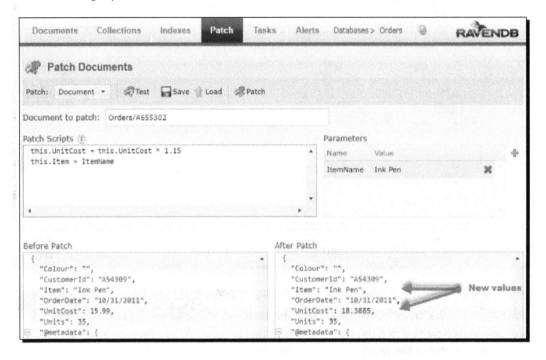

What just happened?

We learned how to patch a document using the Management Studio.

We patched the document with the ID= Orders/A655302 to increase the UnitCost field value by 15 percent and change the Item field value from Pen to Ink Pen.

In steps 1 to 3, we opened the Management Studio and displayed the **Patch** screen. Then we entered the ID of the document that we want to patch.

In steps 4 to 6, we added a new parameter with name= ItemName and value=Ink Pen and entered the patching script.

In this JavaScript code snippet, in the first line of code, the UnitCost property value is increased by 15 percent. In the second line, the value of the parameter named ItemName will be assigned to the Item property.

In steps 7 and 8, we tested the patching script before applying it and visualized the result. Finally, in step 9, we executed the patch script to make the changes permanent.

Have a go hero – patching the Orders collection

In the previous section, you learned to patch a single document. Suppose in a migration scenario when significant structural changes are required by the consuming application, you need to patch more than one document. Of course, you will not process one document at a time. Try to patch the Orders collection and increase all Units values by 10 percent.

Management Studio's Tasks screen

The Management Studio's **Tasks** screen is designed to allow you to perform common administrative tasks for RavenDB databases. Within the Management Studio's **Tasks** screen, you can basically import and export databases between the RavenDB servers. Each database may be exported as a dump file that has a .ravendump extension. On the other hand, you can also use this dump file to import a database into RavenDB.

Also, within the **Tasks** screen, you can create a backup of your database and enable or disable background indexing tasks. This is used basically by developers for debugging purpose and requires database administrator privileges.

You may need to import your data into RavenDB using a CSV file, this task is performed by the **CSV Import** feature. Note that if the imported file contains Unicode characters, it should be encoded using UTF-8.

Also, within the **Tasks** screen, you can insert sample data into your database and populate it for learning or testing purposes (a feature that we used in the previous chapter in order to populate our first RavenDB database).

 The RavenDB's Backup/Restore/Import/Export tasks will be discussed with more detail in *Chapter 7, RavenDB Administration*.

Time for action – importing external data using a CSV file

You will create a new database called `World` and populate it with external data which you will import using a CSV text file.

1. In the Management Studio, click on the **Databases** link to show the **Database** screen.

2. Click on the **New Database** button to open the **Create New Database** wizard form, then create a new database named `World`.

3. Click on the **Tasks** tab to show the **Tasks** screen.

4. Click on the **CSV Import** toolbar button, this will show the **CSV Import** screen which contains a **CSV Import** button.

5. Click on the **CSV Import** button and select the `Cities.csv` file (which is a part of the book companion package files).

6. Click on the **Documents** tab or the **Collections** tab to verify that the database has been populated with new 3051 documents.

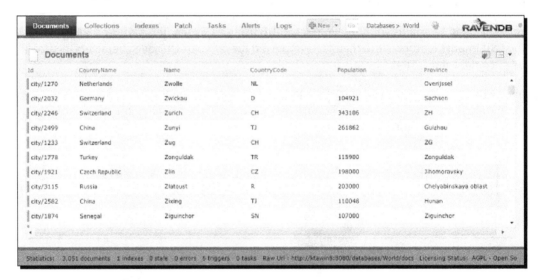

What just happened?

We just created a new database named `World`. Then using the **Import CSV** feature, we imported the `Cities.csv` file and populated the database we just created.

 The `World` database will be used and enhanced throughout the book's chapters.

Have a go hero – exporting documents from different views

Exporting the RavenDB documents to a CSV file is very easy. Depending on the screen you are viewing, you will export different results. Try to export all the documents from each view to a CSV file, where the **Export To CSV** feature is available (**Documents**, **Collections**, and **Index Query Results**).

Management Studio's Alerts screen

The Management Studio's **Alerts** screen is helpful to see the alerts sent from the RavenDB server. At the time of writing this book, in the `RavenDB v2.0.0 Build 2372` only errors in periodic backups will send alerts. If you need to track a specific alert sent by the RavenDB server, you may choose it in the table and mark it as `Observed` and make it `Unobserved` when there is no more need to track it.

You may use the **Alerts** screen's toolbar buttons to perform these actions:

◆ **Hide/Show Observed**: This button will toggle on mouse click between **Show Observed** and **Hide Observed**, this will determine whether the observed alerts will be shown or not.

◆ **Mark as Observed**: This button will mark all the current alerts as `Observed`.

◆ **Mark as Unobserved**: This button will mark all the current alerts as `Unobserved`.

◆ **Delete All Observed**: This button will remove all the observed items from the list.

◆ **Refresh from server**: This button will refresh the alerts table from database. All the changes in the alerts list have to be saved to the server before using this action otherwise these changes will be lost.

◆ **Save Changes**: This button will update the list in the server according to the changes you have made.

Management Studio's Logs screen

RavenDB activity logs can be viewed using the Management Studio's **Logs** screen. The logs journal is limited to the last 500 entries. You can use the filter button on the top-right corner of the Management Studio's user interface and choose to display all tracked events or just the error events entries. When selecting an item in the event logs table, you can see the details of that item in the bottom below the event logs table.

Time for action – exploring the Logs screen

You will learn to explore the Management Studio's **Logs** screen.

1. In the Management Studio, click on the **Logs** tab to show the **Logs** screen.

2. Click on the **All Logs** button to display all the tracked events or click on the **Errors Only** button to show only the error events.

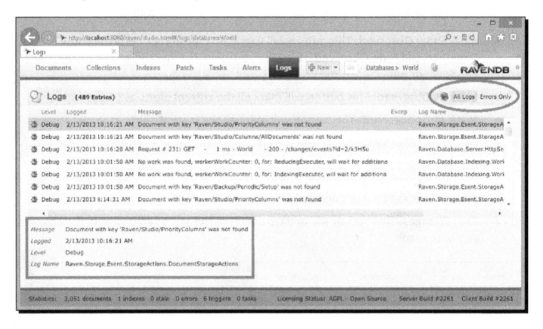

3. Click on any entry in the logs table to view its details in the bottom section.

What just happened?

In steps 1 and 2, we opened the Management Studio and displayed the **Logs** screen.

In step 3, we select a log entry in the logs table and display its details.

Viewing the database settings

The Management Studio provides a complete set of administrative tools that let users fully administer their system and manage all the users and objects in a database. Each RavenDB database has a `Document` database that represents the database. In the **Database Settings** page, you can edit the common databases settings and other options are dependent on the bundles selected for this database.

Time for action – viewing the database's active bundles

We will take a look at the `World` database's **Settings** page.

1. In the Management Studio, click on the **Databases** link to display the **Databases** screen.

2. Select the `World` database and right-click on it to show the contextual menu, then choose **Edit Settings**.

[The **Edit Database Settings** button (the cogwheel button) opens the **Settings** page for the current database.]

| Documents | Collections | Indexes | Patch | Tasks | Alerts | Logs | 🕂 New ▾ |

🗄 Databases ＞ World ＞ Settings

💾 Save Changes

| Database Settings | ✎ Edit |

Periodic Backup

```
{
    "Id": "World",
    "Settings": {
        "Raven/DataDir": "~\\Databases\\World",
        "Raven/ActiveBundles": "PeriodicBackup"
    },
    "SecuredSettings": {},
    "Disabled": false
}
```

What just happened?

We just opened the **Settings** screen for the `World` database and viewed its content.

You can see the different setting parameters as the database folder and active bundles for the database.

When creating a new database, the `PeriodicBackup` bundle is activated by default for the new database. The `Raven/ActiveBundles` metadata key indicates the list of all the activated bundles when the database is created. In this case we did not activate any other bundles.

The System database settings

The settings for the `System` database are different from the other databases. It is possible to edit this document but this is not recommended because this can damage the database. If you need to modify the `System` database settings, you can use the integrated editor which allows you to define the user's access level to a particular database or define the API keys when using RavenDB with the `OAuth` protocol to authorize user and set its privileged access to the database.

Time for action – opening the System database's Settings page

You will open the RavenDB's `System` database in the edit mode.

1. In the Management Studio, click on the **Databases** link to display the **Databases** screen.

2. Click on the **System Databases** button to show the `System` database documents.

3. Click on the **OK** button of the warning window message to confirm the action.

4. Click on the **Edit Database Settings** button (the cogwheel button) to show the **System Database Settings** screen.

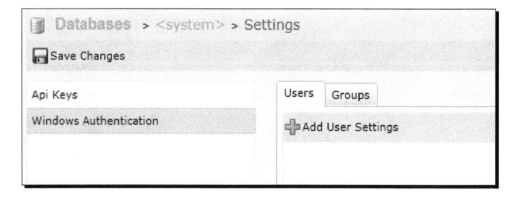

What just happened?

We just opened the **Databases** screen to show the `System` database, then show the **System Database Settings** screen.

The API keys are used when trying to authorize user and has set its privileged access to the database using the `OAuth` protocol, which is an open protocol to allow secure authorization in a simple and standard method from web, mobile, and desktop applications.

Windows Authentication is the process of determining the identity of a user based on the user's credentials. The user's credentials are usually in the form of user ID and password, which is checked against any credentials' store such as database. If the credentials provided by the user are valid then the user is considered an authenticated user. Based on the Windows Authentication, you can set user access for groups and users.

Bundles

RavenDB database supports extensibility and new features can be implemented by a user to meet their needs, if it has not been already implemented by RavenDB. This is where **Bundles** come in. Installing a Bundle is very easy and it is done by dropping the Bundle's files into the `\Plugins` directory of the RavenDB installation, which is the default path. The path to the `Plugins` folder is configurable and can be changed to another location by changing the `Raven/PluginsDirectory` configuration parameter.

You may choose to activate one or more Bundle a when you create a database. You will have to then set up most of the Bundles within the database creation process and they cannot be removed or added afterwards. So, Bundle's strategy has to be considered carefully and adding/removing Bundles is something that can safely happen only when the database is created and does not contain any documents. Usually, Bundles are added within the database creation process and then you configure their behavior by turning them on or off at runtime.

The `Periodic Backup` Bundle is added by default to each database you will create and it needs to be enabled from the **Edit Database Settings** screen, if you want to use this feature.

The next screenshot illustrates the available Bundles within the **Create a New Database** wizard form.

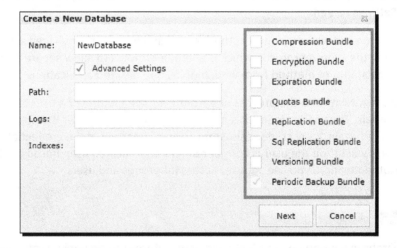

Time for action – enabling the Periodic Backup feature

You will learn to enable or disable the `Periodic Backup` Bundle which is added by default to each new database.

1. In the Management Studio, click on the **Databases** link to display the **Databases** screen.

2. Select the `World` database and right-click on it to show the contextual menu, then choose **Edit Settings**.

3. Select `Periodic Backup` from the list on the left-side to show its settings page and then click on **Activate Periodic Backup** to activate the Bundle.

4. Enter `C:\WorldBackup` as the path where database backups will be stored.

5. Enter 60 minutes for the backup interval.

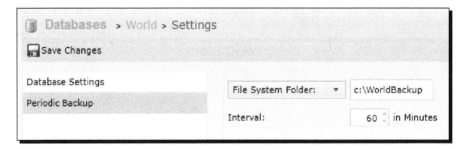

6. Click on the **Save Changes** button to save the new parameters.

What just happened?

We learned how to activate the `Periodic Backups` Bundle for the `World` database.

In steps 1 to 4, we activated the `Periodic Backups` Bundle for the `World` database and in steps 5 and 6, we entered the backup path `C:\WorldBackup` with the backup interval of `60` minutes. RavenDB will use this information to make a backup every `60` minutes and will store this backup in the `C:\WorldBackup` folder.

Doing more with the Management Studio

The RavenDB Management Studio is a great tool with almost everything you need right at your fingertips. Beyond displaying documents, collections, and indexes, it allows you to manage them. You can delete a document, a collection, an index, or copy data to and from the clipboard. Also, you can customize your views by choosing the columns you want to display.

Choosing the columns

Columns are a part of the Management Studio's **Documents** screen which is used to display database documents in the **Details** view mode. You may be familiar with this view type in your **Documents** screen. The Management Studio allows you to add or remove columns to further customize your views (columns are also referred to as fields).

Columns can be bound to properties just like you would in code or a particular item in an array (using an index and square brackets). Also, you can bind column to a document metadata or bind directly to the JSON Document object using an XAML binding syntax.

Time for action – customizing the columns

You will customize the **Documents** screen and choose columns to display.

1. In the Management Studio's **Databases** screen, select the `Sales` database (created in *Chapter 1*, *Getting Started with RavenDB*) and activate it as the current database.

2. Click on the **Documents** tab to display the **Documents** screen.

3. Use the **Switch between views** button to select the **Details** view mode.

4. Right-click on any column header to display the contextual menu and click on **Choose Columns**.

5. In the **Choose Columns** window, select **Custom**.

6. Use **Move Selected Column** (up or down) to move the `AlbumArtUrl` column to be the latest column.

7. Double-click on the **[New-Column]** to add a new column.

8. Enter `Artist.Name` in the **Binding** column and `Artist Name` in the **Title** column.

> Note that while typing, suggestions are displayed.

9. Use **Move Selected Column** to move up the `Artist Name` column to be the third column.

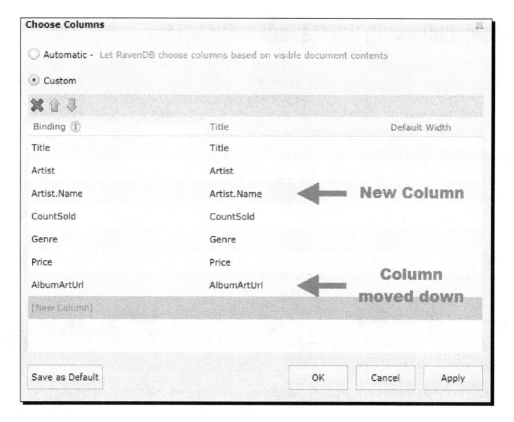

10. Click on the **OK** button to apply changes and return to the **Documents** screen.

What just happened?

We just customized the **Documents Details** view to change the column order and add the `Artist Name` column to the view.

In steps 1 to 5, we selected in the Management Studio the `Sales` database and displayed the **Choose Column** window.

In step 6, we changed the order of display of the `AlbumArtUrl` column.

In steps 7 to 10, we added the `Artist Name` column and changed its order of display to be the third one.

Copying the document to clipboard

The Management Studio supports copying to clipboard feature. This feature is useful especially when someone needs to copy a data document or several data documents from the current database to another application. You can choose to copy the whole document data or only the document ID to the clipboard for the selected item(s) in the documents list.

Time for action – copying the data document to the clipboard

We will take a look at how to utilize the **Copy Document(s) to Clipboard** feature of the Management Studio.

1. In the Management Studio, click on the **Databases** link to display the **Databases** screen.

2. Select the `Sales` database and then click on the **Documents** tab to display the **Documents** screen. (You can also select the **Collections** tab and display the **Collections** screen.)

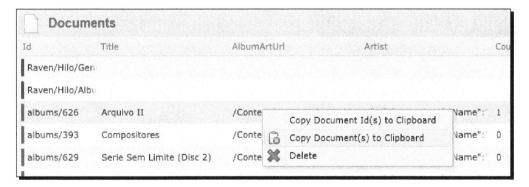

3. Select a document in the list and right-click on it to show the contextual menu and select **Copy Document(s) to Clipboard**. You may need to select multiple documents from the documents list; to do so you can group documents using the *Shift* or the *Ctrl* key.

4. Open the Notepad application (or your favorite text editor).

5. Press *Ctrl* + *V* to paste the document data in the Notepad and view it.

What just happened?

In steps 1 to 5, we copy the data of one document from the Sales database using copy to clipboard Management Studio's feature and paste it in the Notepad application.

Deleting the Documents, Collections, Indexes, or Databases

This topic describes how to delete different objects from RavenDB using the Management Studio. In order to delete any object, you need to select it and then right-click on it and select **Delete**, you can also press the *Delete* key or use the **Delete** toolbar key from the **Documents** screen to delete a document when it is loaded in the editing screen.

You can delete a bulk of documents based on their collection association. Since a collection is just a logical unit in RavenDB, there is no actual meaning in deleting a collection. By deleting a collection, you are telling RavenDB to delete all the documents sharing the same entity name which is equal to the name of the collection you are asking to delete.

You can use the **Delete all Indexes** button in the **Indexes** screen of the Management Studio to delete all the indexes of a given database. When used, all the indexes will be deleted, except from Raven/DocumentsByEntityName which is the index used by the Management Studio.

Time for action – deleting a database using the Management Studio

You will learn how to delete a database from RavenDB using the **Delete** action from the contextual menu in the **Databases** screen.

1. In the Management Studio, click on the **Databases** link to display the **Databases** screen.

2. Select the `Sales` database and right-click on it to display the contextual menu and click on **Delete**.

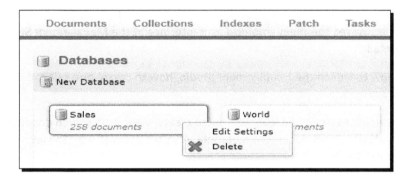

3. Check the option case **Physically delete all database data** to delete all the database data and its folders.

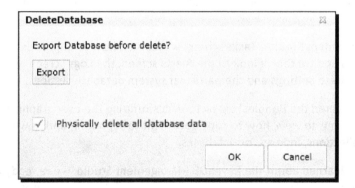

 By clicking on the **Export** button, you can export the database documents before deleting it.

What just happened?

In steps 1 and 2, we selected in the Management Studio the `Sales` database in order to delete it.

In step 3, we deleted the database and all its related files and folders.

By checking the option **Physically delete all database data**, RavenDB will delete all database data and folders containing the database and all its related information, such as logs and indexes, from your computer. Otherwise, the files will remain but you will not be able to access them from the server.

Summary

We learned a lot in this chapter about the RavenDB's Management Studio and its features.

Specifically, we covered the main graphical user interface of the Management Studio and each tab in detail.

We learned how to launch the Management Studio, how to create and select databases from the **Databases** screen.

From the **Documents** screen, we learned how to create, view, edit, search documents, and took a look at the RavenDB document metadata. Also, we covered how to view collections within the **Collections** screen.

We covered the Management Studio's **Indexes** screen and how to create, execute, view, and edit Indexes. Also, we covered the **Query Index** screen and how to create **Dynamic Queries**.

We learned how to patch documents or collections using the Management Studio's **Patch** screen.

From the Management Studio's **Tasks** screen, we learned how to import external data using the CSV text files and we took a look to the **Alerts** screen, the **Logs** screen, viewing and editing the **Database Settings** and the particular system database settings.

Also, we have covered the Bundles' big picture, customizing the user graphical interface by choosing columns to view, how to copy document to clipboard, and how to delete documents, collections, indexes, or databases.

Now that we've learned about the RavenDB Management Studio, we're ready to connect to RavenDB using the .NET framework—which is the topic of the next chapter.

3

RavenDB.NET Client API

RavenDB is written in C# that runs on the Microsoft .NET Framework. The .NET Client API exposes all aspects of the RavenDB server to your application in a seamless manner and can be accessed from any .NET language.

In this chapter, you will learn step-by-step how to connect to RavenDB to interact with the server by writing some C# code and perform various basic operations such as loading, saving, inserting, updating, and deleting documents from the RavenDB server.

In this chapter, we will learn how to use the RavenDB Client API for:

- ◆ Setting up your development environment
- ◆ Connecting to RavenDB
- ◆ Loading a document
- ◆ Creating a document
- ◆ Inserting a new document
- ◆ Updating a document
- ◆ Deleting a document
- ◆ Querying documents in a collection

The RavenDB .NET Client API

RavenDB provides a set of .NET client libraries for interacting with it, which can be accessed from any .NET-based programming languages. By using these libraries, you can manage RavenDB, construct requests, send them to the server, and receive responses.

The .NET Client API exposes all aspects of the RavenDB and allows developers to easily integrate RavenDB services into their own applications.

The .NET Client API is involved with loading and saving the data, and it is responsible for integrating with the .NET `System.Transactions` namespace. With `System.Transactions`, there is already a general way to work transactionally across different resources. Also the .NET Client API is responsible for batching requests to the server, caching, and more.

The .NET Client API is easy to use and uses several conventions to control how it works. These conventions can be modified by the user to meet its application needs.

 It is not recommended to use `System.Transactions`. In fact, it is recommended to avoid it. `System.Transactions` is supported in RavenDB mostly to allow integration while using collaboration tools between services for example, `NServiceBus`.

Setting up your development environment

Before you can start developing an application for RavenDB, you must first set up your development environment. This setup involves installing the following software packages on your development computer:

- Visual Studio 2012 (required)
- RavenDB Client (required)
- NuGet Package Manager (optional)

You may download and install the latest Visual Studio version from the Microsoft website: `http://msdn.microsoft.com/En-us/library/vstudio/e2h7fzkw.aspx`

In order to use RavenDB in your own .NET application, you have to add a reference to the `Raven.Client.Lightweight.dll` and the `Raven.Abstractions.dll` files, (which you can find in the `~\Client` folder of the distribution package) into your Visual Studio project.

The easiest way to add a reference to these DLLs is by using the NuGet Package Manager, which you may use to add the `RavenDB.Client` package.

> NuGet Package Manager is a Visual Studio extension that makes it easy to add, remove, and update libraries and tools in Visual Studio projects that use the .NET framework.
>
> You can find more information on the `NuGet Package Manager` extension by visiting the official website at `http://nuget.org/`.

Time for action – installing NuGet Package Manager

The `NuGet Package Manager` extension is the easiest way to add the RavenDB Client library to a Visual Studio project. If you do not have NuGet Package Manager already installed, you can install it as follows:

1. Start Visual Studio.
2. From the **TOOLS** menu, click on **Extensions and Updates....**
3. In the **Extensions and Updates...** dialog, click on **Online**.
4. If you don't see **NuGet Package Manager**, type `nuget package manager` in the search box.
5. Select the **NuGet Package Manager** extension and click on **Download**.
6. After the download completes, you will be prompted to install the package.
7. After the installation completes, you might be prompted to restart Visual Studio.

What just happened?

We installed the `NuGet Package Manager` extension to Visual Studio, which you will use to add RavenDB Client to your Visual Studio project.

Creating a simple application

Let's write a simple application to learn how to interact with RavenDB.

Time for action – adding RavenDB Client to a Visual Studio project

Let's go ahead and create a new Visual Studio project. You will add the RavenDB Client using the Nuget Package Manager extension to this project to be able to connect to RavenDB and begin using it:

1. Start Visual Studio and click on **New Project** from the **Start** page or from the **File** menu, navigate to **New** and then **Project**.

2. In the **Templates** pane, click on **Installed** and then click on **Templates** and expand the **Visual C#** node. Under **Visual C#**, click on **Windows**. In the list of project templates, select **Console Application**. Name the project as RavenDB_Ch03 and click on **OK**.

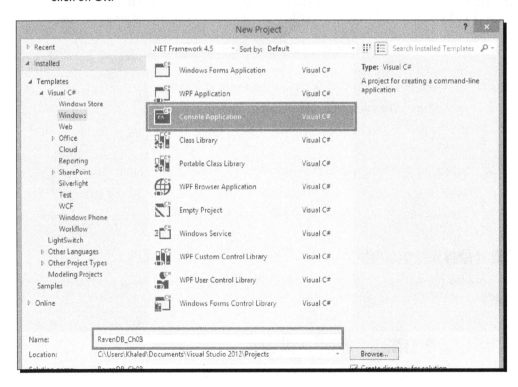

3. From the **TOOLS** menu, click on **Library Package Manager**.

If you do not see this menu item, make sure that the `NuGet  Package Manager` extension has been installed correctly.

4. Click on **Manage NuGet Packages for Solution....**

5. In the **Manage NugGet Packages** dialog, select **Online**.

6. In the search box, type `ravendb`.

7. Select the package named **RavenDB Client**.

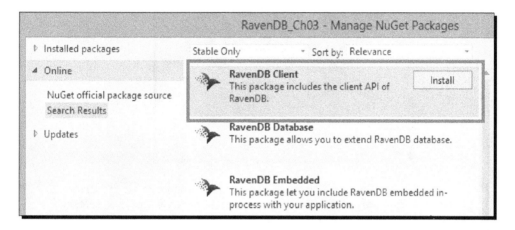

8. Click on **Install** and accept the license.

9. After the package installs, click on **Close** to close the dialog box.

What just happened?

We created the `RavenDB_Ch03` Visual Studio project and added the RavenDB Client to get connected to the RavenDB server.

Once the RavenDB Client is installed, by expanding the **References** node of your project in Visual Studio, you can see the RavenDB DLLs (**Raven.Abstractions, Raven.Client.Lightweight**) added automatically to your project by the Nuget Package Manager extension.

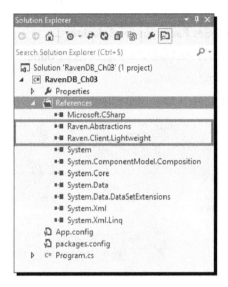

You should ensure that the RavenDB Client version matches the server version you are running. This can lead to some really frustrating runtime errors when the versions don't match.

You can also install RavenDB Client using the Package Manager console (**Visual Studio | Tools | Library Package Manager | Package Manager Console**). To install the latest RavenDB Client, run the following command in the Package Manager console: Install-Package RavenDB.Client or Install-Package RavenDB.Client-Version {version number} to add a specific version.

Connecting to RavenDB

To begin using RavenDB we need to get a new instance of the DocumentStore object, which points to the server and acts as the main communication channel manager.

Once a new instance of DocumentStore has been created, the next step is to create a new session against that Document Store. The session object is responsible for implementing the Unit of Work pattern. A Unit of Work keeps track of everything you do during a business transaction that can affect the database. When you're done, it figures out everything that needs to be done to alter the database as a result of your work.

The `session` object is used to interact with RavenDB and provides a fully transactional way of performing database operations, and allows the consumer to store data into the database, and load it back when necessary using queries or by document ID.

In order to perform an action against the RavenDB store, we need to ensure that we have an active and valid RavenDB session before starting the action, and dispose it off once it ends.

Basically, before disposing of the session, we will call the `SaveChanges()` method on the `session` object to ensure that all changes will be persisted.

To create a new RavenDB session, we will call the `OpenSession()` method on the `DocumentStore` object, which will return a new instance of the `IDocumentSession` object.

Time for action – connecting to RavenDB

Your Visual Studio project now has a reference to all needed RavenDB Client DLLs and is ready to get connected to the RavenDB server. You will add a new class and necessary code to create a communication channel with the RavenDB server:

1. Open the **RavenDB_Ch03** project.

2. Modify the `Main()` method (in `Program.cs` class) to look like the following code snippet:

```
12   static void Main(string[] args)
13   {
14       using (var documentStore =
15               new DocumentStore
16                   {
17                       Url = "http://localhost:8080",
18                       DefaultDatabase = "Orders"
19                   }.Initialize())
20       {
21           //
22           // Examples code goes here
23           //
24       }
25   }
```

3. Press *Ctrl + Shift + S* to save all files in the solution.

What just happened?

We just added the DocumentStore object initialization code to the Main() method of the RavenDB_Ch03 project.

Within the Main() method, you create a new instance of the DocumentStore object, which is stored in the DocumentStore variable. The DocumentStore object basically acts as the connection manager and must be created only once per application.

> It is important to point out that this is a heavyweight and thread safe object. Note that, when you create many of these your application will run slow and will have a larger memory footprint.

To create an instance of the DocumentStore object, you need to specify the URL that points to the RavenDB server. The URL has to include the TCP port number (8080 is the default port number) on which RavenDB server is listening (line **17** in the previous code snippet).

In order to point to the Orders database, you set the value of DefaultDatabase to Orders, which is the name of our database (line **18**).

To get the new instance of the IDocumentStore object, you have to call the Initialize() method on the DocumentStore object. With this instance, you can establish the connection to the RavenDB server (line 19).

The whole DocumentStore initialization code is surrounded by a using statement. This is used to specify when resources should be released. Basically, the using statement calls the Dispose() method of each object for which the resources should be released.

Interacting with RavenDB using the .NET Client API

RavenDB stores documents in JSON format. It converts the .NET objects into their JSON equivalent when storing documents, and back again by mapping the .NET object property names to the JSON property names and copies the values when loading documents. This process that makes writing and reading data structures to and from a document file extremely easy is called Serialization and Deserialization.

Interacting with RavenDB is very easy. You might create a new DocumentStore object and then open a session, do some operations, and finally apply the changes to the RavenDB server.

The session object will manage all changes internally, but changes will be committed to the underlying document database only when the SaveChanges() method is called. This is important to note because all changes to the document will be discarded if this method is not invoked.

RavenDB is safe by default. This unique feature means that the database is configured to stop users querying for large amount of data. It is never a good idea to have a query that returns thousands of records, which is inefficient and may take a long time to process.

By default, RavenDB limits the number of documents on the client side to `128` (this is a configurable option) if you don't make use of the `Take()` method on the `Query` object.

Basically, if you need to get data beyond the 128 documents limit, you need to page your query results (by using `Take()` and `Skip()` methods). RavenDB also has a very useful option to stop you from creating the dreaded SELECT N+1 scenario—this feature stops after 30 requests are sent to the server per session, (which also is a configurable option).

> The recommended practice is to keep the ratio of `SaveChanges()` calls to session instance at 1:1. Reaching the limit of 30 remote calls while maintaining the 1:1 ratio is typically a symptom of a significant N+1 problem.

To retrieve or store documents, you might create a class type to hold your data document and use the `session` instance to save or load that document, which will be automatically serialized to `JSON`.

Loading a document

To load a single document from a RavenDB database, you need to invoke the `Load()` method on the `Session` object you got from the `DocumentStore` instance. Then you need to specify the type of the document you will load from the RavenDB database.

Time for action – loading a document

You will create the `Order` class to hold the order data information and will add the `LoadOrder()` method, which you will call to load an `Order` document from the RavenDB server:

1. Open the **RavenDB_Ch03** project, add a new class and name it `Order`.

2. Add the following code snippet to the Order class:

```
 9 ⊟    class Order
10      {
11          public string Id {get; set;}
12          public string CustomerId {get; set;}
13          public string Item {get; set;}
14          public string OrderDate {get; set;}
15          public double UnitCost {get; set;}
16          public int Units { get; set; }
17      }
```

3. Add the DisplayOrder() method to the Program class using the following code snippet:

```
27 ⊟  private static void DisplayOrder(Order order)
28  {
29      Console.WriteLine(
30      "Id: {0}\tCustomerId: {1}\tItem: {2}\tOrderDate: {3}\tUnitCost: {4}\tUnits: {5}",
31          order.Id,
32          order.CustomerId,
33          order.Item,
34          order.OrderDate,
35          order.UnitCost,
36          order.Units);
37      Console.ReadLine();
38  }
```

4. Add the Load<Order>() method to the Program class using the following code snippet:

```
20  {
21      //
22      // Examples code goes here
23      //
24
25      // Load Example
26      using (var session = documentStore.OpenSession())
27      {
28          var order = session.Load<Order>("Orders/A179854");
29          DisplayOrder(order);
30      }
31  }
```

5. Save all the files and press *F6* to build the solution.

6. Switch to Windows Explorer and go to the RavenDB installation folder and launch RavenDB server using the Start.cmd command file.

7. Return to Visual Studio, once the RavenDB server is running, press *F5* to run RavenDB_Ch03 to see the document information in the output console window.

What just happened?

You just wrote the necessary code to load your first document from the RavenDB server. Let's take a look at the code you added to the RavenDB_Ch03 project.

You added the Order class to the project. This class will hold the data information for the Order document you will load from the server. It contains six fields (lines **11** to **16** in the previous code snippet) that will be populated with values from the JSON Order document stored on the server.

> By adding a field named Id, RavenDB will automatically populate this field with the document ID when the document is retrieved from the server.

You added the DisplayOrder() method to the Program class. This method is responsible for displaying the Order field's values to the output window.

You also added the Load<Order>() method (lines **26** to **30**) to the Program class. This method is surrounded by a using statement to ensure that the resources will be disposed at the end of execution of this method.

To open a RavenDB session you call the OpenSession() method on the IDocumentStore object. This session is handled by the session variable (line **26**).

The Load() method is a generic method. It will load a specific entity with a specific ID, which you need to provide when calling the method. So in the calling code to the Load() method (line **28**), you provide the Order entity and the document ID that we want to retrieve from the server which is Orders/A179854.

Once the Order document with the Id field as Orders/A179854 is retrieved from the server, you send it to the DisplayOrder() method to be displayed (line **29**).

Finally, you build and run the RavenDB_Ch03 project.

Have a go hero – loading multiple documents

You know now how to load any single document from the RavenDB server using the Load() method. What if you have more than one document to load? You can use the Load() method to load more than one document in a single call. It seems easy to do. Well give it a go!

Arrays are very useful!

Inserting a new Document

To insert a new document into a RavenDB database, you need to create a new instance of the object that will hold your data information and then invoke the `Store()` method on the `session` object, which you got from the `DocumentStore` object.

Time for action – inserting a new document

You will add necessary code to the `Main()` method in the `Program` class to create a new `Order` object and insert it into the `Orders` database:

1. Add the following code snippet to the `Main()` method:

```
32   // Store Example
33   using (var session = documentStore.OpenSession())
34   {
35       var order = new Order
36       {
37           Id = "Orders/B279855",
38           CustomerId = "F853998",
39           Item = "Keyboard",
40           OrderDate = "12/20/12",
41           UnitCost = 45.99,
42           Units = 1
43       };
44       session.Store(order);
45       session.SaveChanges();
46   }
```

2. Save all the files, build and run the solution.

3. Switch to your Management Studio, and click on the **Documents** tab to display documents of the `Orders` database and view the newly inserted document.

What just happened?

We just wrote the necessary code to insert a new order into the `Orders` database. Let's take a look at the code we added to the `RavenDB_Ch03` project.

You begin by opening a RavenDB session (line **33** in the previous code snippet). Again, the code is surrounded by the `using` statement in order to release resources when method execution ends.

Then, you create a new instance of the `Order` class and populate its fields with some values (lines **35** to **43**). After that, we call the `Store()` method on the `session` object and pass to it the `new Order` object (line **44**). The data will still be in memory until the `SaveChanges()` method on the `session` object is invoked (line **45**).

Documents						
Id	CustomerId	Item	OrderDate	UnitCost	Units	Colour
Orders/A179854	A54309	Paper Set	11/17/2011	25.99	5	
Orders/A154230	A54309	Pencil	4/18/2010	1.99	75	
Orders/B765760	F843098	Pen	5/12/2011	15.99	20	
Orders/B768920	F843098	Rubber	5/12/2011	1.99	10	
Orders/A655302	A54309	Ink Pen	10/31/2011	18.3885	35	
Orders/C676332	A55689	Mouse Pad	11/3/2011	8.5	10	
ec374ce7-3a5b-4c	B66689	USB Key	1/7/2012	28.5	5	Black
Orders/B279855	F853998	Keyboard	12/20/12	45.9	1	

Updating a document

Updating a document is also very simple in RavenDB, which is responsible for tracking changes you make for an object within your session. This is another reason why the `session` object is important.

To update a document you will load this document first using the `Load()` method on the `session` object, make changes you need to the document and then save the changes to the server using the `SaveChanges()` method on the `session` object. When updating a document, the entire document is sent to the server with the `Id` field set to the existing document value; this means that the existing document will be replaced in the `DocumentStore` object with the new one.

Time for action – updating a document

You will add necessary code to the `Main()` method in the `Program` class to update the `Order` document with the `Id` field as `Orders/B279855`, and save the changes to the `Orders` database.

1. Add the following code snippet to the `Main()` method:

```
48    // Update Exmaple
49    using (var session = documentStore.OpenSession())
50    {
51        var order = session.Load<Order>("Orders/B279855");
52        order.Item = "Wireless Keyboard";
53        order.UnitCost = 59.99;
54        order.Units = 5;
55        session.SaveChanges();
56    }
```

2. Save all the files, build and run the solution.

3. Switch to your Management Studio, and click on the **Documents** tab to display documents of the `Orders` database and view that the document has been updated.

What just happened?

You just wrote the necessary code to update the `Order` document with the `Id` as `Orders/B279855` and save the changes to the `Orders` database.

You begin by opening a RavenDB session (line **49** in the previous code snippet). Then, you load the `Order` document with the `Id` field as `Orders/B279855` by calling the `Load()` method (line **51**). Then you modified its field values (lines **52** to **55**).

After that you call the `SaveChanges()` method on the `session` object to persist changes on the server (line **55**).

> You don't have to call the `Store()` method or track any changes by yourself. RavenDB will do all of that for you.

Documents						
Id	CustomerId	Item	OrderDate	UnitCost	Units	Colour
Orders/A179854	A54309	Paper Set	11/17/2011	25.99	5	
Orders/A154230	A54309	Pencil	4/18/2010	1.99	75	
Orders/B765760	F843098	Pen	5/12/2011	15.99	20	
Orders/B768920	F843098	Rubber	5/12/2011	1.99	10	
Orders/A655302	A54309	Ink Pen	10/31/2011	18.3885	35	
Orders/C676332	A55689	Mouse Pad	11/3/2011	8.5	10	
ec374ce7-3a5b-4dab	B66689	USB Key	1/7/2012	28.5	5	Black
Orders/B279855	F853998	Wireless Keyboard	12/20/12	59.9	5	

Deleting a document

Just like the other operations in RavenDB, deleting a document is very easy to do. First, you will load the document you want to delete using the `Load()` method on the `session` object, and then call the `Delete()` method on the `session` object with the document as a parameter. It is important to note that deletes are final and cannot be rolled back, once committed.

Time for action – deleting a document

You will add necessary code to the `Main()` method in the `Program` class to delete the `Order` with the `Id` field as `Orders/B279855` from the `Orders` database:

1. Add the following code snippet to the `Main()` method:

```
58    // Delete Example:
59    using (var session = documentStore.OpenSession())
60    {
61        var order = session.Load<Order>("Orders/B279855");
62        session.Delete(order);
63        session.SaveChanges();
64    }
```

2. Save all the files, build and run the solution.

3. Switch to your Management Studio, and click on the **Documents** tab to display documents of the `Orders` database, and check that the document is no longer in the `Orders` database.

What just happened?

You just wrote the necessary code to update the `Order` with the `Id` field as `Orders/B279855` and save the changes to the `Orders` database.

You begin by opening a RavenDB session (line **59** in the previous code snippet). Then, you load the `Order` with the `Id` as `Orders/B279855` by calling the `Load()` method (line **61**). Then, you call the `Delete()` method on the `Session` object and pass to it the Order ID you want to delete (line **62**).

Then, you invoke the `SaveChanges()` method on the `session` object to delete the Order document permanently from the database (line **63**).

Querying a documents collection

RavenDB supports many querying types, ranging from simple value comparisons to geo-spatial queries and even full-blown, full-text search queries. To query a RavenDB database, we need to specify the collection we are interested in querying. As RavenDB supports Linq, we can do regular Linq queries. In order to perform a Linq query, we will use the Query() method on the session object and we specify the type of the query object.

Due to RavenDB safe by default feature, only 128 elements will be returned no matter how many there actually are. Also this limit can be changed in the server configuration but it is not recommended.

Time for action – querying a documents collection

You will add the QueryOrder() method to the Program class, which you will call to query the Orders database and retrieve Orders, which match the criteria we specify:

1. Add the following code snippet to the Main() method:

```
66    // Query Exmaple:
67    using (var session = documentStore.OpenSession())
68    {
69        var orders = from order in session.Query<Order>()
70                        where order.UnitCost > 10.0
71                        select order;
72        foreach (var order in orders)
73            DisplayOrder(order);
74    }
```

2. Save all the files, build and run the solution.
3. View the results in the output window.

What just happened?

We want to query the Orders database and retrieve only those Orders whose UnitCost is more than 10.0.

For that, we call the Query() method on the session object using a LINQ query that selects those Orders whose UnitCost value is more than 10.0 (line **70** in the previous code snippet).

Then, the `Orders` documents that match this criteria are stored in the `orders` field. To display each element in the `orders` list, we call the `DisplayOrder()` method and use a `foreach` loop (lines **78** to **88**).

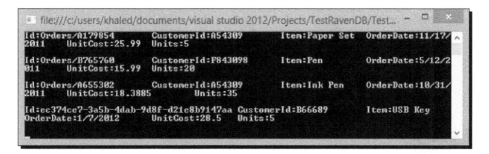

Have a go hero – querying a collection using lambda expression

You learned how to query a documents collection using a regular Linq query. You can get the same results by using a lambda expression. By using lambda expressions, you can write local functions that can be passed as arguments or returned as the value of function calls.

When invoking the `Query()` method, you can load all documents that match your criteria using a lambda expression. Try to rewrite the `QueryOrders()` method and use a lambda expression to retrieve Orders from the `Orders` database.

Use the `Where()` method!

Pop quiz – RavenDB .NET Client API

Q1. When I change a document in RavenDB it will apply changes directly to the database?

1. True.
2. False.
3. Only when the `SaveChanges()` method is called.

Q2. When querying a RavenDB database, RavenDB Client will not return all the documents within the database, why?

1. You must be the server administrator.
2. There is not enough memory to load all documents.
3. RavenDB is "Safe by Default".
4. A query cannot return more than 128 documents.

Q3. You want to display the whole result of this query: `var orders = session.Query<Order>().ToList();` how can you do it?

1. It is not possible.

2. Iterate over orders using a `foreach` loop.

3. Increase memory resources on the RavenDB Client to handle the whole Orders collection.

4. Paging the query result.

Summary

In this chapter, we learned how to use the .NET Client API, which you will probably use often rather than the HTTP API. We created a test project in Visual Studio to cover basic steps to connect and to interact with RavenDB. Specifically, we covered:

◆ How to set up the development environment and how to reference RavenDB Client using NuGet Package Manager.

◆ We learned how to get connected to RavenDB, open a new session, and load a document from RavenDB.

◆ Also, we learned to insert a new document into RavenDB database, update an existing document, and delete documents from RavenDB.

◆ The RavenDB Safe by Default feature and how to query a documents collection.

There are more advanced commands, but we covered only the basic elements that you need to interact with RavenDB in your own .NET application.

In the next chapter, we will learn more about RavenDB Indexes and Queries and how to use them properly in RavenDB.

4

RavenDB Indexes and Queries

Wherever you use a database, you need some queries with search criteria to retrieve your data from this database. This chapter takes us forward towards querying the data in RavenDB.

In this chapter, we will learn how RavenDB indexes work and why we need them. Then, we will cover the different types of indexes and the problem that RavenDB indexes aim to solve.

You will learn about Map/Reduce and how RavenDB indexes implement this paradigm and use it to retrieve data from the server. With a step-by-step approach, we will create some indexes and learn how to query them.

In this chapter, we will cover:

- ◆ RavenDB Map/Reduce implementation
- ◆ RavenDB dynamic indexes
- ◆ RavenDB static indexes
- ◆ RavenDB stale indexes

The RavenDB indexes

All storage systems use indexes to find data quickly when a query is processed. In a database system, an index is a data structure that improves data retrieval operations. Therefore, creating a proper index can drastically increase the performance of an application.

An index in a relational database is very similar to an index in the back of a book. When a database server has no index to use for searching, the result is similar to the reader who looks at every page in a book to find a word. The database engine needs to visit every row in the table. In relational database terminology, we call this behavior a table scan, which becomes slower and more expensive as a table grows to thousands or millions of rows.

RavenDB indexes are used to retrieve data from the server but they do not work the same way as relational database indexes work. The main difference is that relational database indexes are schema-based and RavenDB is a schema-less document-oriented database, which means that a schema definition is not required and therefore not enforced.

RavenDB does not know anything about fields of a document stored in a database on the server, unlike a relational database system where an index is created on columns in the tables or views. Remember that in RavenDB, the whole document is serialized to JSON format when the document is stored and it is deserialized and mapped to a class object. Only at this point, the values of the document fields are copied to the object instance and then you can access these fields in your application code.

As stated, RavenDB has no schema. This is great, except that in practice, there isn't much that we can do with a document. We can display it, and allow the user to edit it, but that is about it. When you ask the server to retrieve all the data with a given field value, it doesn't know how to do that and this is what RavenDB indexes are for.

RavenDB requires an index to solve a query; this is why we need to create indexes in RavenDB. The wonderful thing is that you do not need to manually define indexes, (even if it is highly recommended). This is because the RavenDB database engine can deduct and create required indexes, if not existing, by analyzing the query at runtime.

 RavenDB can make queries on dynamic data and can take care of optimizing this for us on the fly.

In RavenDB an index definition tells Raven how to build the index. The index is held in a separate Lucene index store. At time of query, you either ask RavenDB to use a specific index, or let it try to match against one dynamically—potentially creating a new temporary index in the process. Basically when we create an index, we allow RavenDB to know what fields are in the document and which ones we want to query on this document.

RavenDB indexes can be used to sort or aggregate data together. Indexes define how to transform a document from the basic form to a predictable known format. They retrieve data faster because they organize data in some order that makes it easy to search that data.

RavenDB Map/Reduce implementation

Map/Reduce is a programming model and an associated implementation for processing and generating large datasets. RavenDB indexes are Map/Reduce implementations and allow you to perform aggregations over multiple documents. Indexes use a Map function to specify what to retrieve from the server and optionally use Reduce and Transform functions to specify which results will be returned to the client.

Developer specifies one or more Map function(s) that processes a documents collection to generate a set of intermediate key-value pairs. The intermediate key-value pairs produced by the Map function are buffered in memory.

The Reduce function is not compulsory. An index may have zero or only one Reduce function. The Reduce function reads all intermediate key-value pairs generated by the Map(s) function(s) and aggregates associated values with the same intermediate key. After successful completion, the output of the Reduce function execution is available to the caller and the Transform function if it exists.

The Reduce query must return its result in the same format that it received it.

The Transform function allows constructing queries where the query model is the same type as the Map/Reduce result, but the final query result will be changed to another specified type.

Similar to the Reduce function, only one Transform function is optionally permitted. The Transform function takes its input from two sources, the current database, and the Map query output which is the result of the Map function or the Reduce query output if a Reduce function exists.

The RavenDB Version 2.5 will have result transformers, which is a Transform function's collection, to allow more than one Transform function.

The following figure illustrates the overall flow of a Map/Reduce implementation:

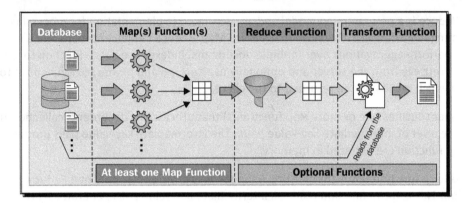

 Indexes in RavenDB are a Map/Reduce implementation. Specifically it is a Map/Reduce implementation that allows one or more Maps (Map versus Multimap), an optional `Reduce` function, and an optional `Transform` function. This makes RavenDB indexes very flexible.

The types of RavenDB indexes

RavenDB doesn't allow unindexed queries, so all the queries that you make using RavenDB will always use an index to return the results. While an index can be defined manually, RavenDB automatically generates an index if you haven't done so when you query a database.

Therefore, there are two types of indexes in RavenDB:

- **Dynamic indexes**: This is the kind of index that RavenDB will use when you want to query data and you haven't explicitly specified a static index. These indexes are created automatically on the fly by RavenDB if no matching index is there to answer the query.

- **Static indexes**: These indexes are created explicitly by the user to tell RavenDB what to index. They use Map functions, and optionally may include Reduce and Transform functions to specify what index entries to create in the index and can be defined using regular Linq expressions.

 In document databases, aggregations are handled using Map/Reduce indexes

RavenDB optimizes itself to handle the type of load presented. Under heavy reads, it will deprioritize the indexing. Under heavy writes, it will self-adjust the batch sizes to reduce the latency to fresh results.

The RavenDB indexing mechanism implements the open source `Lucene.NET` (`http://lucenenet.apache.org/`) library. All indexes in RavenDB are Lucene-based and RavenDB takes advantage of this to provide a very fast, feature-rich and flexible querying system.

Lucene is a full-text search library that makes it easy to add search functionality to an application. It does so by adding content to a full-text index and then searches this index and returns results ranked by either the relevance to the query or by an arbitrary field such as a document's last modified date.

RavenDB creates an index named `Raven/DocumentsByEntityName`, which is the default static index used by the RavenDB Management Studio to access all of the documents stored within a database on the server.

To see the `DocumentsByEntityName` index, open Management Studio and click on the **Indexes** tab to display the Indexes screen where the index can be found.

You can recreate the `DocumentsByEntityName` index by using the RavenDB .NET Client API directly without waiting for the client to open the Management Studio. The index class definition can be found on Github using this link: `https://github.com/ravendb/ravendb/blob/master/Raven.Client.Lightweight/Indexes/RavenDocumentsByEntityName.cs`

RavenDB indexes data in the background whenever it is added or changed and the results are written to the disk. RavenDB indexes are always incrementally built.

RavenDB dynamic indexes

When you make a query to RavenDB, the RavenDB query optimizer will search first for indexes matching that query before performing it. In case there is no matching index found, RavenDB automatically creates a temporary index for this query. When a query is performed often, it will optimize itself based on the actual requests coming in, and can decide to promote a temporary index to a permanent one.

Dynamic indexes are Map/Reduce indexes. They have no reduction function. They are just mapping functions, which allow RavenDB to answer queries by knowing how to traverse the document.

Querying dynamic indexes

Dynamic indexes are created automatically on the fly by RavenDB. When querying the server if there are no matching indexes for this query, RavenDB will create a new temporary index and will use it to query the data on the server.

Time for action – querying a dynamic index

We will query the `World` database and retrieve all `Countries` for which the `Area` field is greater than or equal to `1000000`. Before creating this query, you will import the `Countries.csv` file into the `World` database. After that, you will visualize how RavenDB will perform this task and you will look at the RavenDB logs in the prompt window.

1. In Management Studio, import the `Countries.csv` file into the `World` database.

2. Create a new Visual Studio project, name it `RavenDB_Ch04`.

3. Add a new class, name it `City` and complete it as follows:

```
 9     class City
10     {
11         public string Id { get; set; }
12         public string Name { get; set; }
13         public string CountryCode { get; set; }
14         public long Population { get; set; }
15         public string Province { get; set; }
16         public string CountryId { get; set; }
17     }
```

4. Add a new class named `Country` and make it look as follows:

```
 9     class Country
10     {
11         public string Id { get; set; }
12         public string Name { get; set; }
13         public string Code { get; set; }
14         public long Area { get; set; }
15         public string Capital { get; set; }
16         public string Province { get; set; }
17     }
```

5. Add the RavenDB `DocumentStore` initialization to the `Main()` method using the following code snippet:

```
12  ⊟   static void Main(string[] args)
13      {
14          using (var documentStore =
15                  new DocumentStore
16                  {
17                      Url = "http://localhost:8080",
18                      DefaultDatabase = "World"
19                  }.Initialize())
20          {
21              //
22              // Example  code goes here
23              //
24
25          }
26      }
```

 The `World` database has been created in *Chapter 2, RavenDB Management Studio*.

6. Add this query to the `Main()` method in the `Program` class using the following code snippet:

```
25      // Dynamic Index Query Exmaple
26      using (var session = documentStore.OpenSession())
27      {
28          var countries = from country in session.Query<Country>()
29                          where country.Area >= 1000000
30                          select country;
31
32
33          foreach (Country country in countries)
34          {
35              Console.WriteLine(country.Name);
36          }
37      }
```

7. Save all the files and build the solution.

8. Open the RavenDB installation folder and launch RavenDB server using the `Start. cmd` command file.

9. Return to Visual Studio once the RavenDB server is running, run `RavenDB_Ch04` to see the query results in the output console window.

10. Switch to the RavenDB prompt window and take a look at the RavenDB logs to learn how RavenDB performed the query action.

11. In Management Studio, select the `World` database and click on the **Indexes** tab to display the **Indexes** screen in order to show the new temporary index `Temp/Countries/ByArea_RangeSortByArea`.

12. Open the `Temp/Countries/ByArea_RangeSortByArea` index in edit mode and analyze it.

What just happened?

We just created a new Visual Studio project, `RavenDB_Ch04`, and then added two classes, `City` and `Country`, in order to query the `World` database. Before creating the query you imported the `Countries.csv` file into the `World` database in order to populate it.

The `City` class contains six fields to hold information about a city. These fields are: `Id`, `Name`, `CountryCode`, `Population`, and `Province` (lines **11** to **16**)

The `Country` class will hold information about a country. These fields are: `Id`, `Name`, `Code`, `Area`, `Capital`, and `Province` (lines **11** to **16**).

Then we added a new `Query<Country>()` method, which will filter the `Countries` collection on the `Area` field, to the `Main()` method of the `RavenDB_Ch04` project.

This query returns documents that match the criteria (`Area >= 1000000`) we had specified in the Linq expression (lines **28** to **30**).

We didn't specify any predefined index to be used to retrieve the data. For this reason, RavenDB dynamically creates a temporary index to perform the query.

In the RavenDB logs, we can see that we have a `GET HTTP` method on the `World` database, which addresses the `indexes/dynamic` area structure.

When opening the new added temporary index in Management Studio, you can see that the index code specifies one field to be retrieved from the database which is the `Area` field. This is because in the `Query<Country>()` method we had specified this field to define the query criteria.

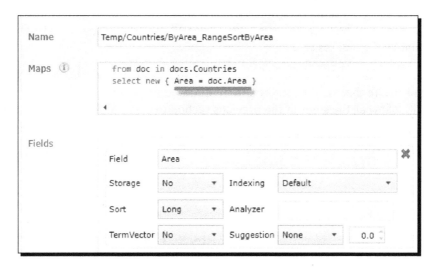

 The specific dynamic index used depends on the version of RavenDB you are using. In RavenDB 2.5 this is different than that in RavenDB 2.0.

Querying temporary indexes

When querying RavenDB collections if there is an existing index that matches the query, it will use it instead of creating a new temporary one. When a temporary index gets significant usage, RavenDB may decide to promote it permanently. Once this happens, the prefix index name changes from `Temp/` to `Auto/` (which is only true for RavenDB 2.0, and not for RavenDB 2.5).

Time for action – querying a temporary index

To illustrate how RavenDB uses existing temporary indexes, we will recall the `Query<Country>()` method we created in the previous section. Also we will create another query using the same parameter, which will use the same temporary index. Then you will analyze the RavenDB logs in the RavenDB prompt window and visualize the Management Studio Indexes screen.

1. Open RavenDB Management Studio, select the **Indexes** tab of the `World` database and ensure that `Temp/Countries/ByArea_RangeSortByArea` index exists. If not, follow all the steps of the previous section to create the temporary index.

2. Open the `RavenDB_Ch04` solution.

3. Add the following code snippet to the `Main()` method in the `Program` class:

```
39    // Query Temporary Index Exmaple
40    using (var session = documentStore.OpenSession())
41    {
42        // 1st Query
43        var countries = from country in session.Query<Country>()
44                        where country.Area >= 1000000
45                        select country;
46
47        foreach (Country country in countries)
48        {
49            Console.WriteLine(country.Name);
50        }
51
52        // 2nd Query
53        countries = from country in session.Query<Country>()
54                    where country.Area <= 1000000
55                    select country;
56
57        foreach (Country country in countries)
58        {
59            Console.WriteLine(country.Name);
60        }
61    }
```

4. Save all the files, build and run the solution.

5. Open the RavenDB prompt window and analyze the RavenDB logs.

6. In Management Studio, select the `World` database and click on the **Indexes** tab to display the Indexes screen and verify that there are no new temporary indexes created.

What just happened?

We modified the Main() method to execute the Query<Country>() method again in order to illustrate that RavenDB will use the existing index if it matches the query. This query returns all the Countries documents for which the Area field is greater than or equal to 1000000 (lines **42** to **45**).

Then you add a second query that uses the same query parameters. This second query retrieves all Countries for which the Area field is less than or equal 1000000 (lines **53** to **55**).

To perform the first Query<Country>() method, RavenDB searched the existing indexes and found that the Temp/Countries/ByArea_RangeSortByArea index matches the query's needs. Then RavenDB will use this index to perform the query on the server instead of creating a new temporary one.

Also as the second query uses the same query parameters, RavenDB will use the same index to perform this query.

In the RavenDB logs, you can see that we have a GET HTTP method on the World database, which addresses the indexes/dynamic area structure. You can see that to perform the first and the second query (**Request #62**, and **#63**) RavenDB uses the same index that is the Temp/Countries/ByArea_RangeSortByArea.

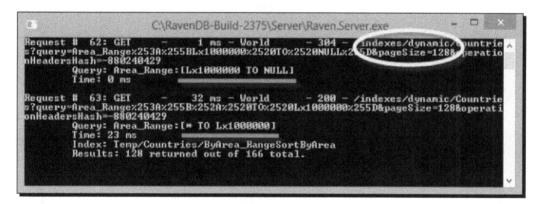

After opening the Management Studio Indexes screen, you can see that there is no new temporary index created, which also indicates that RavenDB uses the existing `Temp/Countries/ByArea_RangeSortByArea` index.

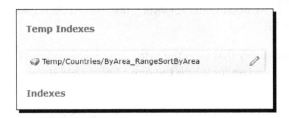

Managing temporary indexes

Now you are familiar with temporary indexes and you have learned how RavenDB generates and uses them. But the question is can you manage those indexes and if yes how you can do that?

Time for action – managing temporary indexes

RavenDB allows you to manage temporary indexes using the server configuration file option. Also, RavenDB will optimize itself by deleting temporary indexes if they have not been used for a given time, or will promote them to permanent indexes if they have been used enough.

These following steps summarize the temporary index management process in RavenDB:

1. RavenDB looks for appropriate index to use in query.
2. If found, it will return the most appropriate index.
3. If not found, it will create an index that will deal with the query.
4. Return that index as temporary.
5. If that index is used enough, promote it into an Auto index

Temporary indexes behavior is controlled by these configuration settings: `Raven/TempIndexPromotionThreshold` and `Raven/TempIndexPromotionMinimumQueryCount`.

By default, the number of times a temporary index has to be queried before becoming a permanent index is 100. You can change these settings by changing the value of the `Raven/TempIndexPromotionMinimumQueryCount` key.

6. If that index is not used enough, delete it.

> The default value before RavenDB a temporary index is 600 seconds (10 minutes). You can change this delay by setting the `Raven/TempIndexCleanupPeriod` key.
>
> The RavenDB's complete configuration options can be found on the official RavenDB website: `http://ravendb.net/docs/server/administration/configuration`

You may decide to promote a temporary index to a permanent index manually at any moment. For that you can select the index in Management Studio and from the contextual menu click on **Promote to auto index** (see *Chapter 2, RavenDB Management Studio*).

Have a go hero – creating projections using Linq queries

Now you know how to query RavenDB using Linq expressions and how to add new methods to the `Program` class to query the server in an efficient manner. It is time to learn about projections.

Projections are specific fields projected from documents using the Linq `Select` method. They are not the original objects but a new object that is being created on the fly and populated with results gathered by the query.

Try to add a new method to the `Program` class that returns one or more fields from the `World` database and displays the result. This seems easy to do. We'll give it a go!

> When you created your first index using Management Studio in *Chapter 2, RavenDB Management Studio* you created a projection.

RavenDB static indexes

RavenDB allows user to manually create and use indexes. These indexes explicitly created are called static indexes or named indexes. A static index allows the use of one or more `Map` functions. It may include a `Reduce` function and/or a `Transform` function. These functions will specify what to retrieve from the server and will be defined using the regular Linq expressions.

Static indexes are more efficient than dynamic indexes. Since dynamic indexes are created on the fly on first user query and are created as temporary indexes, this might be a performance issue on first run. Also, static indexes expose more functionality such as custom sorting, boosting, Full Text Search, Live Projections, spatial search support, and more.

So far we have created some queries so far to retrieve data from the RavenDB server using Linq expression. This can be used the same way to sort or aggregate data and to query specific fields in a document. When using indexes to aggregate data, there are some limitations. RavenDB only supports the `Count()` and `Distinct()` Linq aggregate operators. For more complex aggregations, that use the `SelectMany()`, `GroupBy()`, and `Join()` operators, you will need to create a static index and use `Map/Reduce` functions.

> In RavenDB, every static index is required to have a name and at least one `Map` function but it might have more than one `Map` function.

Creating your first Map function

The Map functions are written using Linq expressions, just like writing a simple query. The Map function does not change any document values, it indicates which ones should be taken into account to index. This way we will be able to perform low cost queries over the stored values.

Time for action – defining a Map function for an index

We will create a new static index and add it to the `World` database (created in *Chapter 2, RavenDB Management Studio*). You will create this index using the `PutIndex()` method. Then you will analyze the RavenDB logs and open the index in Management Studio to view it and execute it.

1. Open the `RavenDB_Ch04` solution in Visual Studio.

2. Add the following code to the `Main()` method to create the static index:

```
64      // Your 1st Map function
65      documentStore.DatabaseCommands.PutIndex("Cities/CountryCode",
66      new IndexDefinitionBuilder<City>
67      {
68          Map = cities => from city in cities
69                          select new
70                          {
71                              CountryCode = city.CountryCode
72                          }
73      }
74      , true);
```

3. Add the following code to the `Main()` method to query the `Cities/CountryCode` index:

```
78    // Querying Cities/CountryCode Index
79    // and retrieve all cities in France
80    using (var session = documentStore.OpenSession())
81    {
82        var cities = from city in session.Query<City>("Cities/CountryCode")
83                     where city.CountryCode == "F"
84                     select city;
85
86        foreach (City city in cities)
87        {
88            Console.WriteLine(city.Name);
89        }
90    }
```

4. Save all the files, build and run `RavenDB_Ch04`.

5. Select the RavenDB prompt window in Windows Explorer and analyze the RavenDB logs to understand how RavenDB created the index.

6. In Management Studio, select the `World` database, click on the **Indexes** tab and open the `Cities/CountryCode` index in edit mode and look at the `Map function` code.

7. In Management Studio, execute the `Cities/CountryCode` index and observe the result.

What just happened?

You just created your first static index `Cities/CountryCode` and defined its `Map` function using a lambda expression.

To create the index you used the `PutIndex()` method on the `DocumentStore` object instance by providing the index name `Cities/CountryCode` to be created. As the index will satisfy queries on the `Cities` collection, we used the `Cities/ {index name}` prefix by convention only (line **65**).

We used the `PutIndex()` method for learning purposes only because it still appears on the official RavenDB website: `http://ravendb.net/docs/2.0/client-api/querying/static-indexes/defining-static-index?version=2.0`

The recommended and preferred way to create RavenDB 2.x indexes is to use the `AbstractIndexCreationTask` class, which is discussed in the next chapter.

The `PutIndex()` method requires the index definition for the index that will be created. You provide this index definition by creating a new instance of the `IndexDefinitionBuilder` class, which requires the document type that in this case is `City` (line **66**).

The `Map` function is defined in the `IndexDefinitionBuilder` class. This `Map` function (which you wrote in a lambda style) reads all documents from the `Cities` collection which is accessible through the `cities` parameter (line **68**). The function selects only one field, the `CountryCode` field and outputs the results as a new anonymous object created by the `select new` statement.

The last parameter of the `PutIndex()` method is a `boolean` value that you set to `true`. This allows RavenDB to overwrite the index if it already exists in the database (line **74**).

To query this index, you call the `Query<City>` object and specify the name of the index to query (`Cities/CountryCode`) (line **82**). Then to get only `Cities` in the given `Country` (France), we apply a filter using the `Where` closure, `city.CountryCode == "F"` (line **83**) and select `City` if it satisfies the filter criteria.

The RavenDB logs show that the RavenDB searches the index first and as it doesn't exist, RavenDB performs a `PUT HTTP` method with the index name to the indexes area.

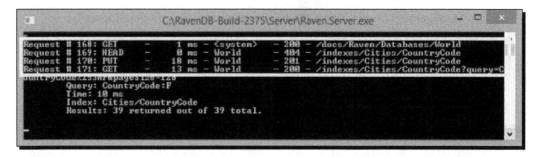

When you open the `Cities/CountryCode` index in Management Studio, you can see that the `Map` function code is very similar to the one you wrote in your code. The main difference is that the `Map` function addresses the special collection `docs` to retrieve documents:

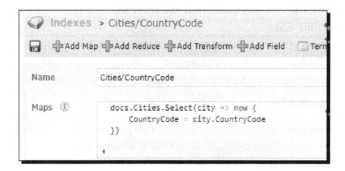

To see the index `Terms` in Management Studio, open the index in edit mode and then click on the **Terms** button.

Note that if you write your `Map` function using a regular Linq expression style, RavenDB will translate it to lambda style automatically.

Creating your first Reduce function

A `Reduce` function is optional and a static index may have zero or only one `Reduce` function. When it exists, the `Reduce` function takes the output of `Map` functions, reduces the values, and aggregates the incoming dataset based on a reduce key (given in `GroupBy` clause). As the `Map` functions, `Reduce` functions are written using Linq expressions. The `Reduce` function is optional and is executed just like the `Map` function, but this time against the mapped results.

Time for action – adding a Reduce function to an index

We will create a new static index and will define its `Map` and `Reduce` functions. You will add this index to the `World` database using the `PutIndex()` method. Then you will modify the `RavenDB_Ch04` project and add a new call to the `PutIndex()` method. After that you will open the index in Management Studio to view it and execute it.

1. Open the `RavenDB_Ch04` solution in Visual Studio.
2. Add the following code snippet to the `Main()` method to create the index:

```
 92     // Your 1st Reduce function
 93     documentStore.DatabaseCommands.PutIndex("Cities/CountryPopulation",
 94     new IndexDefinitionBuilder<City>
 95     {
 96         Map = cities => from city in cities
 97                         select new
 98                         {
 99                             CountryCode = city.CountryCode,
100                             Population = city.Population
101                         },
102
103         Reduce = results => from result in results
104                         group result by result.CountryCode
105                             into g
106                         select new
107                         {
108                             CountryCode = g.Key,
109                             Population = g.Sum(x => x.Population)
110                         }
111     }
112     , true);
```

While writing the `Map` and `Reduce` functions, press *Ctrl +
Space* to display all methods you can set.

3. Add the following code snippet to the `Main()` method to query the index:

```
116    // Querying Cities/CountryPopulation Index
117    // and sum all cities Population in Canada
118    using (var session = documentStore.OpenSession())
119    {
120        var countryPopulation = from city in session
121                    .Query<City>("Cities/CountryPopulation")
122                    where city.CountryCode == "CDN"
123                    select city;
124
125        Console.WriteLine("CountryCode: {0}, Population: {1}",
126                    countryPopulation.FirstOrDefault().CountryCode,
127                    countryPopulation.FirstOrDefault().Population
128                    .ToString());
129    }
```

4. Save all the files, build and run `RavenDB_Ch04`.

5. In Management Studio, open the `Cities/CountryPopulation` index in edit
mode and look at its `Map` and `Reduce` functions code.

6. In Management Studio, execute the `Cities/CountryPopulation` index and
observe the result.

What just happened?

You created the `Cities/CountryPopulation` static index and defined its `Map` and
`Reduce` functions. This index aggregates all `Population` fields in the `Cities` collection and
returns the results.

To create this index you used the `PutIndex()` method (line **92** to **112**) that you used in the
previous section.

The `Map` function defined by the `IndexDefinitionBuilder` class selects the
`CountryCode` and the `Population` fields of all `Cities`.

The `Reduce` function takes the output of the `Map` function (results parameter).

The Reduce function must return its result in the same format that it received from the Map function. If the output fields of the Map function don't match with those of the Reduce function, you will get an error and the index will not be created or saved to the database.

The Reduce function groups the result of the Map function into a group named g (line **105**) and defines its key as the CountryCode value, aggregates all the Population field values, and returns the result (lines **103** to **110**).

Then you added the code to the Main() method to query the index (lines **118** to **129**). The query selects only the Cities documents having the CountryCode == "CDN" (code for Canada) (lines **120** to **123**).

When you open the Cities/PopulationCountry index in Management Studio in edit mode, you can see that the Map/Reduce function's code is very similar to the code you wrote in your Main() method.

When you execute the index in Management Studio, you will get an aggregation of the Population field for each CountryCode. In the query section, you may filter the result by entering CountryCode as "CDN" and click on **Execute** button. You will get only one result line with two columns, CountryCode and Population, which is the aggregation result of the Reduce function.

Using TransformResults in an index

Like Reduce function, the TransformResults function is optional. A static index may have zero or only one TransformResults function. TransformResults is another function on an index that you can access much like Map and Reduce.

As its name suggests, this function aims to transform the result of an index. As the Reduce function's output must be the same as the Map function's output, this format transformation cannot be done using a Reduce function. This is why the TransformResults function exists.

The TransformResults function is useful if you want to get something completely different from the index result. Usually, this is the case when you are using Live Projections. The TransformResults function is not really part of the index, but it is just attached to the index definition and executed at runtime. It provides an easy way to morph the query results on the server-side.

When using the `TransformResults` function, the result that we get back is not of the same type that we query on the index. For that reason, we have to use the `OfType<T>` `(As<T>)` extension method.

 An index may have only one `TransformResults` function.

The `TransformResults` function takes two parameters, `IClientSideDatabase` and `IEnumerable<T>`. The `IClientSideDatabase` interface is purely a data accessor, which gets passed in by RavenDB at runtime. This parameter represents the actual database documents. The second parameter, `IEnumerable<T>` results in the outcome of the `Map(s)` function(s) or the `Reduce` function when it exist.

Time for action – adding a TransformResults to the index

We will modify the `CountryPopulation` index and will define its `Map`, `Reduce`, and `TransformResults` functions. This new index version will aggregate the `Population` for each `Country` and will transform the query result to a new format the shape of which is the same as the `CountryPopulation` class which you will also create. Then you will open the index in Management Studio to execute it and view its result.

1. Open the `RavenDB_Ch04` project in Visual Studio.

2. Add a new class to the `RavenDB_Ch04` project, name it `CountryPopulation` and make it look like the following code snippet:

```
 9    class CountryPopulation
10    {
11        public string Id { get; set; }
12        public string CountryName { get; set; }
13        public long CountryArea { get; set; }
14        public long Population { get; set; }
15    }
```

3. Add the new `CountryPopulation` index definition to the `Main()` method using the following code:

```
132    // CountryPopulation Index version that
133    // implements a TransformResuts function
134    documentStore.DatabaseCommands.PutIndex("Cities/CountryPopulation",
135    new IndexDefinitionBuilder<City>
136    {
137        Map = cities => from city in cities
138                        select new
139                        {
140                            CountryId = city.CountryId,
141                            Population = city.Population
142                        },
143
144        Reduce = results => from result in results
145                            group result by result.CountryId
146                                into g
147                                select new
148                                {
149                                    CountryId = g.Key,
150                                    Population = g.Sum(x => x.Population)
151                                },
152
153        TransformResults = (database, results) =>
154                        from result in results
155                        let country = database.Load<Country>(result.CountryId)
156                        select new
157                        {
158                            Id = result.CountryId,
159                            CountryName = country.Name,
160                            CountryArea = country.Area,
161                            Population = result.Population,
162                        },
163    }
164    , true);
```

4. Add the following code to the `Main()` method to query the `Cities/CountryPopulation` index.

```
168    // Querying Cities/CountryPopulation Index
169    // and sum all cities Population
170    using (var session = documentStore.OpenSession())
171    {
172        var countryPopulation = session
173                    .Query<City>("Cities/CountryPopulation", true)
174                    .OfType<CountryPopulation>()
175                    .ToList();
176
177        foreach (var country in countryPopulation)
178        {
179            Console.WriteLine("Country: {0}, Population: {1}",
180                    country.CountryName,
181                    country.Population
182                    .ToString());
183        }
184        Console.ReadLine();
185    }
```

5. Save all the files, build and run the solution.

6. In Management Studio, execute the `Cities/CountryPopulation` index and observe the result when the **Skip Transform** option is checked and when it is not.

What just happened?

You modified the `Cities/CountryPopulation` index and defined its `Map`, `Reduce`, and `Transform` functions. This index aggregates all the `Population` fields in the `Cities` collection and transforms this aggregation to a four column result: `Id`, `CountryName`, `CountryArea`, and `Population` before returning the result to the client.

 The `TransformResults` function is executed at time of query and provides the other fields.

The `Map` function defined by the `IndexDefinitionBuilder` class selects all `Cities` and returns a two column projection result: `CountryId` and `Population` (lines **137** to **142**).

The `Reduce` function takes the output of the `Map` function (results parameter), groups it into a group named `g`, and defines its key as the `CountryId`. The result of this `Reduce` function is the aggregation of all the `Population` field values for each `CountryId` (lines **144** to **151**).

When querying the index, the `Reduce` query result is sent to the `TransformResults` function which takes two parameters: database which is an accessor for loading documents from the database in the `Transform` function, and results which is the Reduce query result.

In this `Transform` function, we load the related `Country` document from the database using the `CountryId` key by calling the `Load()` method on the database instance. Then we create a four column result that contains the `CountryId`, `CountryName`, `CountryArea`, and `Population` values (lines **153** to **162**).

 The `TransformResults` function will be executed at query time, not indexing time. And the function declared in `TransformResults` will be executed on the results of the queries. That means, we can only query on the output of the `Map/Reduce` function and not the `TransformResults` function.

To query the index, you call the `Query()` method on the `session` object and specify the index name as `Cities/CountryPopulation`. The `Query()` method takes an optional boolean parameter that indicates if we are querying a Map/Reduce index. This will modify how RavenDB treats identifier properties (lines **172** to **175**).

The query returns data in the shape defined in the index. To get the transformed result of the index you have to use `OfType()` method (line **174**).

When you open the `Cities/CountryPopulation` index in Management Studio, you can see that the `Map/Reduce/Transform` function's code is very similar to the code you wrote in the `PutMapReduceTransform()` method.

When you execute the index in Management Studio you got the four column result as we expected from the transform definition function.

Results			
Id	CountryName	CountryArea	Population
country/1067	Kyrgyzstan (Kyrgyz Republic)	198500	630000
country/1136	Peru	1285220	10595921
country/1043	United Kingdom	244820	32650200
country/1149	Western Sahara	266000	0
country/1140	Venezuela	912050	8383739
country/1064	Vietnam	329560	10919549
country/1138	Guyana	214970	170000

You can skip the `TransformResults` function processing by checking the **Skip Transform** option in the **Query Options** menu.

Have a go hero – creating Map/Reduce/Transform index

We need to get the list of all countries in the `World` database. The expected result should be a three column result that contains: `CountryCode`, `CountryName`, and `CountryArea`. You might create a new static index named as `Countries/MapReduceTransform` and specify its `Map`, `Reduce`, and `TransformResults` functions.

Use the `Map` function to return the `CountryId` key, the `Reduce` function to group it, and then load the Country information using the `Load()` method with the `CountryId` key in the `TransformResults` function.

The following screenshot illustrates the expected result:

Results		
CountryName	CountryArea	CountryCode
Kyrgyzstan	198500	KGZ
Lebanon	10400	RL
Western Samoa	2860	WS
Jordan	89213	JOR
Saint Kitts and Nevis	269	KN
Azerbaijan	86600	AZ
Burundi	27830	BI
Central African Republic	622980	RCA
Barbados	430	BDS
Gambia	11300	WAG
Saint Lucia	620	WL
French Guiana	91000	FGU
Belize	22960	BZ
Slovakia	48845	SK

RavenDB stale indexes

RavenDB indexes can be stale. They are eventually consistent and eventually here usually means in under a second. When you query RavenDB to retrieve some data, it will return the data whether or not it has finished indexing this data in the background. RavenDB will let the user know if query results are stale, and can also be told to wait until non-stale results are available, this allows introducing new indexes on the fly. Live index rebuilds is a rare feature.

 Waiting for a non-stale index is not a recommended practice for production systems.

In RavenDB whenever new data is inserted or updated, a background process will perform data indexing. This might be useful to improve the server response time but in this case you may query stale indexes. In a lot of situations, a stale index isn't a problem, and as expressed on the RavenDB site:

Better stale than offline.

When you call the `SaveChanges()` method on the `session` object to persist changes on some objects, and try immediately to get the list of all these objects, the objects won't appear. This is due to background asynchronous thread process which may not have finished yet. Basically, the average latency time observed is about 20 ms.

Checking for stale index results

In some real world scenarios, such as banking, querying a stale index may produce unexpected results. RavenDB allows user to check for stale results and if needed it can wait for non-stale results before returning result to the client. But, it is recommended to avoid waiting for non-stale result because it really hurts performance. Also this means that you have to wait, while generally with RavenDB we avoid waiting.

Time for action – checking for stale index results

You will add a new code snippet to the `Main()` method of the `RavenDB_Ch04` to check if an index result is stale or not.

1. Open the `RavenDB_Ch04` project in Visual Studio.

2. Add the following code to the `Main()` method:

```
187    // Checking for Stale Indexes
188    using (var session = documentStore.OpenSession())
189    {
190        RavenQueryStatistics stats;
191        session.Query<City>("Cities/CountryPopulation")
192            .Statistics(out stats)
193            .Take(0)
194            .ToList();
195
196        if (stats.IsStale)
197        {
198            Console.WriteLine("Index is stale");
199        }
200        else
201        {
202            Console.WriteLine("Index is up-to-date");
203        }
204    }
```

3. Save all the files, build and run the solution.

4. Check the output window for the stale status of the index result.

What just happened?

You added the necessary code to the `Main()` method to check stale index result.

In order to perform stale index result checking, you first declare a new `RavenQueryStatistics` variable that will hold the query statistics information about the query and the index such as the `IndexName`, and the `TotalResults` which indicates the total query results documents count (line **190**).

Then, we query the index using the `Query()` method on the `Session` instance object and specify the index name to check (line **191**). To get back the query statistics, we call the `Statistics()` method (lines **192**).

In this query you don't need to retrieve any document, you want only to get the index state. For that reason, you call the `Take()` method with the 0 parameter, which instructs RavenDB to not extract any document (line **193**).

The index result status is held by the `IsStale` Boolean property. When the `IsStale` property is true, that means probably the data has changed by adding, updating, or deleting a `Country` or a `City` in the `World` database and the indexes haven't had time to fully update before we queried.

> To get the total documents count returned by the query, you can read the `TotalResults` value: `int totalCount = stats.TotalResults`.
>
> As an alternative way, you can also get the stale indexes names by reading the `StaleIndexes` property value: `DocumentStore.DatabaseCommands.GetStatistics().StaleIndexes`

Waiting for non-stale index results

In case you need to query only up-to-date data, you can tell RavenDB to explicitly wait for non-stale data before returning the result to the client. But this isn't the best practice. This can be used for small code samples or unit tests, but it is strongly discouraged in a production environment. Plus, in a lot of situations, a stale index isn't a problem.

To instruct RavenDB to wait for non-stale results, you can call the `WaitForNonStaleResultsAsOf()` method, or if you need to see the most up-to-date results possible you will always have to use `WaitForNonStaleResultsAsOfNow()`.

Time for action – explicitly waiting for a non-stale index result

You will add a new code snippet to the `Main()` method of the `RavenDB_Ch04` project to tell RavenDB to wait for a non-stale result.

1. Open the `RavenDB_Ch04` project in Visual Studio.

2. Add the following code to the `Main()` method:

```
206    // Explicitly Waiting for non-stale index results
207    using (var session = documentStore.OpenSession())
208    {
209        var results = session.Query<City>("Cities/CountryPopulation")
210            .Customize(x => x.WaitForNonStaleResultsAsOfNow(TimeSpan.FromSeconds(5)))
211            .OfType<CountryPopulation>()
212            .ToList();
213    }
```

3. Save all the files, build and run the solution.

What just happened?

You added the necessary code to the `Main()` method to instruct RavenDB to explicitly wait for a non-stale index result.

In order to do that, you call the `Customize()` method on the `Query` object and call the `WaitForNonStaleResultsAsOfNow()` function within a lambda expression. This function takes a `TimeSpan` parameter to specify the time-out waiting delay. In this code snippet, we had specified 5 seconds as the time-out delay.

> Waiting for a non-stale index result is for use only for testing and learning purposes. It is strongly discouraged in a production environment.

Have a go hero – display all index names

Add a new method to the `Program` class and name it `GetIndexesNames()`. This method will display the names of all indexes in the `World` database.

To get the index names you call the `GetIndexNames()` method on the `DatabasesCommand` instance object. This method takes two parameters (`start` and `page size`) to allow the result pagination and returns a string array that contains the indexes names.

Then the index names array is displayed on the output window using a `foreach` loop.

Pop quiz – RavenDB and Map/Reduce

Q1. What is Map/Reduce?

1.   A programming language.
2.   A programming model.
3.   Part of the new .NET framework.
4.   An indexing algorithm.

Q2. A RavenDB dynamic index may contain which function(s)?

1.   Map function.
2.   Map/Reduce functions.
3.   Map/Reduce/Transform functions.
4.   Map/Transform function.

Q3. This `Map` function throws an exception when you execute the index, why?

```
Map = articles => from article in articles select article.Title
```

1.   This is not a regular Linq expression.
2.   There are many documents in the articles database.
3.   Need to upgrade the .NET Framework.
4.   Must always use "select new {...}".

Summary

In this chapter, we have learned about RavenDB indexes, how they work, and their different types. We specifically covered RavenDB's dynamic and static indexes and how to query each type of these indexes using Linq.

Afterward, we continued to discover how RavenDB uses Map/Reduce in static indexes, and how you can best implement it to take advantage of this programming model.

Throughout this chapter, we manually created indexes using the .NET Client API and implemented `Map/Reduce/TransformResults` functions. Then we finished with a sample method to learn how to manage stale indexes.

In the next chapter, we will put our newly learned skills to work and use them to learn another preferred and recommended way to create static indexes in RavenDB. Keep reading!

5
Advanced RavenDB Indexes and Queries

Advanced queries allow you to execute more complex query statements in RavenDB. In this chapter, you will learn a different way to create indexes by inheriting from the AbstractIndexCreatingTask *class.*

We will cover Multi map indexes and learn how to create them. Also you will learn how to register fields to be indexed, how to combine searching option, paging a query result, and some other useful techniques to improve the runtime performance of your queries.

In this chapter, we will cover:

- ◆ Creating indexes using the AbstractIndexCreatingTask class
- ◆ Multi map indexes
- ◆ Full text and exact match searching indexes
- ◆ Paging query results

The RavenDB AbstractIndexCreationTask class

RavenDB has a lot features to create indexes. In the previous chapter, we learned how to create an index and define its Map and Reduce functions using the PutIndex() method and the IndexDefinitionBuilder class. But there is a better way to do this by using the AbstractIndexCreationTask class and using the CreateIndex() method to submit the index to the server.

The AbstractIndexCreationTask class is an abstract generic class. That means no object of this class can be instantiated, but can only make derivations of this class. Also as it is a generic class, it requires the document type to be specified and optionally a ReduceResult type class.

Querying the RavenDB indexes created using the AbstractIndexCreationTask class is the same as the indexes created using the PutIndex() method. You can either let RavenDB decide which index to use, or instruct it to use a specific index by explicitly specifying the index name while querying.

Creating indexes using the AbstractIndexCreationTask class

It is very easy to create indexes using the AbstractIndexCreationTask class. Basically, you will create a new class for the index that will inherit from the AbstractIndexCreationTask class and define the document object type. The index you will create requires at least one map function to be defined. You can define this function in the class constructor directly instead of creating a new instance of the IndexDefinitionBuilder class as we did while using the PutIndex() method.

Time for action – creating indexes using AbstractIndexCreationTask class

Let's take a look and learn how to create a new index by inheriting from the AbstractIndexCreationTask class. To create the index we will create a new project and add a new class that inherits from this class. The index definition is very easy and will contain only one Map function that retrieves the CountryId key. To get all cities in the USA, we will query the index and filter the result. Once the index is created you will execute it in Management Studio and view the result.

1. Start Visual Studio, create a new project and name it RavenDB_CH05.

2. Use the NuGet Package Manager to add a reference to the RavenDB Client.

We need to use the City and Country classes created in the previous chapter, you may make a copy into this project or create a new one.

3. Add a new class to the project, name it `City` and complete it with the following code snippet:

```
 9  class City
10  {
11      public string Id { get; set; }
12      public string Name { get; set; }
13      public string CountryCode { get; set; }
14      public long Population { get; set; }
15      public string Province { get; set; }
16      public string CountryId { get; set; }
17  }
```

4. Add a new class to the project, name it `Country` and complete it with the following code snippet:

```
 9  class Country
10  {
11      public string Id { get; set; }
12      public string Name { get; set; }
13      public string Code { get; set; }
14      public long Area { get; set; }
15      public string Capital { get; set; }
16      public string Province { get; set; }
17      public string ContinentCode { get; set; }
18  }
```

5. Add a new class to the project, name it `Cities_CountryCode` and add the following code snippet:

```
10  class Cities_CountryCode : AbstractIndexCreationTask<City>
11  {
12      public Cities_CountryCode()
13      {
14          Map = cities => from city in cities
15                          select new
16                          {
17                              CountryCode = city.CountryCode
18                          };
19      }
20  }
```

6. Modify the `Program` class in the `Main()` method to make it look like the following code snippet:

```
13 ⊟ static void Main(string[] args)
14   {
15       using (var documentStore =
16           new DocumentStore
17           {
18               Url = "http://localhost:8080",
19               DefaultDatabase = "World"
20           }.Initialize())
21       {
22           // Create Cities/CountryCode Index
23           IndexCreation.CreateIndexes(
24               typeof(Cities_CountryCode).Assembly, documentStore);
25
26           // Query the Cities/CountryCode index
27           using (var session = documentStore.OpenSession())
28           {
29               var cities = session.Query<City>("Cities/CountryCode")
30                   .Where(x => x.CountryCode == "USA")
31                   .ToList();
32
33               Console.WriteLine(cities.Count().ToString());
34           }
35       }
36   }
```

7. Save all files, build and run the `RavenDB_CH5` solution.

8. In Management Studio, execute the `Cities/CountryCode` index to observe the expected result.

What just happened?

You just created your first index using the `AbstractIndexCreationTask` class. This index is very similar to the one we created in the previous chapter. The main difference is that this index is defined as a class rather than within the call of the `PutIndex()` method.

As the `AbstractIndexCreationTask` class is an abstract class it cannot be instantiated directly; you created the `Cities_CountryCode` class that inherits from this class. Inheriting from this class requires the document type to be specified, which you specified as `City` (line **10**).

It is a good practice to name the index class using this naming convention `Collection_IndexName`, which is a good way to know that this is an index that operates on this collection.

The `map` function for the `Cities_CountryCode` index is defined within the class constructor. This function retrieves `CountryCode` for all documents (lines **17**).

In the `Main()` method, you created a new `DocumentStore` that points to the `World` database, and called the `CreateIndexes()` method on the `IndexCreation` class. This method requires at least two parameters, the `Assembly` file to scan for indexing task and the `documentStore` object instance. Basically, this method uses reflection to look in the assembly and look for index creation task type and uses their index definitions to register the indexes into the server (line **24**).

For a single application this is a great and easy way to define indexes through classes because it is more efficient and easier to maintain. In case you have multiple applications that use the same RavenDB database, this can be a problem having indexes in each of your application because they might overwrite each other and you might need other solutions to manage indexes.

To call the `CreateIndexes()` method, you specified a parameter `assembly` that contains the `Cities_CountryCode` index class (line **24**).

To query this index you open a new session, call the `Query()` method, and specify the index name.

Results					
Id	CountryCode	Name	CountryId	Population	Province
city/3387	USA	Honolulu	country/1099	423475	Hawaii
city/1989	D	Aachen	country/1009	247113	Nordrhe
city/2177	RO	Piatra Neamt	country/1028	0	Neamt
city/1333	DK	Aalborg	country/1030	113865	Denmar
city/2273	UA	Horlivka	country/1020	338000	Donetsk
city/1215	CH	Aarau	country/1015	0	AG
city/1534	USA	Pierre	country/1099	11973	South D

Using AbstractIndexCreationTask and ReduceResult

Basically, when you create an index you need to use anonymous type in the map and/or reduce functions. In real world applications, you might need to create a more complex structure and define the data type you want to get back from the Reduce function. A common scenario when you need to define a ReduceResult class is when you have to make a count of elements in a collection.

When inheriting from the AbstractIndexCreationTask class, you can specify an optional generic term that allows you to define the Reduce function result using a concrete class. As the Map and Reduce functions output have to match, this class will be used as the output of the Map function.

Let's go ahead and learn how to create a more advanced index using the AbstractIndexCreationTask class with a ReduceResult class.

Time for action – creating indexes using the ResultReduce class

We will create a new index which will aggregate the World database to make a count of Cities that have the same name in different countries and return the CountryId key for each city as a single document. The following screenshot illustrates the expected result:

```
Projection                              Projection                              Projection
[{"CountryId":"country/1043...          [{"CountryId":"country/1099...          [{"CountryId":"co
{                                       {                                       {
  CityName: "London"                      CityName: "Manchester"                  CityName: "Meri
  Count: "2"                              Count: "2"                              Count: "3"
  CountriesId: [                          CountriesId: [                          CountriesId: [
    {                                       {                                       {
      CountryId: "country/1043"               CountryId: "country/1099"               CountryId: "c
    },                                      },                                      },
    {                                       {                                       {
      CountryId: "country/1098"               CountryId: "country/1043"               CountryId: "c
    }                                       }                                       },
  ]                                       ]                                       {
}                                       }                                         CountryId: "c
                                                                                }
```

1. Start Visual Studio and open the RavenDB_CH05 solution.

2. Add a new class to the project, name it `Cities_SameName` and add the following code snippet:

```
10    class Cities_SameName :
11        AbstractIndexCreationTask<City, Cities_SameName.ReduceResult>
12    {
13        public class ReduceResult
14        {
15            public string CityName { get; set; }
16            public int Count { get; set; }
17            public List<SingleCountryId> CountriesId { get; set; }
18
19            public class SingleCountryId
20            {
21                public string CountryId { get; set; }
22            }
23        }
```

We named the embedded class `ReduceResult` by convention. You can choose any other name for this class and place it outside the index class.

We could use a `String` type in the `ReduceResult` class to store the document ID `CountriesId` (which is a `string` type), but we choose to create a second embedded class, for learning purposes and show that it is possible to create more complex structure.

3. Add a default constructor to the `Cities_SameName` class and within this constructor add the index `Map` function using the following code snippet:

```
25    public Cities_SameName()
26    {
27        Map = cities => from city in cities
28                        select new
29                        {
30                            CityName = city.Name,
31                            Count = 1,
32                            CountriesId = new[] { new { CountryId = city.CountryId } }
33                        };
```

4. Within the `Cities_SameName` class constructor add the index `Reduce` function using the following code snippet:

```
35    Reduce = results => from result in results
36              group result by result.CityName into g
37              select new
38              {
39                  CityName = g.Key,
40                  Count = g.Sum(x => x.Count),
41                  CountriesId = from country in g.SelectMany(x => x.CountriesId)
42                                group country by country.CountryId into gp
43
44                                select new
45                                {
46                                    CountryId = gp.Key,
47                                }
48              };
```

5. Modify the `Main()` method in the `Program` class using the following code snippet:

```
32    ...
33        Console.WriteLine(cities.Count().ToString());
34    }
35
36    // Create Cities/SameName Index
37    IndexCreation.CreateIndexes(
38        typeof(Cities_SameName).Assembly, documentStore);
39
```

6. Save all the files, build and run the solution.

7. In Management Studio, execute the `Cities/SameName` index to get the expected result.

 You can query this index directly in Management Studio to get only cities for which the name appears more than a single time by applying the `[2 TO *]` filter on the `Count` field in query edit box.

What just happened?

You just created the `Cities_SameName` index class that inherits from the `AbstractIndexCreationTask` class and specifies a concrete class to define the `Reduce` function result, which will be also used as the `Map` function output. We called this class `ReduceResult` and specified that we want to use it to return data when inheriting from the `AbstractIndexCreationTask` class (line **10** to **11**).

 We define the type we are working with and the type we want to return.

In this index class, the embedded `ReduceResult` class definition is very simple and contains three properties: `CityName`, a `string` property which will hold the name of the city, `Count`, an `integer` property which will hold the aggregation count of cities names, and the `List<Countries>` a string collection which will hold all `CountriesId` where the city name appears. As stated, we choose to implement a `List<Countries>` list instead of a `List<String>` list for learning purposes only (lines **13** to **23**).

The `Map` function populates the `ResultReduce` fields using values from the `Cities` collection. The `CityName` field will get the `city.Name` value, a new `List<Countries>` collection is created and a new entry is added to this list using the actual `CountryId` value. The `Count` field is set to `1` to count each city name from the `Cities` collection (lines **27** to **33**).

The `Reduce` function takes the `Map` function output and groups it by the `CityName` field value. For each group created, the `ReduceResult` fields are populated with the `Reduce` function values; `CityName` will hold the city's name which is the aggregation key, `Count` will hold the number of elements of the group and `CountriesId` field is populated with all the `CountriesId` values found in each group (lines **35** to **48**).

Have a go hero – query the Cities_SameName index

Add a new method to the `Program` class and name it `QueryCities_SameName()`.

In this method, add the necessary code to call the `Query()` method on the `Session` object to retrieve and display all city names that appear more than one time.

Using the TransformResults function

The `TransformResults` function has already been discussed in the previous chapter. You can implement the `TransformResults` function the same way you did when creating your index using the `PutIndex()` method. Remember that an index may have only one `TransformResults` function.

Time for action – using the TransformResults function

You will create a new index class, then add a Map and TransformResults function. The index definition will contain only one Map function that retrieves the city population. Once the index is created you will execute it in Management Studio and view the result.

1. Open the RavenDB_CH05 project in Visual Studio.

2. Add a new class, name it TransformationResult and complete it with the following code snippet:

```
 9  class TransformationResult
10  {
11      public string Name { get; set; }
12      public string Province { get; set; }
13      public long Population { get; set; }
14  }
```

3. Add a new class, and name it Cities_ByPopulation and complete it with the following code snippet:

```
10  class Cities_ByPopulation : AbstractIndexCreationTask<City>
11  {
12      public Cities_ByPopulation()
13      {
14          Map = cities => from city in cities
15                          select new
16                          {
17                              Population = city.Population
18                          };
19
20          TransformResults = (database, cities) =>
21                          from city in cities
22                          select new
23                          {
24                              Name = city.Name,
25                              Province = city.Province,
26                              Population = city.Population
27                          };
28
29      }
30  }
```

4. Add the following code snippet to the `Main()` method in the `Program` class:

```
40   IndexCreation.CreateIndexes(
41       typeof(Cities_ByPopulation).Assembly, documentStore);
42
43   using (var session = documentStore.OpenSession())
44   {
45       var cities = session.Query<City, Cities_ByPopulation>()
46           // Filter based on 'City' fields
47           .Where(x => x.Population > 2000000)
48
49           .OfType<TransformationResult>()
50
51           // Filter based on 'TransformationResult' fields
52           .Where(x => x.Population < 3000000)
53           .ToList();
54
55       Console.WriteLine(cities.Count().ToString());
56   }
```

5. Save all the files, build and run the solution.

6. In Management Studio, execute the `Cities/ByPopulation` index and observe the result.

What just happened?

You just created the `Cities_ByPopulation` index and implemented its `Map` function and `TransformResults` functions in order to transform the `Map` function result and get something different from the original `Map` result.

We begin by creating the `TransformationResult` class, which will hold the transformation output data. This class contains three fields: `Name`, `Province`, and `Population` (lines **9** to **14**).

Then, we created the index `Cities_ByPopulation` definition. This index contains one `Map` function. This function retrieves the `Population` field from the `Cities` Collection (lines **14** to **18**).

To perform transformation, the `TransformResults` function will take the `Map` query output and will get a data accessor from RavenDB pointing on the actual documents. This is a regular Linq expression in which we read all the `Map` function outputs and use each entry to create a new anonymous object. This new object has three fields: `Name`, `Province`, and `Population` (lines **20** to **27**).

You can query the `Cities_ByPopulation` index the same way you query any other index. To get a result of the same type as `TransformationResult`, you need to use the `.OfType<TransformationResult>()` (line **49**). The advantage you get by using `TransformResults` is that you have an access to the executed index query and the collection of all returned results. In this code example, note that you can query on both, `city.Population` and `TransformationResult.Population`.

When you execute the index `Cities_ByPopulation` in Management Studio, you may choose to apply the `TransformResults` function or to skip it in order to visualize the index output before and after the transformation applied.

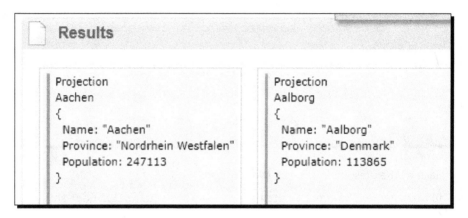

Creating multimap indexes

RavenDB allows you to define more than one `Map` function for static indexes. In this case such indexes are called Multi map indexes. When using a Multi map index, we are looking to take information from different documents. A single map index has only one `Map` function, while a Multi map index has more than one `Map` function. A Multi map index will get its data from multiple sources. It may have no or only one `Reduce` function, and no or only one `TranformResults` function.

If the index has a `Reduce` function, then the `multi map`(s) function(s) output is sent to the `Reduce` function. The only requirement that we have is that the output of all of the `Map` functions should be identical (and obviously, matches the output of the `Reduce` function). Then we can just treat this information as normal Map/Reduce index, which means that you can use all usual index features of RavenDB.

To create a `multi map index` class, we have to inherit from the `AbstractMultiMapIndexCreationTask` class instead of the `AbstractIndexCreationTask` class (as we have done while creating single map indexes class). To add a `Map` function in a multi map index, we basically call the `AddMap()` method and specify each `Map` function definition.

Time for action – creating multimap indexes

We will create a new index class that aggregates the `World` database and makes a count of `Cities` in each country using a multi map index.

1. Start Visual Studio and open the `RavenDB_CH05` solution.

2. Add a new class to the project, name it `Cities_MMapCitiesByCountry` and add the following code snippet:

```
10   class Cities_MMCitiesByCountry :
11       AbstractMultiMapIndexCreationTask<Cities_MMCitiesByCountry.ReduceResult>
12   {
13       public class ReduceResult
14       {
15           public string Name { get; set; }
16           public int CitiesCount { get; set; }
17           public string CountryId { get; set; }
18           public string Capital { get; set; }
19       }
```

3. Add a default constructor to the `Cities_MMCitiesByCountry` class and within this constructor add two `Map` functions using the following code snippet:

```
21   public Cities_MMCitiesByCountry()
22   {
23       AddMap<City>(cities => from city in cities
24                           select new
25                           {
26                               Name = (string)null,
27                               CitiesCount = 1,
28                               CountryId = city.CountryId,
29                               Capital = (string)null,
30                           });
31
32       AddMap<Country>(countries => from country in countries
33                           select new
34                           {
35                               Name = country.Name,
36                               CitiesCount = 0,
37                               CountryId = country.Id,
38                               Capital = country.Capital,
39                           });
```

4. Within the `Cities_MMCitiesByCountry` class constructor add the index `Reduce` function using the following code snippet:

```
41   Reduce = results => from result in results
42                       group result by result.CountryId into g
43                       select new
44                       {
45                           CountryId = g.Key,
46                           CitiesCount = g.Sum(x => x.CitiesCount),
47
48                           Name = g.Select(x => x.Name)
49                                    .Where(x => x != null)
50                                    .FirstOrDefault(),
51
52                           Capital = g.Select(x => x.Capital)
53                                      .Where(x => x != null)
54                                      .FirstOrDefault(),
55                       };
```

5. Modify the `Main` method in the `Program` class using the following code snippet.

```
59   // Create Cities/MMCitiesByCountry Index
60   IndexCreation.CreateIndexes(
61       typeof(Cities_ByPopulation).Assembly, documentStore);
62
63   using (var session = documentStore.OpenSession())
64   {
65       var citiesbyCountry = session.Query<Cities_MMCitiesByCountry.ReduceResult,
66                                     Cities_MMCitiesByCountry>()
67                                .ToList();
68
69       Console.WriteLine(citiesbyCountry.Count().ToString());
70   }
```

6. Save all files, build and run the solution.

7. In Management Studio, execute the `Cities/MMCitiesByCountry` index.

What just happened?

You just created the multi map `Cities_MMCitiesByCountry` index class. This index aims to aggregate the `World` database and get the cities count in each country.

The `Cities_MMCitiesByCountry` class inherits from the `AbstractMultiMapIndexCreationTask` class and specifies the `ReduceResult` class as the `Reduce` function result (lines **10** to **11**).

The embedded `ReduceResult` class, which is used to specify the `Reduce` function output, defines four fields (lines **13** to **19**):

- `Name`: It is a `string` field that will hold the country's name
- `CitiesCount`: It is an `integer` field to hold the number of cities in each country
- `CountryId`: It is a `string` field to hold the country's ID
- `Capital`: It is a string field to hold the country's capital

The first `Map` function reads all of the `City` collection and retrieves each city's `CountryId` and sets the `CitiesCount` to `1`. The `Name` field will hold the country's name and we don't need it while reading the `Cities` collection, so its value is set to null. A single `City` document doesn't contain any `Capital` field, so its value is set to `null` (lines **23** to **30**).

The second `Map` function will read the `Countries` collection and retrieve the `Name`, the `CountryId` and the `Capital` field values. The `CitiesCount` field will be summarized from the `Cities` collection, so its value is set to `zero` (lines **32** to **39**).

The `Reduce` function will aggregate the projections from the two `Map` function's output and group documents by the `CountryId` value. Then for each group created it populates the `ReduceResult` class fields with values from the current group. The `Reduce` function gets the values from two different collections, `Cities` and `Countries`. We need to make sure that `Map` functions are actually using the same output, which is what caused us the null casting for `Name` and `Capital` fields and the filtering that we needed to do on the `Reduce` function (lines **41** to **55**).

The multi map index `Cities_MMCitiesByCountry` is created within the `Main()` method (line **60**). Also in this method, you query this index to retrieve the documents and display the count of elements returned by the server (lines **63** to **70**).

When opening the index in Management Studio, you can observe that for each `Country` we get four columns (one column represents one field), the `CountryId`, `Name`, `Capital`, and the `CitiesCount`.

Name	Capital	CitiesCount	CountryId
Results			
Afghanistan	Kabul	1	country/1044
Albania	Tirane	6	country/1000
Algeria	Algiers	14	country/1142
Andorra	Andorra la Vella	1	country/1004
Angola	Luanda	18	country/1150
Antigua and Barbuda	Saint Johns	1	country/1092

Using indexes to search over documents

Providing a search feature is a common functionality in real world applications. RavenDB indexes can be used to look up search terms and find their corresponding values in one or more documents. When we create an index based on documents, we can query the index to find out what documents match our search terms.

In order to optimize queries over indexes, RavenDB processes queries in the background against the stored documents and persisting the results to a `Lucene` index. Lucene is a full-featured text search engine library available for JAVA and .NET platform.

 The Lucene official website can be reached at `www.lucene.net`.

Lucene comes with several analyzers, which are used to process and convert field text to their most fundamental unit for searching called terms. Term is composed of two elements: the text of the word and the name of the field in which the text occurs.

These terms are used to determine which documents match searching criteria. Each analyzer differs in the way it splits the text stream and in the way it processes it. Splitting the text stream is called Tokenization process.

By default, RavenDB uses a custom Lucene analyzer called `LowerCaseKeywordAnalyzer` for all content. This analyzer will convert all characters to lowercase and behaves like Lucene's `KeywordAnalyzer`. The Lucene's `KeywordAnalyzer` will perform no tokenization, and will consider the whole text stream as one token.

Basically, the `Where()` closure is used to perform simple text field search. We can perform more complex searching by calling the `Search()` method on the `Query()` object. This method will send back `Hits` which represents the search results and basically we iterate over the search result to obtain each individual `Hit` object.

To register a field to be indexed you might add it to the `Indexes` list (member of the `AbstractIndexCreationTask` class) which requires two parameters: the field name to be indexed and the field indexing option which can take one of four values:

- ◆ `No`: This field will not be indexed. This field cannot be searched, but can still access its contents.

- ◆ `Analyzed`: RavenDB will index the tokens produced by running the field's value through an analyzer. This is useful for common text.

- ◆ `NotAnalyzed`: RavenDB will index this field's value without using an analyzer and its value will be stored as a single term, so it can be searched. This is useful for unique IDs for example, product numbers.

 This is important if you want to search in a case sensitive manner.

- ◆ `Default`: This field will be indexed using the default internal analyzer: `LowerCaseKeywordAnalyzer`.

 A query is broken up into terms and operators. We call `Single Term` a single word such as hello and `Phrase` is a phrase or a group of words usually surrounded by double quotes such as "Hello World".

Full-text and exact matching search

Searching using indexes in RavenDB lets users (and applications) run full-text queries against character-based data. Each index indexes one or more fields from a document and can use a specific language to perform linguistic searches against text data by operating on words and phrases based on rules of a particular language such as English or Japanese.

Exact matching queries cause RavenDB to make an exact (and case sensitive) match to a field value. Full-text queries can include simple words and phrases or multiple forms of words or phrases. A full-text query (and exact matching query) returns any documents that contain at least one match (also known as a hit). A match occurs when a target document contains any of the terms specified in the full-text query, and meets any other search conditions.

Usually to create a simple condition or for simple text field search a `Where` closure is enough to create condition. By default, RavenDB uses case insensitive match to compare values. You can change this behavior and tell RavenDB to compare a field value as it is and perform a case sensitive exact matching search. In order to implement this behavior, you need to add the field to be indexed to the `Indexes` collections and specify the `NotAnalyzed` option `Field Indexing`.

Time for action – creating a full-text searching index

We will create a new full-text index searching class using a single search term. This index will search matching text over the `Cities` collection based on the city name field value.

1. Start Visual Studio and open the `RavenDB_CH5` solution.

2. Add a new class to the project, name it `Cities_FullTextSearch` and add the following code snippet:

```
10    class Cities_FullTextSearch :
11        AbstractIndexCreationTask<City, Cities_FullTextSearch.ReduceResult>
12    {
13        public class ReduceResult
14        {
15            public string Name { get; set; }
16        }
17
18        public Cities_FullTextSearch()
19        {
20            Map = cities => from city in cities
21                            select new
22                            {
23                                Name = city.Name
24                            };
25
26            // Enable full text searching on 'Name' field
27            Index(x => x.Name, Raven.Abstractions.Indexing.FieldIndexing.Analyzed);
28        }
29    }
```

3. Modify the `Main()` method in the `Program` class using the following code snippet:

```
73    // Create Cities/FullTextSearch Index
74    IndexCreation.CreateIndexes(
75        typeof(Cities_FullTextSearch).Assembly, documentStore);
76
77    using (var session = documentStore.OpenSession())
78    {
79        var cities = session.Query<Cities_FullTextSearch.ReduceResult,
80                                   Cities_FullTextSearch>()
81            //.Where(x => x.Name.Contains("San")) Is not supported
82            .Search(x => x.Name, "San Los") //we used .Search instead
83            .ToList();
84
85        Console.WriteLine(cities.Count().ToString());
86    }
```

The `Contains()` method is not supported, performing a substring match over a text field is a very slow operation, and is not allowed using the LINQ API. The recommended method is to use the `.Search()` method to query it. (The field has to be marked as `Analyzed`).

4. Save all the files, build and run the solution.

What just happened?

You created the `Cities_FullTextSearch` index class to allow single term full-text searching over the `city.Name` text field.

The `Cities_FullTextSearch` class inherits from the `AbstractIndexCreationTask` class and specifies a `ReduceResult` class as the `Reduce` function result (lines **10** to **13**).

The embedded `ReduceResult` class defines one field only: `Name` a string field that will hold the city name (lines **13** to **16**).

The `Map` function reads the `Cities` collection and retrieves only the `city.Name` field. Then in order to allow full-text searching on its value, we need to add it to the `Index` list and declare it as `Analyzed` using the `FieldIndexing` option (line **27**).

The `Cities_FullTextSearch` index is created within the `Main()` method by calling the `CreateIndexes()` method (line **74**).

To perform the full-text search when querying the index, we used the .Search() method (which is the recommended method). The .Search() method accepts two parameters: the field selector, and the text criteria to be searched over this field. You set the field to Name, and set the search criteria explicitly to "San Los".

When querying the index, the .Search() method will return all cities which have San or Los in their name (lines **77** to **85**).

> The Contains() method on the String object is not recommended to perform full-text searching. An attempt to use string. Contains() method a condition of Where closure will throw a NotSupportedException. That is because the search term as *term* (note wildcards at the beginning and at the end) can cause performance issues. Due to RavenDB's safe by default paradigm such an operation is forbidden.

Have a go hero – adding exact matching searching index class

You learned how to create a full-text search index class. Creating exact matches index class is very similar to what you did to create the full-text search index class. The main difference is the option you will choose to specify how to index the field when registering it.

Add a new class to RavenDB_Ch05 project and name it Cities_ExactMatchSearch. Define a single term Map function which will return a city's name. Then register this field to be indexed and choose NotAnalyzed for the Field indexing option.

Modify the Main() method in the Program class to create the index and to query it. Try different search terms and observe the result sent back by the server.

Multiple field searching and search options

RavenDB allows the registration of one or more than one field for indexing when creating the index class definition. While querying such index you can use the .Search() method consecutively more than one time to look for multiple indexed fields.

When querying the index using consecutive .Search() method, you can specify the logic of search expression and choose how to combine search results. The .Search() method accepts an optional SearchOptions parameter, which can be combined through logic operators, with the following values:

- Or: This operator divides the query into several optional terms.
- And: This operator means that all terms in the AND group must match some part of the searched field(s).

- **Not**: This operator excludes documents that contain the term after NOT. But an AND group which contains only terms with the NOT operator gives an empty result set instead of a full set of indexed documents.

- **Guess**: (The default value). By default RavenDB attempts to guess and match up the semantics between terms. If there are consecutive searches, the OR semantic will be used, otherwise AND will be used by default.

Time for action – creating multifields searching index

You will create a new index class and register three fields to be indexed. This index will perform search over the `Cities` and `Countries` collections. To query this index you will use consecutive `.Search()` method and specify `SearchOptions` for each method.

1. Start Visual Studio and open the `RavenDB_CH05` solution.

2. Add a new class to the project, name it `Cities_MultiFieldsSearch` and it inherits from `AbstractIndexCreationTask` class:

```
10      class Cities_MultiFieldsSearch :
11          AbstractIndexCreationTask<City>
12      {
```

3. Add a default constructor, and then add the `Map` function within the class constructor using the following code snippet:

```
15   Map = (cities => from city in cities
16                    select new
17                    {
18                        Name = city.Name,
19                        CountryCode = city.CountryCode,
20                        Population = city.Population,
21                    });
```

4. Add Indexes field's registration to the class constructor using the following code snippet:

```
23   //Indexing CityName field for Exact Matching search
24   Index(x => x.CountryCode, Raven.Abstractions.Indexing.FieldIndexing.NotAnalyzed);
25
26   //Indexing CountryName field for Full-Text search
27   Index(x => x.Name, Raven.Abstractions.Indexing.FieldIndexing.Analyzed);
28
29   Index(x => x.Population, Raven.Abstractions.Indexing.FieldIndexing.Default);
```

5. Add the following code snippet to the `Main()` method in the `Program` class:

```
88    // Create Cities/FullTextSearch Index
89    IndexCreation.CreateIndexes(
90        typeof(Cities_MultiFieldsSearch).Assembly, documentStore);
91
92    using (var session = documentStore.OpenSession())
93    {
94        var cities = session.Query<City, Cities_MultiFieldsSearch>()
95       //Get all CoutryCode that match with two terms: F, USA
96      .Search(x => x.CountryCode, "F USA", options: SearchOptions.Or)
97
98      // Wilcard searching is not recommanded,
99      // this is for learning purpose only
100     .Search(x => x.Name, "van*", escapeQueryOptions:
101                             EscapeQueryOptions.AllowPostfixWildcard,
102                             options: SearchOptions.Guess)
103
104     // Population Range condition
105     .Where(x => x.Population > 200000 && x.Population < 5000000)
106     .As<City>()
107     .ToList()
108     ;
109
110      Console.WriteLine("{0} elements returned by the query",
111                      cities.Count.ToString());
112    }
```

6. Save all the files, build and run the solution.

What just happened?

You created the `Cities_MutliFieldsSearch()` index class to search over multiple indexed fields.

This index will define one `Map` function that inherits from the `AbstractIndexCreationTask` class and specifies the `City` document type (lines **10** to **11**).

The `Map` function reads from the `Cities` collection and retrieves the city's `Name`, city's `CountryCode` and city's `Population` field's values (lines **15** to **21**).

Within the class constructor we registered the following three fields to be indexed: (lines **23** to **29**):

- `CountryCode`: This field is registered using the `NotAnalyze` field indexing option to allow exact matching search over this field.

- `CityName`: This field is registered using the `Analyze` field indexing option to allow full-text search only over this field.

- `Population`: This field is registered using the `Default` field indexing option, which convert strings to lowercase but as this field contains numeric values this has no effect on it.

The index is created by calling the `CreateIndexes()` method within the `Main()` method (line **89**).

To perform the multi filed search, we use two consecutive `.Search()` method and one `Where()` closure.

The first `.Search()` call will perform an exact matching search over the `CountryCode` field using two terms: `F` (or) `USA`. It will return all documents that `F` (or) `USA` are a part of the country's code (line **96**).

The second `.Search()` method performs full-text search over the city `Name` and allows to use post wildcards (line **100** to **102**).

> The `EscapeQueryOptions.AllowPostfixWildcard` searching option enables searching against a field by using a search term that ends with wildcard character
>
> This query is for learning purposes only. It is not recommended to use wildcard to search over string value. RavenDB allows to search by using such queries but you have to be aware that leading wildcards drastically slows down searches, which is due to the underlying Lucene.NET implementation.

The `Where()` closure defines a range condition and will retrieve only cities where the `Population` is greater than `2000000` and less than `5000000` (line **105**).

As we have used consecutive `.Search()` method, we define the logic of the search expression to be inclusive (`Or` operator).

Using a custom analyzer for searching

When creating RavenDB documents, you may populate them with other language than English. Therefore, you need to query these document's content in the same language when storing them into the database.

As discussed in the previous section, RavenDB processes queries in the background against the stored documents and persists the results to a `Lucene` index. Lucene comes with several analyzers which include different language's analyzers.

RavenDB allows you to specify a custom analyzer to be used while searching document's content. The custom analyzer has to be registered while creating the index that you will query to perform searching.

The analyzer you will use has to be referenced into your application and has to be available to the RavenDB server instance. When using custom analyzers, you need to drop all the necessary DLLs into the `~\Analyzers` folder of the RavenDB server directory, and use their fully qualified type name (including the assembly name).

Time for action – using a custom analyzer

You will create a new index class and register one field that will use a specific analyzer, the `FrenchAnalyzer`. This index will perform search over the `Cities` collections on the `Name` field. To query this index you will use a `.Search()` method and specify a `Where` closure.

1. Start Visual Studio and open the `RavenDB_CH05` solution.

2. Use the NuGet Package Manager to add a reference to the **Lucen.Net Contrib** package:

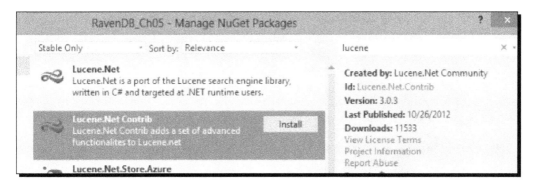

3. Add a new class to the project, name it `Cities_CustomAnalyzer` that inherits from `AbstractIndexCreationTask` class:

```
10        class Cities_CustomAnalyzer :
11            AbstractIndexCreationTask<City>
12        {
```

4. Add a default constructor, and then add the `Map` function within the class constructor using the following code snippet:

```
15        Map = cities => from city in cities
16                    select new
17                    {
18                        Id = city.Id,
19                        Name = city.Name,
20                        CountryCode = city.CountryCode
21                    };
```

5. Under the `Map` function, add `Analyzer` field's registration to the class constructor using the following code snippet:

```
23      // Setting analyser for French language
24      // You can find FrenchAnalyser in this Lucene package
25      // http://nuget.org/packages/Lucene.Net.Contrib/
26
27      Analyze(x => x.Name, typeof(Lucene.Net.Analysis.Fr.FrenchAnalyzer)
28                          .AssemblyQualifiedName);
```

6. Add the following code snippet to the `Main()` method in the `Program` class:

```
151    // Create Cities/CustomAnalyzer Index
152    IndexCreation.CreateIndexes(
153        typeof(Cities_CustomAnalyzer).Assembly, documentStore);
154
155    using (var session = documentStore.OpenSession())
156    {
157        var cities = session.Query<City, Cities_CustomAnalyzer>()
158
159            // Wilcard searching is not recommanded,
160            // this is for learning purposes only
161            .Search(x => x.Name, "B*", escapeQueryOptions:
162                                EscapeQueryOptions.AllowPostfixWildcard)
163
164            // Only Cities in France
165            .Where(x => x.CountryCode == "F")
166            .ToList();
167
168        Console.WriteLine("{0} elements returned by the query",
169                        cities.Count.ToString());
170    }
```

7. Save all the files.

8. Open the `RavenDB_Ch05` output folder and copy `Lucene.Net.Contrib.Analyzers.dll` to the `\Analyzers` folder under the `RavenDB \Server` folder.

9. Restart RavenDB server.

10. In Visual Studio, run the `RavenDB_Ch05` solution.

What just happened?

You created the `Cities_CustomAnalyzer()` index class to allow searching using a custom analyzer in order to search a language other than English.

In order to use the `Lucen.Net FrenchAnalyzer`, which is part of the `Lucene.Net Contrib` package, you used the NuGet Package Manager to add this package to the `RavenDB_CH05` project.

> You may directly install `Lucene.Net Contrib` package using the Package Manager Console using this command line:
> `Install-Package Lucene.Net.Contrib`

Then you created the `Cities_CustomAnalyzer` index definition. The `Map` function output selects three fields from each `City` document: `Id`, `Name`, and `CountryCode`.(lines **15** to **21**).

The custom analyzer is registered using the `Analyze()` method. This method takes two parameters, the field name to be analyzed and the analyzer name that will be used (lines **27** to **28**).

The `FrenchAnalyzer` that we want to use has to be available to the RavenDB server instance. For that, you copied the `Lucene.Net.Contrib.Analyzers.dll` to the `\ Analyzers` folder under the `RavenDB \Server` folder and restarted the server.

The `Cities_CustomAnalyzer` index can be queried as any other index. To perform searching on the `Name` field you call the `.Search()` method and specify the `Name` field and the search criteria.

Paging a query's results

Paging a query result is the process of returning the results of a query in smaller subsets of data, or pages. Nowadays implementing pagination is a very common scenario for displaying results to a user in small, easy to manage chunks.

RavenDB allows query's result pagination and supports both `Skip` and `Take` LINQ operators, making paging through a collection easy. To perform paging you will call the `Take` and `Skip` operators on the `Query` object to return a given number of elements and/or to skip over a given number of elements and then return the remainder.

As RavenDB is safe by default, it protects itself and user applications from overload scenarios and limits the number of documents to be returned to the client from the server. In large dataset scenarios it makes paging mandatory. This means that we need to ensure that we limit the result sets to reasonable sizes.

By default, the number of documents on the client side is 128 (but you can change that) and 1024 for the server side no matter how many documents there actually are. This limit can be changed in the server configuration but it is strongly recommended not to do so.

Time for action – paging a query's results

Now let's take a look at how to implement paging in RavenDB. You will add two new methods to the `Program` class: the first one will query the `Countries` collection using `Skip()` and `Take()` methods, the second one will display the query's result pages.

1. Start Visual Studio and open the `RavenDB_Ch05` solution.

2. Add the following code to the `Main()` method in the `Program` class:

```
114    // Paging QueryResult
115    using (var session = documentStore.OpenSession())
116    {
117        //number of elements per page
118        int pageSize = 30;
119
120        // hold the query satistics
121        RavenQueryStatistics stats;
122
123        // we want to get query statistics only
124        session.Query<Country>()
125            .Statistics(out stats)
126            .Take(0).ToList();
127
128        // get the total elements count and
129        // calculate how many pages we have
130        var totalNumberOfItems = stats.TotalResults;
131        int PageCount = (int)Math.Ceiling((double)stats.TotalResults / pageSize);
132
133        // simulate 1-based index to display all query's pages
134        for (int pageIndex = 1; pageIndex < PageCount + 1; pageIndex++)
135        {
136            //will use "Countries/ByName" index
137            var countries = session.Query<Country>()
138            .Skip((pageIndex - 1) * pageSize)
139            .Take(pageSize) // load elements
140            .ToList();
141
142            // get page's elements and order them by Country.Name (optional)
143            foreach (var item in countries.OrderBy(x => x.Name))
144            {
145                Console.WriteLine(item.Name);
146            }
147        }
148        Console.ReadLine();
149    }
```

3. Save all the files, build and run the solution.

What just happened?

We just queried the `Countries` Collection and implemented paging on the query result. By design RavenDB limits the number of returned documents to the client to 128 no matter how many there actually are.

In the code snippet (line 121), we declare a `RavenQueryStatistics` field to hold the output of the `Statistics` extension method, which will allow you to read the number of `TotalResults`.

While the only thing we wanted to do is to get the document count. So making `Take(0)` call will explicitly tell RavenDB not to load any entities at all. Why? Because on the next line (line 126) we are calling `ToList()`, which would fetch all of the documents you are querying for (128 with standard RavenDB client configuration). So as the effect of this call, the `TotalResults` property will be set, allowing us to get the number of total documents in the `Countries` collection.

> Basically, `TotalResults` contains the total count of matching documents. When executing a `Distinct` query it will not take into account any results that were skipped as a result of the `Distinct` operator. You have to check the `SkippedResults` value and whenever it is greater than 0 it implies that there are skipped results in the index.

Then a `for` loop is used to display query's result pages. The interesting point in this method is how to fix the loop bounds to loop over the query result pages.

To page the query result you call the `Skip()` and `Take()` Linq operators on the `Query` object (lines **137** to **140**). Basically, the page number requested by the user is normally 1-based, hence the need to do `pageIndex - 1` in the code snippet. To go to the first element in a given page you need to skip `(pageIndex - 1) * pageSize` documents worth of countries (line **138**). Once you are positioned on the first element on a given page you use the `Take` operator to take documents in the page size (line **139**) and then return the result to the caller.

Pop quiz – searching the right way

Q1. How do we load the 190th document only from a collection?

1. `Session.Query<T>().Take(190).`

2. `Session.Query<T>().Skip(190).`

3. `Session.Query<T>().Skip(190).Take(0).`

4. `Session.Query<T>().Skip(189).Take(1).`

Q2. We registered the `Name` field to be indexed and use the `NotAnalyzed` option. What will RavenDB do while searching this field?

1. The field is indexed but it cannot be searched.

2. The field is registered and full-text searching is allowed.

3. The field is registered and exact matching searching is allowed.

4. The field is registered but it cannot be used with LuceneQuery.

Q3. We need to search the "San" term, which method is not supported?

1. `Session.Query<T>().Where(x => x.Name.Contains("San")).`

2. `Session.Query<T>().Where(x => x.Name.Equals("San")).`

3. `Session.Query<T>().Where(x => x.Name ==."San").`

4. `Session.Query<T>().Where(x => x.Name.ToLower().Equals("San")).`

Q4. By default Lucene searches multiterms using?

1. AND operator

2. OR operator

3. Both a and b

4. Neither a or b

Summary

In this chapter, we learned some advanced techniques to execute more complex query statements in RavenDB, which will help us to use RavenDB in an efficient way. Specifically we covered how to create indexes using the `AbstractIndexCreatingTask` class, what are multi map indexes and how to create them.

Also we learned how to register fields to be indexed and how to combine searching options.

Then we presented paging and how to page query's results using `Skip()` and `Take()` LINQ operators to return small data chunks to the user.

In the next chapter, we will talk about RavenDB documents attachment, about handling documents relationships and some useful techniques to patch a single document or a set of documents using a JavaScript. So let's go!

6
Advanced RavenDB Document Capabilities

Beyond storing a single document in RavenDB, there are many scenarios where you need to do more. The good thing is that RavenDB allows you to do more than just storing documents in its document store. In this chapter, you will learn different advanced techniques which you can apply to use RavenDB documents in an efficient way.

We will learn how to store and retrieve documents' attachment, how to handle documents' relationship, and how RavenDB can help you to do that in an easy way. Also you will learn how to patch, server side, a document or a set of documents using a simple syntax and discover how amazing ScriptedPatchRequest *method is.*

In this chapter we will cover:

- RavenDB attachments
- Handling documents relationships
- Patching documents

RavenDB attachments

Your application might require the storage of binary data in the database. For that you can choose to store this binary data in a field as part of a document in your database. In this case, the data will be stored and loaded with the document; this can work fine with a small binary data chunk. Large binary data is not recommended because it can increase the document size significantly. This is a result of increased I/O from disk and over the network.

The alternative is to use RavenDB attachments, which allows storage of large chunks of binary data such as video, audio, and images. Attachments are basically **BLOB**s (**binary large object** is a data type that can store binary data).

> If binary data is stored as part of a document, RavenDB will store this binary data base64-encoded in the document.
>
> Storing attachments in RavenDB may not be the best choice for binary data. A better choice might be to store those data in a cloud environment or on dedicated servers.

Attachments are completely decoupled from documents. They don't participate in transactions and are not tracked for changes. They can be updated and changed independently from the documents.

Storing attachments

To store or to get attachments you don't require a session. This can be done directly by calling the `DatabaseCommands` object on the `DocumentStore` object.

Storing attachments requires four parameters: the attachment key, which you can freely specify, the attachment `Etag`, which is used for versioning, the data stream to be stored in RavenDB, and metadata information to describe the attachment.

Time for action – using attachments to store images

We want to add a flag image to a `Country` document and we want to store this image as an attachment. You will modify the `Country` class and add a new property to hold the `FlagId` value. Then you will add necessary code to store the attachment and modify a `Country` document to populate the `FlagId` property in order to refer the attachment. Once it is done, you will observe RavenDB logs to learn how RavenDB stores the attachment.

1. Start Visual Studio, create a new project and name it `RavenDB_Ch06`.

2. Add a new class, name it `Country`, and make it look like the following code snippet:

```
 9 ⊟     class Country
10        {
11            public string Id { get; set; }
12            public string Name { get; set; }
13            public string Code { get; set; }
14            public long Area { get; set; }
15            public string Capital { get; set; }
16            public string Province { get; set; }
17            public string ContinentCode { get; set; }
18            public string FlagId { get; set; }
19        }
```

3. Add the following code to the `Main()` method:

```
14 ⊟   static void Main(string[] args)
15     {
16         using (var documentStore =
17             new DocumentStore
18             {
19                 Url = "http://localhost:8080",
20                 DefaultDatabase = "World"
21             }.Initialize())
22     {
23         // We want to attach a flag image to a country
24         // We choose freely: Canada
25
26         // We load flag image for Canada .
27         var flag = File.OpenRead(@"\Flags\flag-ca.png");
28
29         // PutAttachmnt method is called to store files as attachment
30         // Canada country Id: country/1098, Attachment Id:flag/1098
31         documentStore.DatabaseCommands.PutAttachment("flag/1098",
32             null, // ETag
33             flag, // Stream to be stored as attachment
34             // metadata informations
35             new RavenJObject { { "Description", "Canada flag" } });
36
37         using (var session = documentStore.OpenSession())
38         {
39             // We load Canada Country document.
40             var country = session.Load<Country>("country/1098");
41
42             // We set the flag Id
43             country.FlagId = "flag/1098";
44
45             session.SaveChanges();
46         }
47         Console.WriteLine("Attachement has been stored succefully.");
48     }
49     }
```

4. Save all the files, build and run the solution.

5. In Windows Explorer, switch to the RavenDB prompt window and look at the RavenDB logs.

6. In Management Studio, use the **Go To document "country/1098"** to view this document with its new `FlagId` property.

What just happened?

We aim to attach a flag image file to a `Country` document from the `Countries` collection (we choose randomly: `Canada`). You stored the image file in RavenDB as attachment and modified the `Country` class to hold a reference to the attached file.

You added a new string property to the `Country` class named it `FlagId`. This property will hold the flag ID which is the attachment ID (`Country` class, line **18**).

To store the attachment, you call the `PutAttachment()` method on the `DatabaseCommands` object. This method stores the attachment file as a byte array and assigns a specified key to this attachment. This method requires the following four parameters (lines **31** to **35**):

- ◆ `key`: This is the attachment ID. We choose freely `"flag/1098"`.

- ◆ `Etag`: The `Etag` is used for versioning. We set it to null when creating a new attachment.

 When set, it makes sure that the data we send is not persisted using this key unless the current attachment's `Etag` has that value `set`. This ensures you don't overwrite an attachment by accident. So set it to `null` whenever putting a new attachment, or when you want to forcibly overwrite an existing one.

- ◆ `data`: To store the stream, we used the `flag-ca.png` bytes stream.

- ◆ `metadata`: The attachment metadata is key-value collection which lets you specify information about the attachment. We choose to define one key: `"Description"` with `"Canada flag"` as value.

 To store metadata we need to create a new instance of `RavenJObject` which will convert metadata to JSON format.

The last step is to populate the `FlagId` field for the `Canada` document with the attachment ID. This is very easy. You call the `Load()` method on the `Session` object and specify the document ID, which in this case is `country/1098`. Once the document is loaded you populate the `FlagId` field (`flag/1098`) and save the changes to the server (lines **37** to **46**).

Let's take a look at the RavenDB logs and see how RavenDB stored this attachment:

To store the attachment, RavenDB performs a `PUT` command on the `static` endpoint with the attachment ID.

In Management Studio, you can see in the document that the ID is `country/1098` and has a property `FlagId` set to `"flag/1098"`.

Retrieving attachments

Retrieving attachments from RavenDB is simple. All you need is to call the `GetAttachment()` method on the `DatabaseCommands` object which doesn't require a session.

This method requires the attachment key you want to retrieve to be specified when you call it. It will return an `Attachment` object which contains five properties: the four properties you used to store the attachment (`key`, `Etag`, `data`, and `metadata`) and the `Size` property which holds the size of the attachment.

Time for action – retrieving stored attachments

We want to retrieve the flag image we stored early as an attachment. You will add a code snippet to the `Main()` method to retrieve the attachment.

1. Start Visual Studio and open the `RavenDB_Ch06` solution.

2. Add the following snippet of code to the `Main()` method:

```
49    // Get Attachment
50    using (var session = documentStore.OpenSession())
51    {
52        // GetAttachment method is called to retrive attachment
53        // Attachment Id = "flag/1098"
54        var attachement = documentStore.DatabaseCommands
55                            .GetAttachment("flag/1098");
56
57        Console.WriteLine("Description: {0}, \tSize: {1}",
58                            attachement.Metadata["Description"],
59                            attachement.Size.ToString());
60        Console.ReadLine();
61    }
```

3. Save all the files, build and run the solution.

4. In Windows Explorer, switch to the RavenDB prompt window and look at the RavenDB logs.

What just happened?

We aim to retrieve the flag image file stored earlier as an attachment.

Within the `Main()` method you called the `GetAttachment()` method on the `DatabaseCommands` object and specified the attachment ID to retrieve, which in this case is `flag/1098`.

This method returns an `Attachment` object that contains all data and metadata used to store the attachment.

To retrieve the attachment RavenDB performs a `GET` command on the static endpoint using the attachment ID:

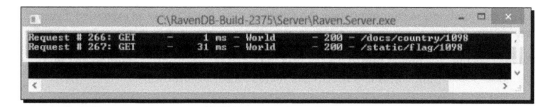

Have a go hero – retrieving country flag image attachment

Write a new method to retrieve the attachment using the ID stored earlier in `FlagId` property and display its metadata information in the following three steps:

- ◆ Loading the document
- ◆ Retrieving the attachment
- ◆ Printing out the metadata information.

Update and delete attachments

We have covered storing and retrieval of attachments in RavenDB. It is time that we learn how we can update or delete an attachment.

Deletes are performed by the `DeleteAttachment()` method on the `DatabaseCommands` object. Only the attachment ID to be deleted needs to be specified.

RavenDB doesn't provide a particular method to update an attachment. To update an attachment, we simply use the `PutAttachment()` method, again providing just the attachment ID.

RavenDB provides a way to update or retrieve metadata information. To perform such update you call the `UpdateAttachmentMetadata()` method which takes the following three parameters:

- The attachment `key`
- The attachment `Etag`
- The attachment `metadata` (as opposed to four parameters used in the `PutAttachment()` method)

Using this method you cannot retrieve the attached data. It will throw an exception if you attempt to do so.

To retrieve the attachment metadata, you call the `HeadAttachment()` method on the `DatabaseCommands` object and specify the metadata key to retrieve.

Time for action – retrieving and updating an attachment's metadata

You will write two new methods to the `Program` class: the first method will retrieve the metadata information for a given attachment based on its key, the second method will update the metadata information for an attachment.

1. Start Visual Studio and open the `RavenDB_Ch06` solution.
2. Add the following code to the `Main()` method:

```
63    // Retrieve attachment metadata
64    string key = "flag/1098";
65    var head = documentStore.DatabaseCommands.HeadAttachment(key);
66
67    Console.WriteLine("Description: {0}, \tSize: {1}",
68                      head.Metadata["Description"],
69                      head.Size.ToString());
70    Console.ReadLine();
71
72    // Update attachment metadata
73    documentStore.DatabaseCommands.UpdateAttachmentMetadata(key,
74        null, //etag
75        new RavenJObject // metadata information
76    {
77        { "Description", "Canada flag" },
78        { "Format", "png"} // new key-value pair
79    });
80
81    Console.WriteLine("Attachement {0} metadata has been updated.", key);
82    Console.ReadLine();
```

3. Save all the files, build and run the solution.

What just happened?

We just retrieved the metadata information for the attachment with the ID as `flag/1098` and updated them.

To retrieve the attachment metadata you call the `HeadAttachment()` method and specify the attachment key. This method returns the attachment header through which you can get its field values (line **65**).

To update the metadata you called the `UpdateAttachmentMetadata()` method and provided the new metadata values (lines **73** to **79**).

Have a go hero – updating and deleting attachments

Write two new methods to the `Program` class to update and delete an attachment.

The first method takes one parameter named `key` (`string` type), and uses this parameter to delete the attachment identified by this key.

The second method takes three parameters: `key` (`string`), `data` (`stream`), `metadata` (`RavenJObject`) and calls the `PutAttachment()` method to update an existing attachment using new values.

Handling documents relationships

Relational databases allow the user to create relationships between tables while in document databases the basic idea is that documents are independent.

Most of the advantages of document databases come from the document-oriented modeling. In a document-oriented model, data objects are stored as documents; each document stores your data and enables you to update the data or delete it. Analogous to the relational approach, complex parts (separate document(s)) can be implemented in a document, which will refer to these parts by a unique identifier.

However, in the document-model it is also possible to add a part as a property or collection inside the document representing the owner. In this case, if the owner is removed, the part will be removed with it automatically.

This approach is called data denormalization, where the owner document contains the actual value of the referenced entity in addition (or instead) to the foreign key. Therefore, this approach may help to reduce number of requests to the database, but updating and deleting operations may become more complex.

 Denormalization is a viable solution for rarely changing data, or for data that must remain the same despite the underlying referenced data changing over time.

But often, we need to make relationships even in a document database. That means when you load a document you also need to load the referenced document. The first idea is to fetch related documents by their IDs and make two separate roundtrips to the database.

Using Include to preload documents

The RavenDB `Include` feature aims to optimize this and offers an elegant way to pre-load the referenced document at the same time as the original document. To use this feature it is necessary, in a given root document, to hold a reference to the second document. Then RavenDB instructs to preload the referenced document at the same time the root document is retrieved.

Time for action – using Include to reduce query calls

Now let's take a look at how to handle document relationships while reducing query calls. You will make a call to the `Load()` method and the `Include()` method on the `Session` object to retrieve a `City` from the `Cities` collection and preload the `Country` referenced by the `City.CountryId` field. Then you will take a look at the RavenDB log and analyze its entries.

1. Open the `RavenDB_Ch06` project in Visual Studio.

2. Copy the `City` class you created previously and make it a part of the `RavenDB_Ch06` project.

3. Add the following code snippet to the `Main()` method:

```
84     // Loading Related Documents
85     using (var session = documentStore.OpenSession())
86     {
87         var city = session
88             //pre-load the document referenced
89             //by the CountryId field
90             .Include<City>(x => x.CountryId)
91             // Load the city with the Id= city/3242 (Montreal)
92             .Load<City>("city/3242");
93
94         // this call will not require querying the server
95         // a second time !
96         var country = session.Load<Country>(city.CountryId);
97
98         Console.WriteLine("Country Name: {0}", country.Name);
99         Console.ReadLine();
100    }
```

[
You can specify more than one ID in the Load() method. In this case RavenDB will preload all related documents once and this will not require querying the server again.
]

4. Save all the files, build and run the solution.

5. In Windows Explorer, switch to the RavenDB prompt window and observe the RavenDB logs.

What just happened?

You just learned how to handle related documents in RavenDB. You called the Load() and Include() methods on the Session object in order to load a City document and preload its related Country document in a single database call.

To instruct RavenDB to preload a document, you call the Include() method before you call the Load() method.

In the code snippet (line **90**) you call the Include() method on the Session object and then call the Load() method. You specify the City type and the ID of the city you want to load (line **92**). This is similar to a single call to the Load() method, except that in this case you will get both the documents in one trip to the database.

We use a special syntax to include the related document. On the Session object, before calling the Load() method you call the Include() method and specify the type which is City and use a lambda expression to specify the key of the related document (CountryId). So you load the city document (Montreal ID as city/3242) which contains a CountryId reference (Canada ID = country/1098). This is similar to the foreign key in relational databases. By running this code you load both the documents, City and Country, in one time.

In the code snippet (line **96**), you load the Country document referenced by the CountryId field by calling the Load() method on the Session object.

Let's take a look at the RavenDB log entries and see what happened when you called the Include() method.

When you call the Include() method, RavenDB calls the queries endpoint and specifies the include parameter to load the document with the specified ID (city/3242). In the code snippet (line **96**), you call the Load() method to load the Country document. But RavenDB fetches this document in its session cache and does not make a new call to the database. As you can see in the following screenshot, this call is not logged, which indicates that the document has been preloaded and retrieved from the RavenDB cache:

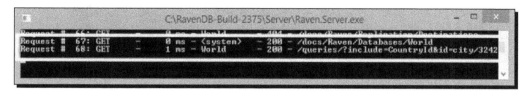

 Using `Include` feature can save database resources and is more efficient.

To make the `Include` feature work, RavenDB needs to know the object type you want to preload (or to include). Neither option will work for includes if we don't specify a `Raven-Clr-Type` in the metadata of the included document.

Raven throws an `InvalidCastException` when loading a preloaded document if the document has no `Raven-Clr-Type` metadata. In our case, this may happen when you try to load the `Country` document. This is due to documents being imported via a CSV file.

At the time of writing this book, a `@Raven-Clr-Type` metadata column is not available in a CSV file. This will be done in the next RavenDB Version (2.5+).

You can work around this by loading the document and just flush it to the database by calling the `SaveChanges()` method to persist the `Raven-Clr-Type` metadata.

```
session.Load<Country>("country/1098");
session.SaveChanges();
```

You can also set the metadata manually for a specified document using the Management Studio.

```
country/1098

Data    Metadata

{
    "Raven-Entity-Name": "Countries",
    "DNT": "1",
    "Raven-Clr-Type": "RavenDB_Ch07.Country, RavenDB_Ch07"
}
```

There is another way to preload related documents. You can use the `Include()` method on the `Query` object instead of the `Session` object. The syntax is a little bit different than you have done in the previous section.

You need to use the `Customize()` method and within this method you can call the `Include()` method. Try to rewrite `IncludeRelatedDocuments()` and load related document using this new method.

Indexing related documents

This is another great feature of RavenDB. This feature aims to simplify loading related documents such as a customer and its invoices. RavenDB allows you to load a document and its related documents during the index process, thereby reducing the number of `Map` and `Reduce` functions needed to load all related documents.

In order to load documents during the index process, you need to call the `LoadDocument()` method which takes one parameter, the document ID to be loaded.

Time for action – indexing related documents

You will create the `Cities_RelatedCountry` index which will implement the `LoadDocuement()` method. Then you will query this index while running the `RavenDB_Ch06` project using the Management Studio.

1. Open the `RavenDB_Ch06` project in Visual Studio.

2. Add a new class and name it `Cities_RelatedCountry`.

3. Complete the `Cities_RelatedCountry` class definition using the following code snippet:

```
10      class Cities_RelatedCountry
11          : AbstractIndexCreationTask<City, Cities_RelatedCountry.Result>
12      {
13          public class Result
14          {
15              public string Name { get; set; }
16              public long Population { get; set; }
17              public string CountryName { get; set; }
18          }
```

4. Add the index's `Map` function within the class constructor using the following code snippet:

```
21    public Cities_RelatedCountry()
22    {
23        Map = cities => from city in cities
24                        let country = LoadDocument<Country>(city.CountryId)
25                        select new
26                        {
27                            Name       = city.Name,
28                            Population = city.Population,
29                            CountryName = country.Name,
30                        };
31
32        Index(x => x.CountryName, FieldIndexing.Analyzed);
33    }
```

5. Add the following code snippet to the `Main()` method:

```
104    // Index Related Documents
105    // Create Cities/RelatedCountry Index
106    IndexCreation.CreateIndexes(
107        typeof(Cities_RelatedCountry).Assembly, documentStore);
108
109    // Query the Cities/RelatedCountry index
110    using (var session = documentStore.OpenSession())
111    {
112        var cities = session.Query<Cities_RelatedCountry.Result,
113                                    Cities_RelatedCountry>()
114            .Customize(x => x.Include<City>(y => y.CountryId))
115            .Where(x => x.CountryName == "France")
116            .OfType<City>()
117            .ToList();
118
119        // this call will not require querying the server
120        var country = session.Load<Country>(cities.First().CountryId);
121
122        Console.WriteLine(cities.Count().ToString());
123    }
```

6. Save all the files, build and run the solution.

What just happened?

You just learned how to index related documents in RavenDB. In order to implement this feature, you called the `LoadDocument()` method within the `Cities_RelatedCountry` index's `Map` function.

The index's `Map` function defines three fields: `Name`, `Population` which will hold values from the `City` document, and `CountryName` which will hold information from the `Country` document. To load the current `City`'s related `Country`, you call the `LoadDocument()` method and specify the `city.CountryId` as the document key to be loaded. The returned document is saved in the local variable `country` (line **24**). Then the `CountryName` field is populated with the value you read from the `country.Name` value (line **29**).

As we want to be able to apply a filter on the `CountryName` field while querying the index, we registered the `CountryName` field to be indexed (line **32**).

To create the `Cities_RelatedCountry` index, you call the `CreateIndexes()` method within the `Main()` method (lines **106** to **107**).

Now, you are able to search for `Cities` using `CountryName` as a parameter.

The `Include()` method call aims to preload the related `Country` documents data without requiring a second trip to the database.

When querying the index in Management Studio, you can apply a filter to the query such as `CountryName: Canada`.

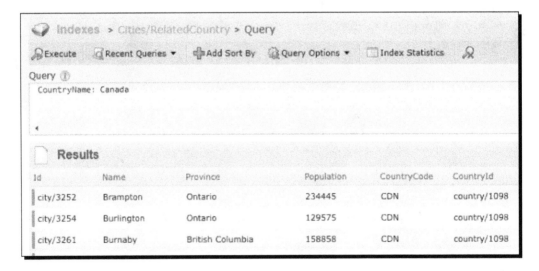

Patching documents

Document patching is the way to modify a document on the server side without having to load it on the client side and saving it back. This is a great way to improve read and write performance. There are no documents sent to the client and no network bandwidth is used. Basically, a patch is a dedicated command that transforms server-side documents directly in the store.

RavenDB allows you to patch documents on the server side by sending either a JavaScript function to the server, or a command to the server with some instructions about how to modify a document (or a set of documents). This feature can be used to update a single document without the need to load the entire object or replacing its entire content.

You can apply patches on a document for creating, renaming, deleting a property, setting values, and so on.

There are many different types of patches supported by RavenDB. To apply a patch you need to call the `Patch()` method on the `DatabaseCommands` (on the `Store` object). This is an overloaded method and requires two parameters: the document key ID to patch and either a JavaScript patch script to use (`ScrptedPatchRequest`) or a `PatchRequest` array.

Patching documents using ScriptedPatchRequest

The purpose of this feature is to allow arbitrary code execution on the server. It allows great level of freedom in how to patch a document. To apply a `ScriptedPatchRequest`, you create your patch using JavaScript and pass it as a string parameter to the `Patch()` method.

RavenDB supports batch operations while they are not supported by NoSQL databases. To patch a set of documents, you need to specify a static index, and a query to send to it.

Time for action – applying a ScriptedPatchRequest

We will add the Language property to a Country document. This property will be set to EN (English) if the country's ContinentCode is NA and ES (Espagnol) if ContinentCode is SA. We want to apply this on all documents in the Countries collection.

1. Start Visual Studio and open the RavenDB_Ch06 project.

2. Add the following code snippet to the Main() method:

```
126         // ScriptedPatchRequest
127         // Add Language Property and populate it
128         // based on the ContinenentCode
129         documentStore.DatabaseCommands.UpdateByIndex(
130             "Raven/DocumentsByEntityName",
131             new IndexQuery { Query = "Tag:Countries" },
132             new ScriptedPatchRequest()
133             {
134                 Script = @"
135                 if (this.ContinentCode == 'NA')
136                     this.Language = 'EN';
137                 else if (this.ContinentCode == 'SA')
138                     this.Language = 'ES';
139                 else
140                     this.Language = '';
141                 "
142             });
```

3. Save all the files, build and run the solution.

What just happened?

You just updated the Countries collection using a ScriptedPatchRequest written in JavaScript. During this update operation, you added a new property named language and populated it with values: EN or ES based on the country's ContinentCode.

To apply the update on Countries collection, you call the UpdateByIndex() method on the DatabaseCommands object (lines **129** to **142**). This method performs a set-based update using the specified index and will not allow the update operation on a stale index.

This method requires the following three parameters:

◆ Index name: The index name specified in the code snippet is `Raven/DocumentsByEntityName` (line **130**).

◆ `Query`: You create a new instance and specify the name of the collection to use: `Countries` (line **131**).

◆ `ScriptedPatchRequest`: The JavaScript patch to use. This script is created as a string and it is very simple script. It checks the value of the `ContinentCode` and assigns a value to the `Language` property. If the `Language` property doesn't exist, it will be created (lines **132** to **141**).

Patching documents using PatchRequest

This method is the second overload of the `Patch()` method, which you may also use to patch a document. It accepts three parameters: the document key, an array of `PatchRequests` which means you can specify more than one patching operation to be performed on the same document, and an optional parameter Etag.

The `PatchRequest` object is used to specify the operation you want to apply and the target of this patch is adding a new field to a single document or to the entire collection. It has several properties but when creating a `PatchRequest` instance at least two properties have to be specified: `Name` and `Type`. The different command keys you might specify are:

◆ `Type`: This represents an operation type. The following patch operations are supported:

  ❏ `Set`: Set a property to a new value (Optionally creating the property)

  ❏ `Inc`: Increment a property value by a given value (Optionally creating the property)

  ❏ `Unset`: Remove a property

  ❏ `Add`: Add a value to an existing array

  ❏ `Insert`: Insert a value to an existing array at the specified position

  ❏ `Remove`: Remove a value from an existing array at a specified position

  ❏ `Modify`: Apply nested patch operation to an existing property value

  ❏ `Copy`: Copy a property value to a new property

  ❏ `Rename`: Rename a property

◆ `Name`: This is a property name

◆ `Position`: This specifies position in array.

- ◆ `Value`: This specifies new value
- ◆ `PrevVal`: This specifies old property value
- ◆ `Nested`: This provides more patch operations
- ◆ `AllPositions`: Set to `true` if you want to modify all items in a collection
- ◆ `FromJson`: Create an instance from a JSON object
- ◆ `ToJson`: Translate instance to JSON format

Time for action – using PatchRequest to add a new field to a document

We aim to add a new string field named `FlagId` to a document from the `Countries` collection. We arbitrarily choose the document with the ID as `country/1005` (France) to apply the patch command. For that you will add the `PatchingDocument()` method to the `Program` class and then execute it.

1. Start Visual Studio and open the `RavenDB_Ch06` project.

2. Add the following code to the `Main()` method:

```
144        // call the Patch method and specify the document Key
145        string docId = "country/1005";
146        documentStore.DatabaseCommands.Patch(docId,
147            new[] // array of PatchRequest objects
148        {
149            new PatchRequest
150            {
151                // operation type: Set,
152                // add a property if it does not exist
153                Type = PatchCommandType.Set,
154                Name = "FlagId",// the property name
155                Value= String.Empty,// the property value
156            }
157        });
158
159        Console.WriteLine("FlagId field added to {0} ", docId);
160
```

3. Save all the files, build and run the solution.

4. In Windows Explorer, switch to RavenDB prompt window to look at its logs.

What just happened?

You just patched one item from the `Countries` collection by calling the `Patch()` method on the `DatabaseCommands` object. This patch operation aims to add the `FlagId` property to the `Country` field with the ID as `country/1005`.

In the previous code snippet (line **146**) you call this method providing the document key (`country/1005`) to patch.

The `Patch()` method requests an array of `PatchRequest` object, you create a new array (line **147**) and add a new `PatchRequest` instance (line **149**).

Within the `PatchRequest` instance, we specified the following three parameters:

◆ The operation patch `Type`, we defined to `Set`. It means to set the property value to a new one, but if it doesn't exist it will create a new one (line **153**).

◆ The property `Name`, which we named `FlagId` (line **154**).

◆ The property `Value`, which we set to empty string (line **155**).

When you run the `Patch()` method, RavenDB calls the `bulk_docs` endpoint and sends a patch request on `country/1005`.

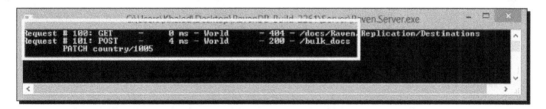

When you open the `country/1005` document in Management Studio, you will see that a new property named `FlagId` has been added to the document with an empty string value.

```
country/1005

Data       Metadata

    {
       "Name": "France",
       "Code": "F",
       "Area": 547030,
       "Capital": "Paris",
       "Province": "Ile de France",
       "FlagId": ""
    }
```

Have a go hero – adding a FlagId field to the Countries collection

Now, you learned how to patch a set of documents (collection) and a single document in a given collection. What if you try to patch the entire `Countries` collection and add the `FlagId` property to each document?

To perform a patch command over a collection you need to call the `UpdateByIndex()` method on the `DatabaseCommands` object. This method requires three parameters, the index `Name` which you can specify as the `Raven/DocumentsByEntityName`, the `Query` index to update which you can set to a new instance, and the `ScriptedatchRequest` object which you can fill using what you learned in the previous section.

Summary

In this chapter, we learned some advanced techniques which will help you use RavenDB documents in an efficient way. Specifically we covered RavenDB attachments and how to store them on the server and retrieve them back.

We also covered the `Include` feature and how to use it to preload related documents and optimize the read and write operations.

Finally, we covered RavenDB patching and how to update documents on the server side without the need to load them on the client side.

In the next chapter, we will talk about administrating RavenDB, its configuration options and some useful tasks such as customizing the RavenDB server using bundles and importing and exporting data. Keep reading!

7
RavenDB Administration

Wherever you have a server, it needs to be managed. RavenDB's database management involves monitoring, administration, and maintenance of these databases. RavenDB includes several features and provides external tools whose main purpose is to help administrators manage datafiles, add and remove databases, drop databases, and backup and restore databases.

This chapter covers RavenDB basic administration functionalities to help RavenDB beginner administrators get started with the help of simple step-by-step instructions.

We aim to provide a comprehensive overview of how to administer a RavenDB server, explaining the fundamental features and tools so that new administrators can feel familiar with them. Specifically, we explain key features and functionalities such as backing up and restoring databases, and exporting and importing data. Also we will learn how to extend RavenDB server features using bundles and how to secure it using replication.

In this chapter, we will learn how to:

- Configure a RavenDB server
- Backup and restore RavenDB databases
- Export and import RavenDB databases
- Activate replication and authorization bundles
- Enable RavenDB logging
- Upgrade a RavenDB server

RavenDB configuration options

The goal of a good system configuration is to configure the system elements needed to keep it running as securely as possible while delivering maximum performance. System administrators must strive to keep systems set up, configured, and patched properly with the latest software from the vendors. This includes not only maintaining the hardware layers by installing cumulative updates and service packs, but also correctly configuring the software layers to get the best performance.

In this section we will focus on some RavenDB configuration options based on best practices and experience. We will only focus on the basics, and therefore there is a lot more to do and learn from the RavenDB configuration file.

RavenDB uses XML configuration files that can be changed as needed. Developers and administrators can use these configuration files to change the settings that affect how RavenDB runs on their computers.

Basically, when you first install a RavenDB server you need to configure it so it works properly in your environment. First, you will check the TCP port number, the data directory, and the security access level to define what you can do on the server. Then you may check for index and log storage locations. Storing logs and indexes on different disk volumes will improve disk time response.

Depending on the RavenDB running mode, you have to select the appropriate configuration file. When running RavenDB as a website through **IIS (Internet Information Server)** or in Embedded mode, the configuration file is `web.config`, located in the `~\Web` folder; otherwise it is the `Raven.Server.exe.config` file, located in the `~\Server` folder. After changing a configuration setting in the `Raven.Server.exe.config` file, you might need to restart the server so that the changes will take effect. Changing the `web.config` file will cause IIS to automatically restart RavenDB.

The following table shows a non-exhaustive list of the configuration keys that you will use most in order to configure a RavenDB server. The complete list of configuration keys can be found on the official RavenDB website at `http://ravendb.net/docs/2.0/server/administration/configuration`:

Key	Description	Default value
`Raven/DataDir`	Sets the path for the database directory. Can use ~\ as the root, in which case the path will start from the server base directory.	`~\Data`
`Raven/Port`	Sets the port to use. Allowed values: 1 to 65536 or * (find first available port from 8080 and upward).	`8080`
`Raven/Esent/LogsPath`	Sets the path for the `Esent` logs. You can use it to store logs on another disk to improve performance.	`~/Data/ Logs`
`Raven/Esent/LogFileSize`	Sets the size of the database log file. This value is specified in megabytes.	`64`
`Raven/IndexStoragePath`	Sets the path for the indexes. You can use it to store indexes on another disk to improve performance.	`~/Data/ Indexes`
`Raven/AnonymousAccess`	Determines what actions an anonymous user can do: ◆ `Get`: read only ◆ `All`: read and write ◆ `None`: allows access to only authenticated users ◆ `Admin`: must be used for testing only It grants read and write and administrative actions.	`Get`
`Raven/MaxPageSize`	Defines the maximum page size (number of documents) that can be specified on the server side.	`1024` Minimum: `10`
`Raven/ ResetIndexOnUncleanShutdown`	Determines whether to reset the index or to check it when the database is shut down rudely. Checking indexes may take some time on large databases.	`false`
`Raven/RunInMemory`	This is mostly useful for testing. Determines whether the database should run purely in-memory. When running in-memory, nothing is written to disk and if the server is restarted all data will be lost.	`false`

Key	Description	Default value
`Raven/VirtualDirectory`	Sets the virtual directory for the RavenDB server when running in IIS mode.	`/`
`Raven/PluginsDirectory`	Sets the location of the plugins directory for this database.	`~\Plugins`
`Raven/ActiveBundles`	A list of bundle names separated by a semicolon, such as `Replication;Versioning`. If the value is not specified, none of the bundles are activated.	`none`

 It is good practice to change the server settings when it is empty and it doesn't contain any data. Otherwise this may cause unexpected stability or security issues.

RavenDB optimizing key concepts

Every administrator wants their servers to run efficiently and is always monitoring the servers and finding different ways of improving their performances. Like other servers, when using RavenDB, you need to observe some points to ensure there are no processing delays or any long response times:

- **Hardware improvements**: When the hardware is not able to support the work load, many delays will occur. This can be enhanced by using more RAM, more CPU, SSD hard drives, write cache, network bandwidth, and so on.

- **Index storage and log paths**: Make sure to store indexes and logs on different storage volumes. This would avoid disk bottlenecks and optimize disk space usage.

- **Initialization delay**: Initializing a document store is one of the most expensive operations and most of the launching delay would be when starting the server. Reducing this delay means that you keep the `IDocumentStore` object in your client applications as a singleton. There should only ever be one instance of this in your application, and it should be created on startup and disposed on shutdown.

- **Storing delay**: When storing documents, RavenDB needs an identifier for each document. If you don't provide your own, RavenDB will auto-generate one for each document using its HiLo generation algorithm, which may increase storing time. This delay may be perceptible when inserting a large volume of documents. Optimizing this time means you will supply your own valid ID property, which would reduce storing delay because RavenDB will skip over the key generation.

◆ **Querying delay**: Always use static indexes instead of dynamic indexes. When querying a collection for the first time, if you did not specify a static index, RavenDB will try to create a dynamic index that matches the query expression, which will increase response delay.

Time for action – optimizing RavenDB performances

Here, you will make some changes to the `Raven.Server.exe.config` configuration file and set new values to four configuration keys: `IndexStoragePath`, `Esent/LogsPath`, `PluginsDirectory`, and `ResetIndexOnUncleanShutdown`, in order to optimize your server performance and disk space:

1. In Windows Explorer, go to the `\Server` folder of your RavenDB installation folder (we installed the RavenDB package earlier in `c:\ RavenDB-Build-2375`).

2. Open the `Raven.Server.exe.config` file using the Notepad application or use your favorite text editor.

3. Modify the configuration file to make it look like the following code snippet:

```xml
<?xml version="1.0" encoding="utf-8" ?>
<configuration>
<appSettings>
    <add key="Raven/Port" value="*"/>
    <add key="Raven/DataDir" value="c:\RavenDB\Data"/>
    <add key="Raven/AnonymousAccess" value="All"/>
    <add key="Raven/IndexStoragePath" value="d:\RavenDB\Data\Indexes" />
    <add key="Raven/Esent/LogsPath" value="e:\RavenDB\Data\Logs" />
    <add key="Raven/PluginsDirectory" value="c:\RavenDB\Plugins"/>
    <add key="Raven/ResetIndexOnUncleanShutdown" value="true"/>
</appSettings>
    <runtime>
        <loadFromRemoteSources enabled="true"/>
        <assemblyBinding xmlns="urn:schemas-microsoft-com:asm.v1">
            <probing privatePath="Analyzers"/>
        </assemblyBinding>
    </runtime>
</configuration>
```

4. Restart the RavenDB server to allow the changes to take effect.

 You can also restart the RavenDB server using the `Raven.Server.exe /restart` file.

What just happened?

In order to optimize your RavenDB server performance and disk space, you just modified the `Raven.Server.exe.config` configuration file and set new values to four configuration keys:

Key	Value
Raven/IndexStoragePath	d:\RavenDB\Data\Indexes
Raven/Esent/LogsPath	e:\RavenDB\Data\Logs
Raven/PluginsDirectory	c:\RavenDB\Plugins
Raven/ResetIndexOnUncleanShutdown	True

These keys are used to store indexes and logs on another disk volume than the data location. This will help to improve disk time response. When the server needs to log the activity, it will use another disk volume and the volume where data is stored is dedicated to answering data requests:

- ◆ Raven/IndexStoragePath: It is used to store indexes in another location
- ◆ Raven/Esent/LogsPath: It is used to store logs in another location
- ◆ Raven/PluginsDirectory: It sets the location of the plugins directory for this database
- ◆ Raven/ResetIndexOnUncleanShutdown: It determines whether to reset the index or to check it when the database is shut down rudely

Backing up RavenDB databases

To ensure that your sensitive data remains secure at all times against viruses, user errors, and computer crashes, and to prevent loss of important data, you need to backup the data. Backups make it simple for you to protect your data by copying and storing it somewhere other than your computer hard drive. Therefore, it is crucial to secure your files regularly so that in cases of emergency, your computer data is still accessible.

RavenDB supports backup and restore data. Backup operations are done asynchronously and can be performed while the database is online and accepting read and write requests. Using RavenDB backup and restore features has some benefits such as backing up index results, while backward compatibility is not supported and it is strict about OS compatibility between the machine on which the backup was created and the machine it was restored to.

When performing RavenDB backups, you need to observe backward compatibility. RavenDB relies on operating system services to manage data storage and backups. Those services are forward compatible, which means you cannot restore your backup on an earlier system version than the backup system version.

Two principal methods of backing up your data are possible. You can choose either to back up your data using your system backup services, which require **VSS (Volume Shadow Copy Service**) support, or you can use RavenDB's backup system. Whichever you choose, it is essential to observe and consider ease of use, speed, and backup media reliability (and may be its price).

It is also important to define what you want to backup. You may choose to make full backups or incremental backups, which store all files changed since the last full (or incremental) backup. The advantage of an incremental backup is that it takes the least time to finish.

Incremental backup requires a special configuration setting. You need to set the `Circular logs` key to `false` (`Circular logs = false`) in the RavenDB configuration file.

The disadvantage is that during a restore operation, each increment is processed and this could result in a lengthy restore job. You might back up all logs, indexes, and datafiles of a database, or choose only datafiles and indexes. Storing logs, indexes, and datafiles on separate drives gives you a number of benefits such as optimizing performance by reducing the disk contention, giving you a better visibility into usage for each type of folder, and allowing you to scale each independently.

To configure RavenDB to use multiple drives, you might change the `Raven/DataDir`, `Raven/IndexStoragePath`, and `Raven/Esent/LogsPath` configuration settings.

Backing up databases using the RavenDB backup tool

RavenDB provides its own backup system. In order to perform a backup, you need to run the command line tool `Raven.Backup.exe`, which will proceed to perform a full backup of the database's data to a specified directory. During the backup procedure, the database remains online and can respond to read and write requests. However, the backup will reflect the state of the database at the start of the backup.

The `Raven.Backup.exe` tool requires at least two parameters: the database URL to backup, which is the server root URL followed by `/databases/<database_name>` and the backup destination, which has to be writable.

> Providing the server root URL (`http://localhost:8080/`) will perform a backup of the system database.

Time for action – backing up the World database

Here, you will make a full backup of the `World` database using the `Raven.Backup.exe` tool and store this backup into `c:\RavenBackups\World`. Then you will analyze the RavenDB logs and explore stored backup files:

1. Ensure that the RavenDB server is running and open a new command prompt window using administrator privileges.

2. Go to the `~\Backup` folder of your RavenDB installation folder.

3. Run the backup tool `Raven.Backup.exe`.

> You may need to copy the `Raven.Abstractions.dll` file from the `~\Client` folder in order to launch `Raven.Backup.exe`.

4. When prompted to enter the RavenDB server URL, enter the URL of your server followed by `/databases/World` and press *Enter*.

```
Enter RavenDB server URL:
http://localhost:8080/databases/World_
```

5. When prompted to enter the backup destination, enter the following `c:\RavenBackups\World` path and press *Enter*:

```
Enter RavenDB server URL:
http://localhost:8080/databases/World
Enter backup destination:
c:\RavenBackups\World
```

6. Wait until the backup completes and close the prompt windows.

You can perform only one backup operation at a time.

What just happened?

You just created a full backup of the `World` database and stored this backup into `c:\RavenBackups\World`. To perform this backup, you used the `Raven.Backup.exe` tool, which is the RavenDB command-line backup tool provided with the RavenDB package and located in the `~\Backup` folder of the package.

Once `Raven.Backup.exe` is launched, it requires the RavenDB server URL followed by the database name that you want to backup (`http://localhost:8080/databases/World`) and the backup destination which you specified (`c:\RavenBackups\World`). While performing backup, `Raven.Backup.exe` will output the progress to the console window.

Let's take a look at the RavenDB log. It shows that a `POST` command is performed by RavenDB to the special `area/admin/backup` to initiate the backup operation and then a `GET` operation is sent to the `Raven/Backup` area to get the operation status.

 You can view the backup status in Management Studio by opening the special document `Raven/Backup/Status` in the `World` database.

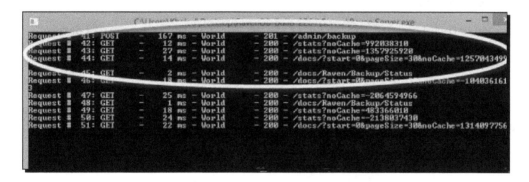

By exploring the `c:\RavenBackups\World` folder, you can see the `World` database backup files which contain all the database's data and indexes.

Have a go hero – creating an incremental backup

Incremental backup provides a faster method of backing up data than repeatedly running full backups. During an incremental backup, only files changed since the most recent backup are included. That is where it gets its name: each backup is an increment for a previous backup.

The `Raven.Backup.exe` tool allows you to create incremental backups. Try to modify some documents in the `World` database or your own database and make an incremental backup using the right parameter options.

> For incremental backups to work, the configuration option `Raven/Esent/CircularLog` has to be set to `false`.

Backing up a database using VSS

RavenDB supports VSS backups, which is a Windows service for capturing and creating snapshots called shadow copies. It operates at the block level of the filesystem and provides a backup infrastructure for Microsoft operating systems.

Installing Windows Server Backup Tools to create backups is out of the scope of this book. If you want to learn more about how to install those tools, you can find more information on the Microsoft website (`http://technet.microsoft.com/en-us/library/cc732081.aspx`).

Basically to create backups, you can either use the Windows Server Backup GUI or the Wbadmin command-line tool, which enable you to backup and restore volumes, files, folders, and applications from a command prompt.

Let's assume that the RavenDB package and the `World` database's data are located in `C:\RavenDB-Build-2261\Server\Database\Databases\World` and we want the backup to be stored on the `E:` drive. Then, to start a full backup you just need to run:

```
wbadmin start backup -backupTarget:e: -include:C:\RavenDB-Build-
    2261\Server\Database\Databases\World
```

In this command-line, you ask the Wbadmin tool to backup the content of the `C:\RavenDB-Build-2261\Server\Database\Databases\World` folder, store this backup on the `E:\` drive, and to start backup immediately. The following screenshot illustrates the Wbadmin execution log:

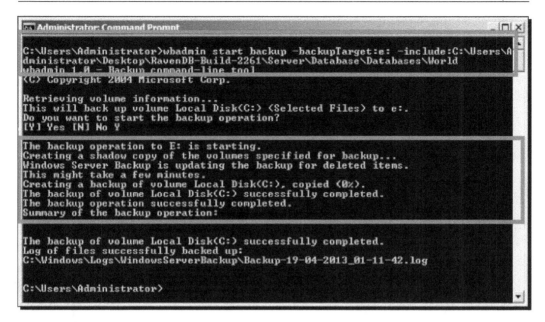

 Making regular backups using VSS tools is preferred by administrators. Often they use incremental backups, which can be performed hourly, daily or weekly, to save disk space rather than making a full backup each time.

Backing up a database using Management Studio

As an alternative method to RavenDB's backup tools, you may use RavenDB Management Studio to create full backups of a particular database. You only need to provide the path to the backup location.

Time for action – backing up the World database using Management Studio

Here, you will make a full backup of the World database using Management Studio and store this backup into c:\RavenBackups\UI\World. Then you will analyze the RavenDB on-screen logs and explore stored backup files:

1. Ensure that the RavenDB server is running and open Management Studio.

2. Select the World database as the current database.

3. Select the **Tasks** tab screen and click on the **Backup Database** button in the tasks toolbar.

4. In the **Location** textbox, enter the path to the backup: `c:\RavenBackups\UI\World`

5. Click on the **Backup Database** button to perform the backup.

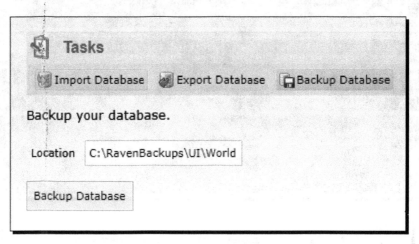

6. Go to the `c:\RavenBackups\UI\World` folder and verify that the backup files are present in the folder.

What just happened?

You just created a full backup of the `World` database using Management Studio and stored this backup into `c:\RavenBackups\UI\World`.

To perform this backup, you activated the `World` database as the current database and from the **Tasks** screen you clicked on the **Backup Database** button in the tasks toolbar.

Then you provided the backup destination location path `c:\RavenBackups\UI\World`. To launch the backup process, you clicked on the **Backup Database** button.

While performing the backup, Management Studio will output the task progress on the **Tasks** screen.

When opening the backup destination folder, you can observe that all the `World` documents data, indexes, and index definitions have been saved.

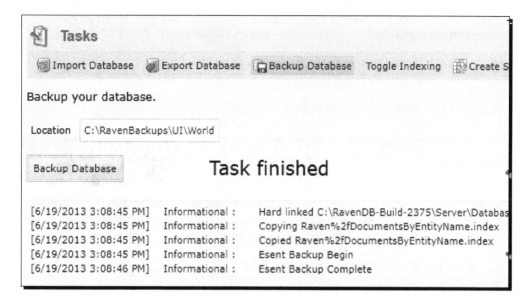

Restoring RavenDB databases

A restore data process is performed in order to return backup files from a secondary storage location to its original condition if files have been damaged or to copy or move data to a new location.

To restore data from a given backup, you will need all of the files of this backup. In case of incremental backups, you need any incremental backup files created after the initial backup was taken.

Unlike backups, RavenDB restores are offline operations at the database level, while the server continues to operate normally. When restoring a database, you must first shut down the database instance and then after the restore process completes, restart the database instance.

Restoring databases using the command line

RavenDB includes features that allow you to restore a database. To perform a restore using command line, you will need to run the `Raven.Server.exe` tool and specify at least the following three parameters:

- `--src`: It is used to specify the backup location files
- `--dest`: It is used to specify the restore location
- `--restore`: It is the action to be performed

Time for action – restoring the World database using the command line

Here, you will make a restore of the `World` database (you made the backup in the previous section) to a new installed RavenDB package. Then, you will restart the RavenDB server to explore the restored database using Management Studio:

1. If it is running, shut down the RavenDB server.

2. Unpack the RavenDB package to a new location, let's say, `C:\RavenDB-NewInstance`.

3. Open a new command prompt window and change the path to the `C:\RavenDB-NewInstance\Server` folder.

4. Run the `Raven.Server.exe` tool using the following parameters:

```
Raven.Server.exe --src=C:\RavenBackups\World --dest=C:\RavenDB-
   NewInstance\Server\Database\Databases\World --restore
```

> You cannot restore to an existing database data directory, the restore operation will fail if it detects that the restore operation will overwrite existing data.

5. Press *Enter* to perform database restore:

6. Start the RavenDB server and use Management Studio to explore the `World` database.

What just happened?

You restored the backup of the `World` database created earlier to a new RavenDB server location.

To perform the restore, you shut down the RavenDB server and unpacked the RavenDB package to a new folder `C:\RavenDB-NewInstance\Server`. Then from a command prompt window, you launched RavenDB and specified three parameters in the command line:

- ◆ `--src: C:\RavenBackups\World`, which is the backup location
- ◆ `--dest: C:\RavenDB-NewInstance\Server\Database\Databases\World`, which is the restore location
- ◆ `--restore`, which is the operation to perform

 If the restore location doesn't exist, RavenDB will create it.

Restoring databases using Management Studio

Management Studio allows you to restore a database from a previous backup. In order to restore a previous backup, you need to activate the system database to see the restore feature button. When restoring a database, you need to specify the backup location, an optional location for the database restore, and a (optional) name for the database.

Time for action – restoring the World database using Management Studio

Here, you will restore the `World` database using Management Studio:

1. In Management Studio, click on the **Databases** hyperlink to display the **Databases** screen and then click on **System Database** to activate the System database.
2. Click on the **Tasks** tab to display the **Tasks** screen then click on the **Restore Database** button on the tasks toolbar.
3. In the **Backup Location** textbox, enter `c:\RavenBackups\UI\World`.
4. Leave the **Database Location** and the **Database Name** field empty (optional parameters) and click on the **Restore Database** button.

You cannot restore to an existing database. If the target database already exists, RavenDB will throw an exception. You may provide a new name and location to the target database.

What just happened?

You restored the `World` database from a previous backup using Management Studio.

In Management Studio, the **Restore Database** button will only appear in the system database **Tasks** screen.

In order to perform the database restore, you activated the **System** database, then you displayed the **Tasks** screen and click on the **Restore Database** button. As there is no need to change the database location or give a new database name to the target database, you left these fields blank.

While restoring, Management Studio displays the progress on the **Tasks** screen.

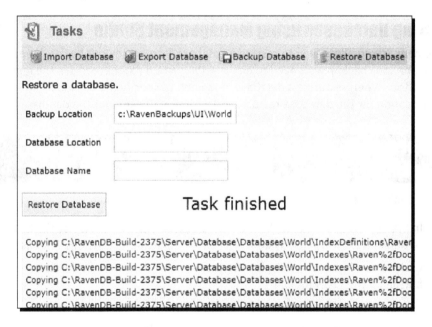

Exporting and importing RavenDB databases

Another option is not to perform a backup but make an export of the database. In *Chapter 2, RavenDB Management Studio*, you learned how to import/export documents using RavenDB Management Studio. There is also another way to perform database import/export using a command-line tool named Raven.Smuggler.exe, which is part of the RavenDB distribution package and located under the ~\Smuggler folder.

 There is no difference between the RavenDB Smuggler utility and Import/Export performed using Management Studio. Both use the same Smuggler API code.

The Raven.Smuggler.exe utility works over HTTP and it is necessary when trying to move a RavenDB data folder between servers. Simply copying is not supported and can result in server errors.

 An export is good if you need to move data between systems.

The Raven.Smuggler.exe utility has several command-line optional parameters. Basically, to perform an Export or an Import operation it requires you to specify the operation way by using the command-line parameter in to perform an import operation or out to perform an export operation. Also it requires the database URL and the dump filename, which is created when performing a database export.

Exporting RavenDB databases

When using Raven.Smuggler.exe to export a database, the output is a zipped JSON document which contains all database elements. This dump file allows to store documents, indexes, and database attachments, unlike a CSV file, which allows storing only document data.

 RavenDB backups are binary files, whereas exports are straight JSON dumps.

Time for action – exporting the World database using Smuggler

Here, you will export the `World` database using the RavenDB `Smuggler` utility and store the output dump file to a new location:

1. If it is not running, launch the RavenDB server.

2. Create a new folder on your primary disk and name it `RavenExports`.

 RavenDB `Smuggler` will not create the destination folder and it will throw an exception if it does not exist.

3. Open a new command prompt window and change the path to the `C:\RavenDB-Build-2261\Smuggler` folder.

4. Run the `Raven.Smuggler.exe` utility using the following parameters:

   ```
   Raven.Smuggler.exe out http://localhost:8080/databases/world
       c:\RavenExports\World.raven
   ```

```
C:\RavenDB-Build-2261\Smuggler>Raven.Smuggler.exe out http://localhost:8080/data
bases/world c:\RavenExports\World.raven
Reading batch of  14 indexes, read so far:            14
Done with reading indexes, total: 14
Reading batch of 1024 documents, read so far:       1,024
Reading batch of 1024 documents, read so far:       2,048
Reading batch of 1024 documents, read so far:       3,072
Reading batch of 174 documents, read so far:        3,246
Done with reading documents, total: 3246
Reading batch of   1 attachments, read so far:          1
Downloading attachment: flag/1098
Done with reading attachments, total: 1

C:\RavenDB-Build-2261\Smuggler>
```

What just happened?

You exported the `World` database with all its contents and stored the output dump file into the `C:\RavenExports` folder using the RavenDB `Smuggler` utility.

To perform the `export` operation, you run the `Raven.Smuggler.exe` utility located in the `~\Smuggler` folder of the RavenDB distribution package and specify the following three parameters:

- ◆ `out`: It means that this is an `Export` operation
- ◆ `http://localhost:8080/databases/world`: It is the URL of the `World` database
- ◆ `c:\RavenExports\World.raven`: It is the destination folder and the name of the output dump file

The dump file will also include documents that were added during the export process, so you can make changes while the export is executing.

By looking at the RavenDB `Smuggler` utility logs, they show the `World` database statistics (**14** indexes, **3246** documents, and **1** attachment) and we can see that RavenDB performs multiple `GET` operations to retrieve the **3246** documents by retrieving 1024 elements each time (the default server configuration is 1024 elements per page, which will change in later RavenDB versions).

To export a single collection call, RavenDB Smuggler uses the `metafilter` parameter. In this example, we export the `Countries` collection only:

```
Raven.Smuggler.exe out http://localhost:8080/
databases/World
    c:\RavenBackups\Countries.raven.dump --metadata-
filter=Raven-
    Entity-Name=Countries --operate-on-types=Documents
```

Importing RavenDB databases

Whenever you use a RavenDB database server, you will sooner or later need to import some data into it. Basically, developers use data imports for testing purposes and administrators use them to move data between new folders or machines.

The `Raven.Smuggler.exe` utility (used in the previous section) is a great way to quickly import a RavenDB dump file into the server with many different options and customizations. To perform the import, it requires at least three parameters: the `in` keyword parameter, the database URL, and the dump filename to import.

> To restore a periodic backup, run `Raven.Smuggler.exe` using this command line:
>
> `Raven.Smuggler.exe in http://raven-db:8080 c:\path-to-backup --`
>   `database=db-name --incremental`

Time for action – importing the World database using Smuggler

Here, you will import the `World` database dump file created in the previous section into RavenDB using the RavenDB `Smuggler` utility:

1. If it is not running, launch the RavenDB server.

2. Open a new command prompt window and change the path to the `C:\RavenDB-Build-2261\Smuggler` folder.

3. Run the `Raven.Smuggler.exe` utility using the following parameters:

    `Raven.Smuggler.exe in http://localhost:8080/databases/world`
      `c:\RavenExports\World.raven`

```
C:\RavenDB-Build-2261\Smuggler>Raven.Smuggler.exe in http://localhost:8080/datab
ases/world c:\RavenExports\World.raven
    1: Wrote 1,024 in  1,111 ms (1.11 ms per doc) (total of 1,024) documents [36
5.35 kb compressed to 38.56 kb]
    2: Wrote 1,365 in  1,816 ms (1.33 ms per doc) (total of 2,389) documents [49
5.07 kb compressed to 50.76 kb]
    3: Wrote 857 in  1,152 ms (1.34 ms per doc) (total of 3,246) documents [311.
49 kb compressed to 32.71 kb]
14 indexes, distance: 2,222 - latency: 3 seconds ago - batch: 512
Importing attachment flag/1098
Imported 3,246 documents and 1 attachments in 4,939 ms

C:\RavenDB-Build-2261\Smuggler>_
```

What just happened?

You imported the `World` database (including all indexes and attachments) into RavenDB using the RavenDB `Smuggler` utility.

To perform this `import` operation, you run the `Raven.Smuggler.exe` utility located in the `~\Smuggler` folder of the RavenDB distribution package and specified the following three parameters:

- ◆ `in`: It is used to specify an `Import` operation
- ◆ `http://localhost:8080/databases/world`: It is the URL of the `World` database

> A database named `World` must exist to perform this `import` operation, otherwise RavenDB may throw an exception.

- ◆ `c:\RavenExports\World.raven`: It is the source folder and the name of the input dump file

> An `Import` operation will overwrite any existing document on the local instance. While importing data into your instance, it is not locked and you can continue using it.

Have a go hero – importing/exporting using the Client .NET API

You may prefer to perform an import/export using the RavenDB Client .NET API rather than from the command-line utility. In order to do that you need to give a reference to the `Raven.Smuggler.exe` utility into your Visual Studio project and then use the `SmugglerApi` class which contains the following two main methods:

- ◆ `ExportData()`: This method is used to perform an export of a given database
- ◆ `ImportData()`: This method is used to import a dump file into a database instance

Deleting RavenDB databases

At times, it becomes necessary to remove obsolete information from a database. RavenDB allows you to delete documents from a database and/or delete the database itself.

We have already presented how to delete a given database and/or documents from a database in *Chapter 2, RavenDB Management Studio*, while presenting RavenDB Management Studio. Depending on your needs you may want to:

- Delete all documents from a given collection, then you can use the Delete command in the contextual menu when viewing it in the **Collections** tab in Management Studio.

- Remove the entire database permanently, then you can use the Delete command in the contextual menu when viewing it in the **Databases** screen and by checking **Physically delete all database data**.

RavenDB server bundles

The default RavenDB distribution package includes basic features. More advanced functionality can be installed with bundles. RavenDB bundles are used to plugin new features to the RavenDB server and enhance the server capabilities. They can be used to adjust many aspects of the server behavior to meet a user's needs. RavenDB bundles enable those features and extensions dynamically without the need to rebuild the server or require any specific knowledge in bundle development.

RavenDB package distribution includes several out-of-the-box bundles such as authorization, documents versioning, documents expiration, or cascade delete functionality, as well as many others which are shipped in the `~\Bundles` folder of the package. Basically, RavenDB bundles can be added selectively to a specific database and are activated while creating a new database, and they cannot be removed afterward.

RavenDB bundles are .NET assemblies and are easy to install. By default, RavenDB searches for bundles in a `~\Plugins` folder next to the RavenDB server location. To install an out-of-the-box bundle, simply copy its assembly and dependent files to the `~\Plugins` folder (by default inside the `~\Server` folder) and modify the configuration file `Raven.Server.exe.config` when needed and then restart the server. By modifying the `Raven/PluginsDirectory` value in the server configuration file, you can specify a new location for bundles.

> The RavenDB distribution package includes two scripts which you can use to get new bundles or update the bundles you already have: `Raven-GetBundles.ps1` and `Raven-UpdateBundles.ps1`.

Replication bundles

Database replication is the process of copying a database from one environment to another and keeping the subsequent copies of the data in sync with the original source so that all users share the same data.

RavenDB replication allows you to have an exact copy of a database from a master server to (one or more) other server called slave. All updates to the database on the master server are immediately replicated to the database on the slave server so that both databases stay synchronized. The following figure illustrates basic RavenDB replication configuration:

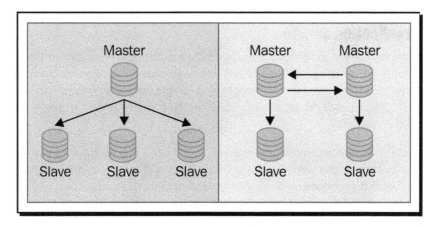

All replications in RavenDB are unidirectional, which means the replication works from one server to another (master to slave). The key to create a (master to master) relationship is to create two unidirectional associations (master1 to slave1, slave1 to master1).

In a (master to slave) configuration, any changes made to the master server will be propagated to the other server(s). However, if you make any changes to the documents on a slave server, those changes will not be reflected on any other servers. Slave servers are effectively read, write local–only, and this may be exactly what you want.

In a replicating system, RavenDB tries to replicate databases against each other, and it is possible that two writes to the same document will occur on two different servers. What happens when two documents are changed on two separate database servers? This means we have two authentic versions of the same document saying different things. This occurrence is called a conflict.

If this occurs, the replication bundle will mark these documents as conflicting, store all the conflicting documents in a safe place, and set the documents' contents to point to the conflicting documents.

In a multiple master configuration scenarios (master to master), any changes to any of the master servers will be replicated to the other master servers (and slaves if they exist). This may be ideal if you wish to have geo-localized servers, and have users connected to the nearest server to them.

Replication should not be considered as a backup strategy because a DELETE command (accidental or otherwise) will also be replicated out from the master on the slave. In some cases, replication may protect against hardware failures. One possible scenario to prevent server failover is by creating a hot spare server. Any changes to the backup server will be synchronized back to the primary server once the failed one comes back online.

RavenDB replication bundle

RavenDB has a replication embedded feature which you can activate when creating a new database. Enabling the replication bundle will inform the RavenDB server to track master database instance documents for any changes and will create several system documents, such as Raven/Replication/Destinations, which contains the list of servers involved in the replication process.

Creating a database replication relation requires at least one master database and one slave, which can be located on the same RavenDB server. RavenDB instances must be running to perform the replication process and must be able to communicate together.

 The replication bundle will exclude any system documents (whose key starts with Raven/) from the replication process.

Time for action – creating a master to slave database replication

Here, you will create a (master to slave) replication relation between two new databases, ReplMaster and ReplSlave, that you will create and configure to allow replication. Then you will populate the ReplMaster database and observe the replication result process on the ReplSalve database:

1. Launch the RavenDB server and open Management Studio.

2. Create a new database, name it ReplMaster and ensure that the **Replication Bundle** checkbox is checked.

3. Create a new database, name it ReplSlave and ensure that the Replication Bundle checkbox is checked.

4. Right-click on the ReplMaster database and select Edit Settings to open the database settings screen.

5. Click on the `Replication` node and then click on **Add Replication** to add a new replication configuration.

6. In the **Url** textbox, enter the RavenDB database instance URL: `http://localhost:8080`

7. In the **Database** textbox, enter the name of the Slave replication instance: **ReplSlave**.

8. Click on the **Save Changes** button to save the replication configuration settings.

> After saving the new replication, RavenDB will add a new system document to the `ReplMaster` database named `Raven/Replication/Destinations` which contains the replication configuration settings.

9. From the **Databases** screen, select the **ReplMaster** database and import the `Countries.csv` file using the **Csv Import** button from the **Tasks** screen.

10. Return to the **Databases** screen and open the **ReplSlave** database, you can see that it contains replicated **ReplMaster** database documents.

> During the replication process, RavenDB will add a new system document to the `ReplSlave` database named `Raven/Replication/Sources/<replication source>` which contains the replication source URL.

What just happened?

You just created a (master to slave) replication relation between two databases, `ReplMaster` and `ReplSlave`, that you have created and configured to allow replication.

Then you selected the master replication database `ReplMaster` and added a new replication destination. In the replication settings dialog, you specified the URL and the name of the slave replication database as `ReplSlave`.

After configuring the replication settings, you imported the `Countries.csv` file to populate the master database `ReplMaster` with some data and observed that the `ReplSlave` database contained replicated documents from the `ReplMaster` database.

Have a go hero – creating World database replication

When we created the `World` database in previous chapters, we didn't activate the replication bundle. What if we need to create a replication database for the `World` database? How can we activate the replication bundle afterwards?

 It is recommended to activate bundles while database creation, but it is good to learn how you can do it afterward.

In Management Studio, create a new database and name it `WorldReplica`, and ensure to activate the **Replication Bundle** for this database. Then open the `World` database settings in edit mode to modify the `Raven/ActiveBundles` key by adding `Replication` to the active bundles list and save your changes.

Once it is done, the `Replication` node will appear and now you can create a new (master to slave) replication to replicate the `World` database's documents to the `WorldReplica` database.

```
World

Data     Metadata

{
    "Settings": {
        "Raven/DataDir": "~\\Databases\\World",
        "Raven/ActiveBundles": "PeriodicBackup;Replication"
    },
    "SecuredSettings": {},
    "Disabled": false
}
```

SQL replication bundle

The SQL Replication bundle is part of the RavenDB server package and can be activated when creating a new database. With this bundle, you have the ability to replicate a RavenDB collection to a table on a Relational Database Management System (RDMS). Basically, it retrieves a document's fields that you specify to be mapped to a relational database table and then performs the replication process for each document in the RavenDB collection.

It is important to note that the bundle does not replicate the collection itself, it only replicates changes to the documents made once the configuration is set.

 You can force the replication of all the documents in the collection by deleting all the rows in the `LastReplicatedEtags` array in the `Raven/SqlReplication/Status` document.

To perform the replication process, this bundle needs to be configured and requires mandatory parameters. The SQL Replication bundle needs to connect to a relational database and it requires an appropriate connection string. Also it requires the data provider to be specified, which you may choose from a supported provider list. The last step to configure the SQL Replication bundle is to tell it which collection to replicate and how to do it. Then the replication settings are stored in the database and we do that by creating a replication definition document, which contains at least the following fields:

- `ID`: This is the replication identifier (`Raven/SqlReplication/ Configuration/<replication name>`)
- `Name`: This is the replication name
- `RavenEntityName`: This is the name of the collection to be replicated
- `Script`: This contains the field's mapping definitions
- `FactoryName`: This is the data provider to be used
- `ConnectionString`: This is the connection string to be used to connect to the RDBMS

 The replication document definition can be created using the RavenDB Client API or by using Management Studio.

Time for action – replicating to Microsoft SQL Express

Here, you will create a database replication between RavenDB and Microsoft SQL Express in order to replicate the RavenDB Countries collection to the Countries table in Microsoft SQL Express. To perform this replication process, you will create a new database in RavenDB and a new one in Microsoft SQL Express then configure the RavenDB database to enable SQL replication:

 To be able to follow these instructions, we assume that Microsoft SQL Server Express is installed and operational. Also you should have a basic knowledge of Microsoft SQL Server and the Management Studio and know how to create a new database and/or create a new table. You may find more information about how to download and install Microsoft SQL Server Express on this page: http://www.microsoft.com/En-us/download/details.aspx?id=29062

1. Open Microsoft SQL Express Management Studio and connect to the database engine using your credentials.

2. Create a new database, name it RavenDBReplica.

3. Add a new table to the RavenDBReplica database using the following column definitions and name it Countries:

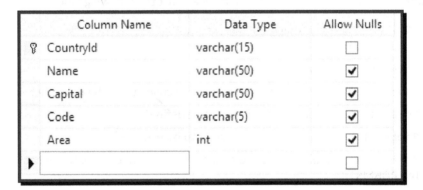

	Column Name	Data Type	Allow Nulls
🔑	CountryId	varchar(15)	☐
	Name	varchar(50)	☑
	Capital	varchar(50)	☑
	Code	varchar(5)	☑
	Area	int	☑
▶			☐

4. Open RavenDB Management Studio and create a new database, name it SQLReplica and ensure that the **SQL Replication Bundle** checkbox is checked.

5. Import the Countries.csv file into the SQLReplica database.

6. Open the SQLReplica database settings and select the **SQL Replication** node.

7. Click on the green plus sign to add a new replication and name it CountriesReplication.

8. Select **System.Data.SqlClient** as the factory name.

9. Enter the **Connection string** as follows: `Data Source=.\SQLEXPRESS;Initial Catalog=RavenDBReplica;Integrated Security=SSPI`

10. Select **Countries** from the **Source Document Collection** drop-down list.

11. Click on the green plus button to add a new entry to the **SQL Replication Tables** and enter `Countries` and `CountryId` for the `Table Name` and `Document key` fields.

12. In the **Script** area, enter the following code snippet:

```
Script: ⓘ
    var country = {
        CountryId: documentId,
        Name: this.Name,
        Capital: this.Capital,
        Code: this.Code,
        Area: this.Area
    };

    replicateToCountries(country);
```

13. Click on the **Save Changes** button to save the replication definition, which should look like the following:

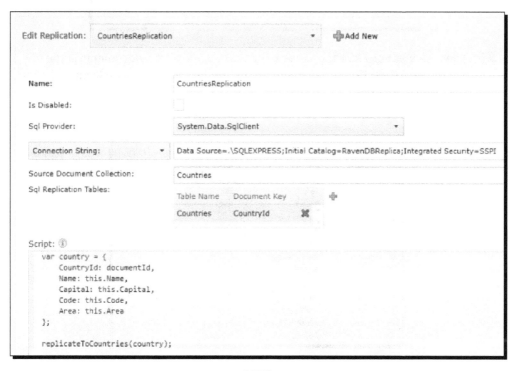

> After saving the new replication, RavenDB will add two new system documents to the SQLReplica database named `Raven/SqlReplication/Configuration/CountriesReplication`, which contains the replication definition, and `Raven/SqlReplication/Status`, which is added after a replication completes.

14. Open any document in edit mode and click on the **Save Document** button to replicate the document to the SQL table.

15. To enforce the replication of all documents in the `Countries` collection to Microsoft SQL Server, open the `Raven/SqlReplication/Status` document and delete all `Etags` rows in the `LastReplicatedEtags` array.

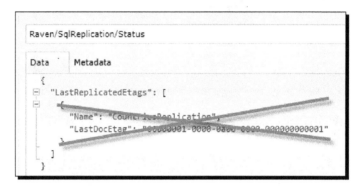

16. Then, save `Raven/SqlReplication/Status` and all the documents in the `Countries` collection should be replicated to the `Countries` table on Microsoft SQL Server.

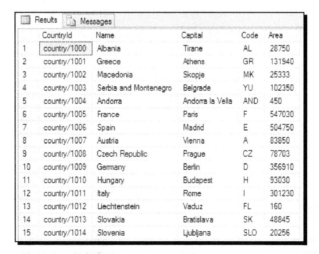

	CountryId	Name	Capital	Code	Area
1	country/1000	Albania	Tirane	AL	28750
2	country/1001	Greece	Athens	GR	131940
3	country/1002	Macedonia	Skopje	MK	25333
4	country/1003	Serbia and Montenegro	Belgrade	YU	102350
5	country/1004	Andorra	Andorra la Vella	AND	450
6	country/1005	France	Paris	F	547030
7	country/1006	Spain	Madrid	E	504750
8	country/1007	Austria	Vienna	A	83850
9	country/1008	Czech Republic	Prague	CZ	78703
10	country/1009	Germany	Berlin	D	356910
11	country/1010	Hungary	Budapest	H	93030
12	country/1011	Italy	Rome	I	301230
13	country/1012	Liechtenstein	Vaduz	FL	160
14	country/1013	Slovakia	Bratislava	SK	48845
15	country/1014	Slovenia	Ljubljana	SLO	20256

What just happened?

You created a database replication between RavenDB and Microsoft SQL Express server in order to replicate the RavenDB Countries collection to the Countries table in Microsoft SQL Express.

A database replication needs at least two databases, the first database is RavenDBReplica on the MSSQL Express server and the second database is SQLReplica on the RavenDB server. On the RavenDBReplica database, there is nothing special to do, but on creating the RavenDB SQLReplica database, you activated the SQL Replication bundle.

After the creation of the databases, you populated the SQLReplica database by importing the Countries.csv file. Then you opened the database settings to configure the SQL Replication bundle and created a new replication definition which you named CountriesReplication.

The SQL Replication bundle requires the data source, the data provider, the connection string, and the field mapping function to be specified. You set the following parameter values:

- **Name**: The name of the Replication you are creating.
- **Sql Provider**: The data provider, set to System.Data.SqlClient, which is the appropriate provider to interact with MSSQL Express Server.
- **Connection string**: It is used to connect to MSSQL Express server, set to Data Source=.\SQLEXPRESS;Initial Catalog=RavenDBReplica;Integrated Security=SSPI
- **Source Document Collection**: This is the data source, set to Countries.
- **Sql Replication Tables**: The table name in MSSQL Express and the identification column name. You set these values to Countries and CountryId.
- **Script**: Or the mapping function is used to define field mapping between RavenDB documents and the MSSQL Express server table.

You created a country object and set its field values for each column you need to map to the SQL table, you specified the column name and the RavenDB field name from where to get the value. Then you called the replicateToCountries() method which requires the object to replicate.

This script will be called once for each document in the Countries collection, with this representing the document and the document ID available as documentId.

It is not mandatory to map all fields of a given document, you can map only fields that you need to be replicated.

During the replication process, RavenDB will apply this script function on each concerned document in the Countries collection.

Once the replication definition is saved, RavenDB added new system documents to the SQLReplica database. Raven/SqlReplication/Configuration/CountriesReplication, which contains the replication definition, and Raven/SqlReplication/Status are added after a replication completes.

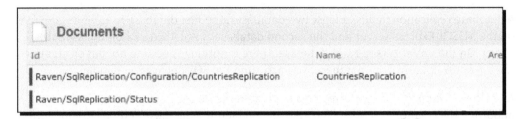

The bundle will not replicate all of the collection's documents by default; it will replicate only modifications to the SQL server table. But, you can enforce the replication of all documents by deleting all rows in the LastReplicatedEtags array in the Raven/SqlReplication/Status document.

Have a go hero – activating and using the IndexReplication bundle

The IndexReplication bundle is an out-of-the-box bundle provided with RavenDB and located in the ~\Bundle folder of the distribution package. This bundle allows replicating an index to a table in a relational database. You may use the same SQL database and table you used for the SQL Replication bundle.

Install the IndexReplication bundle and configure its connection string to connect to the RavenDBReplica database on SQL Express. Create a new RavenDB database and name it IdxReplication and populate it using the Countries.csv file. You need to create a new index (AllCountries) which will return two fields, Name and Capital.

Then add a replication definition document to the IdxReplication database and define the PrimaryKeyColumnName and column mapping.

To make it work, you may need a little hint: modify the replication Metadata as follows:

```
{
  "Raven-Entity-Name": "IndexReplicationDestinations",
  "Raven-Clr-Type":
    "Raven.Bundles.IndexReplication.Data.IndexReplicationDestination,
     Raven.Bundles.IndexReplication",
  "DNT": "1"
}
```

Open any document in edit mode and save it and it will be immediately replicated to the SQL server.

Voilà!

RavenDB authorization bundle

By default, RavenDB authentication is based on Windows authentication. That means you must have a valid Windows account on the machine or the domain that RavenDB is running on to authenticate the RavenDB server. The default settings specify that all users that have a valid account are able to access the RavenDB server, but you may want to limit access to specific users. In this case, to avoid creating users twice (in RavenDB and in Windows), you must specify only users allowed to access the special group `Raven/Authorization/Windows/RequiredGroups`.

For anonymous users, RavenDB allows by default a read-only access to the server and the `Raven/AnonymousAccess` configuration key is set to `Get`. If you set this key to `All`, that means users are able to perform both read and write operations. When the value is set to `None`, only authenticated users will have access to the RavenDB server (read and write).

RavenDB supports custom authentication using `OAuth`, which is an open protocol to allow secure authorization in a simple and standard method from web, mobile, and desktop applications, this allows you to make identity credentials or API keys. RavenDB supports `OAuth` on both server side and client side.

Time for action – authenticating and authorizing

RavenDB comes with built-in authentication functionality. Here, you will learn how to set it and how to grant groups or users access to the RavenDB server. Then, you will open the `Raven/Authorization/WindowsSettings` system document and analyze its content:

1. In Management Studio, open the system database settings.

2. Select the **Windows Authentication** node and then click on the **Groups** tab to show the Groups screen.

3. Click on **Add Group Settings** to add new group settings.

4. Select **IIS AppPool\DefaultAppPool** from the **Name** drop-down list and check the **Enable** checkbox.

5. Click on the green plus sign to add a database access, under **Databases**, select the `World` database from the drop-down list.

6. Save your settings.

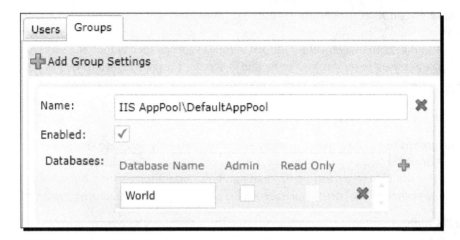

These settings are written to the `Raven/Authorization/WindowsSettings` system document.

What just happened?

You just set group authorizations to allow access to the RavenDB `World` database.

In order to set authorization, you open the system database settings and select the **Windows Authentication** node and add a new group setting.

Then, you select the **IIS AppPool\DefaultAppPool** group from the list and grant access to all group members to the `World` database and save your changes.

When opening the `Raven/Authorization/WindowsSettings` system document, you can see that the special group `RequiredGroups` allows access to the group you selected.

```
Raven/Authorization/WindowsSettings

Data    Metadata

  {
    "RequiredGroups": [
      {
        "Name": "IIS AppPool\\DefaultAppPool"
        "Enabled": true,
        "Databases": [
          {
            "Admin": false,
            "TenantId": "World",
            "ReadOnly": false
          }
        ]
      }
    ],
    "RequiredUsers": [
      {
        "Name": "IIS AppPool\\DefaultAppPool",
        "Enabled": true,
        "Databases": [
```

Have a go hero – activating the authorization bundle

Why not try to activate the authorization bundle and learn how to define Role and User permissions? The authorization bundle is part of the RavenDB package. It extends RavenDB features to allow document-level permissions. Also it allows you to define permissions for a specific user, a group, or using arbitrary tagging.

You will now learn how to activate the authorization bundle and how to define Role and User permissions. The bundle authorization logic can be described as follows:

♦ If the current user performs a query over a set of documents but does not have the permission to do this operation, those documents are filtered out from the query result

♦ If the current user doesn't have the permission to load a document (by ID), an error is raised

♦ If the current user tries to write to a document (either PUT or DELETE) but does not have the permission to do so, an error is raised

Install `Raven.Bundles.Authorization.dll` and restart the RavenDB server. Then open the `World` database settings and add the bundle name to the `Raven/ActiveBundles` key, save your settings, and when you click on the `Authorization` node you should get a screen that looks like the following screenshot:

Enabling RavenDB logging

RavenDB logs its activity and creates several different log files to help you see what activity is taking place. You may want to backup and remove old log files from time to time and tell RavenDB to start logging to new files. By default, RavenDB log files are located in the `~\Server\Logs` folder.

 However, you must clean up these files regularly to ensure that the logs do not take up too much disk space.

When using RavenDB in console mode, the server activity is printed out in the command prompt window and you may need to monitor the server activity with more details. RavenDB has extensive support for debug logging, enabling you to figure out exactly what is going on in the server. By default, logging is turned off but you can enable it at any time by creating a file called `NLog.config` in Raven's base directory.

Time for action – enabling RavenDB logging

We will now create the `NLog.config` configuration file, which is an XML file, in order to enable RavenDB logging:

1. Using the Notepad application or your favorite text editor, create a new file and name it `NLog.config`.

2. Add the XML namespaces and root node elements to the `NLog.config` file:

```
1  <nlog xmlns="http://www.nlog-project.org/schemas/NLog.netfx35.xsd"
2        xmlns:xsi="http://www.w3.org/2001/XMLSchema-instance">
3    <targets>
4
5    </targets>
6    <rules>
7
8    </rules>
9  </nlog>
```

3. Add these three targets to the `<targets>` node:

```
4  <target xsi:type="AsyncWrapper" name="AsyncLog">
5    <target xsi:type="SplitGroup">
6      <target name="File" xsi:type="File"
7                       fileName="${basedir}\Logs\${shortdate}.log">
8        <layout xsi:type="CsvLayout">
9          <column name="time" layout="${longdate}" />
10         <column name="logger" layout="${logger}"/>
11         <column name="level" layout="${level}"/>
12         <column name="message" layout="${message}" />
13         <column name="exception" layout="${exception:format=tostring}" />
14       </layout>
15     </target>
16   </target>
```

4. Add these rule to the `<rules>` node:

```
20     <logger name="Raven.*" writeTo="AsyncLog"/>
```

5. Save your `NLog.config` file.

What just happened?

You just enabled RavenDB activity by logging in, which is based on NLog (http://nlog-project.org/), which is a free logging platform for .NET, Silverlight, and Window's Phone with rich log routing and management capabilities.

In order to enable logging, you need to create an XML file which represents the configuration file for the NLog platform.

In steps 1 and 2, you create the `NLog.config` configuration file with the `<nlog />` element as its root. The use of namespaces is optional, but it enables the Intellisense in Visual Studio.

 Note that the `NLog config` file is case-insensitive when not using namespaces and case-sensitive when you use them. Intellisense only works with case-sensitive configurations.

The root element of the `NLog` configuration file has two elements that are required to be present in the `NLog` configuration file:

- `<targets />`: It defines the log target's outputs
- `<rules />`: It defines the log routing rules

In step 3, you define three targets:

- `AsyncWrapper`: It provides asynchronous, buffered execution of target writes. You set the buffer name to `AsyncLog`.
- `SplitGroup`: It is used to write log events to all targets.
- `File`: It is used to write log messages to one or more file.

The output filename is set to the current date in short format and will be stored in the `\Logs` folder under the `\Server` folder of the RavenDB server. It will log messages in a `CSV` file format having five columns: `time`, `logger`, `level`, `message`, and `exception`.

In step 4, you add the routing rule where you define the source of messages, set to `Raven.*`, and the logger target, set to `AsyncLog`.

Upgrading the RavenDB server

The emergence of a new version gives you an opportunity of taking advantage of new features and functionalities implemented in this version

Before you can start your migration planning, you may need to answer two important questions: when should you migrate, and how much will it cost in terms of money and effort.

Basically before upgrading a RavenDB to a new version, ensure that the server version is stable. It is not recommended to attempt an upgrade to a new unstable version.

Also, it is not recommended to upgrade to a stable new version if your actual server is undergoing a period of intense change.

Upgrading a large real-world application may take several weeks. During this time, if users are also making changes to current databases, then you have to either make changes in both databases or re-synchronize the databases at a later time by upgrading the changed database again.

Time for action – upgrading the RavenDB server

RavenDB is a .NET-based application and upgrading to a new version is very simple. Basically, we replace all its binary files with those from the new version.

 Before proceeding with any upgrade always ensure to make a backup of your databases and your configurations file.

These are some of the important concerns you should review after you have decided to upgrade to a new version which may help you to save a couple of hours:

1. Make a backup of your databases and your configuration files.

2. Shut down the RavenDB server.

3. Replace the binaries including any bundles (their version has to match the server version).

4. Ensure that the RavenDB client DLLs in the applications that connect to RavenDB also match with the server version numbers.

5. Make sure not to delete your actual ~\Data folder if you didn't specify another location in the server configuration file Raven.Server.exe. config or web.config.

6. Restore your data and your configuration files to the new version.

Once you make sure all the above points are checked, then upgrade your server to a new version and you may restart the server again!

Pop quiz – RavenDB administration

Q1. How do you restore a periodic backup?

1. `raven.smuggler.exe in http://raven-db:8080 c:\path-to-backup --incremental`.

2. `raven.smuggler.exe out http://raven-db:8080 c:\path-to-backup --database=db-name --incremental`.

3. `raven.smuggler.exe in http://raven-db:8080 c:\path-to-backup --database=db-name --incremental`.

4. `raven.smuggler.exe in http://raven-db:8080 --database=db-name --incremental`.

Q2. You have a local database and you would like to export the data of one collection only. How can you do it?

1. `Raven.Smuggler.exe out http://localhost:8080/databases/MyDatabase c:\export.raven.dump --metadata-filter=Raven-Entity-Name=MyCollection --operate-on-types=Documents`.

2. `Raven.Smuggler.exe out http://localhost:8080/databases/MyDatabase c:\export.raven.dump --Raven-Entity-Name=MyCollection --operate-on-types=Documents`.

3. `Raven.Smuggler.exe out http://localhost:8080/databases/MyDatabase c:\export.raven.dump --MyCollection`.

4. `Raven.Smuggler.exe in http://localhost:8080/databases/MyDatabase c:\export.raven.dump --Raven-Entity-Name=MyCollection --operate-on-types=Documents`.

Q3. What are the main RavenDB replication characteristics? Select all that apply:

1. One-way.
2. Push-based.
3. Asynchronous.
4. Secure.
5. Batched.

Q4. To make incremental backups work, you need to set this configuration key:

1. `Raven/Esent/CircularLog =true`.
2. `Raven/Esent/CircularLog =false`.
3. `Raven/IncrementalBackups =true`.
4. `Raven/Backups =Incremental`.

Summary

In this chapter, we covered RavenDB basic administration functionalities and presented a step-by-step illustration with an overview of how to administer the RavenDB server.

Specifically, we covered the RavenDB configuration options and presented a non-exhaustive list of configuration keys that you may use to configure the RavenDB server.

We presented backup and restore RavenDB functionalities and learned how to export data to use outside RavenDB and how to import data to RavenDB.

Also, we covered RavenDB bundles and how they extend RavenDB server features. We presented the three most-used bundles: the Replication bundle, which is used to replicate RavenDB databases to other databases, the SQL Replication bundle, which is used to replicate a given RavenDB collection to an SQL table, and the Authorization bundle, which is used to secure RavenDB database access.

Finally, we learned how to enable RavenDB logging and how to upgrade a RavenDB server.

In the next chapter, we will talk about RavenDB deployment strategies and look at guidelines to choose a strategy.

8
Deploying RavenDB

Using RavenDB outside the development environment implies the need to know how to deploy RavenDB to this new environment. This chapter provides an overview of the deployment strategies you might plan for the RavenDB server.

Every organization is unique. This chapter aims to provide information to help you define the best deployment strategies and plans for your organization and gives a description of each deployment approach, associated benefits, assumptions, and risks.

In this chapter, we will cover how to run RavenDB:

◆   As a Windows Service
◆   As an IIS application
◆   In Embedded mode

RavenDB deployment strategies

Until now, to launch the RavenDB server, we used the `Start.cmd` command file or executed the `Raven.Server.exe` file directly in Windows Explorer. This running mode is called console mode, and it might be good for testing and developing purposes; however, this running mode is not recommended for a production environment.

RavenDB gives you three other deployment options for getting your data from the server. The first option is the ability to run as a Windows Service, the second option is the ability to be hosted in **Internet Information Server (IIS)**, and the last option, called Embedded mode, allows you to embed the RavenDB server into your application or to run it completely in the memory.

RavenDB Version 2.5 will provide an MSI installer which will allow efficient installation and configuration of RavenDB.

Running RavenDB as a Windows Service

RavenDB offers the possibility to run as a Windows Service. Windows Services are designed to allow long-running executable applications that run in their own Windows sessions.

When running RavenDB as a Windows Service, it doesn't show any user interface and can be automatically started when the computer boots; it can also be stopped and restarted. After a RavenDB service is installed, it must be started, and it will remain active until it is manually stopped or the computer on which it is running is shut down.

A RavenDB service can be set up to start automatically or manually. Starting automatically means that it will be started when the computer on which it is installed is rebooted or first turned on. If RavenDB is set up to start manually, that means it must be started (manually) by a user.

You can run a RavenDB service in a security context of a specific user account that is different from the logged-on or the default computer account. Also, it can be installed on a computer other than the one users are working on.

Installing the RavenDB service

To install the RavenDB service under Windows, we use the command-line parameter `/install` when launching `Raven.Server.exe`. Once the service is installed, it can be configured and managed like any other service on Windows.

Installing RavenDB in this mode doesn't use much memory, and it is a preferred way when developing an application and hosting a production version of the application on the same machine.

Time for action – running RavenDB as a Windows Service

You will now manually install and run RavenDB as a Windows Service using the command line. Then, you will verify that it appears in the Windows Services Management Console, from where you can stop and restart it:

1. Ensure that RavenDB is not running.
2. Open a new command prompt window using administrator privileges.
3. Change your current directory to the `~\Server` folder of the RavenDB installation directory.

4. Run the `Raven.Server.exe` file using the `/install` parameter in the command line:

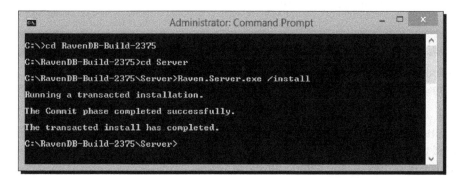

5. When the install process completes, enter `services.msc` to open the Services Management Console.

6. Locate the **RavenDB** service and ensure it is successfully installed and running:

The RavenDB service will start automatically after the install process terminates. To change the startup type (**Automatic** or **Manual**), double-click on the **RavenDB** service in the Services Console Management and change it to the desired type from the **Startup Type** drop-down list.

7. Open RavenDB Management Studio and verify that the server is responding and runs as expected so you can access your RavenDB databases.

What just happened?

You just installed and ran the RavenDB server as a Windows Service manually from the command line.

In order to perform this install, you opened a new command prompt window with administrator privileges and launched a RavenDB server using the `/install` command-line parameter, which will install and run the RavenDB service.

Then, you opened the Windows Services Management Console to change the service startup type if needed, and finally you launched the RavenDB Management Studio to verify that you have access to the RavenDB server and your databases.

Have a go hero – setting a particular host name to RavenDB

Some administrators want to name their server to simplify and optimize their server's management. Why not try to name your RavenDB server when running as a Windows Service?

To define your RavenDB server name, add a `Raven/HostName` key to the RavenDB configuration file. To let Windows find your named RavenDB server over your network, you may need to add a new entry to your `~\Windows\System32\Drivers\etc\hosts` file to point to the IP address of the named RavenDB server.

Uninstalling the RavenDB service

An installed RavenDB service can be quickly uninstalled from the system. To uninstall the RavenDB service, you launch `Raven.Server.exe` using the command-line parameter `/uninstall`. Before uninstalling the service, it will be automatically stopped and then removed from the Windows Services configuration list and will no longer appear in the Services Management Console. Removing the RavenDB service will not remove or delete any RavenDB storage or indexes, and they will remain in their locations.

Time for action – uninstalling the RavenDB service

You will now manually uninstall the RavenDB service using the command line and then open the Services Management Console to verify that it has been removed from the Windows Services list:

1. Open a new command prompt window using administrator privileges.

2. Change your current directory to the `~\Server` folder of the RavenDB installation directory.

3. Run the `Raven.Server.exe` file using the `/uninstall` parameter in the command line.

4. Once the uninstall process completes, enter `services.msc` to open the Services Management Console to verify that the RavenDB service has been removed.

What just happened?

You used the `/uninstall` command-line parameter to manually uninstall the RavenDB service from the Windows Services list.

To perform the service uninstall, you launched `Raven.Server.exe /uninstall`, which will stop the RavenDB service and remove it from the Windows Services list.

RavenDB and IIS

RavenDB supports running as an IIS application, or from an IIS virtual directory under an IIS application. IIS stands for Internet Information Services, and it is a secure and scalable web server provided with Windows operating systems.

When running RavenDB as an IIS application or from a virtual directory, it can be managed from the IIS Manager, and you may use the IIS management tool to configure, start, stop, and restart the web application.

Running RavenDB on IIS offers the full benefits of being managed in IIS, which allows you to set memory limits, monitor via standard tools, use SSL, and so on.

In IIS mode, RavenDB uses configuration from the `Web.config` file in the physical directory to which the directory is mapped as well as in any child directories in that physical directory.

Running RavenDB from an IIS virtual directory

A virtual directory is a path that you specify in IIS and map to a physical directory on a local or remote server. Then, this path becomes a part of the application's URL, and users can request the URL from a browser to access content in the physical directory. It is good practice to specify a different name for the virtual directory than the physical directory to avoid users discovering the actual physical file structure on the server because the URL does not map directly to the root of the site.

Basically, to run RavenDB from an IIS virtual directory, you need to create a new virtual directory, specify the appropriate application pool, and define a binding port. Once the virtual directory is created, you map it to point to the `~\web` folder in the RavenDB package. Then, you need to assign an application pool for this virtual directory that runs at least under .NET Framework v4.0. An application pool is a grouping of URLs that is routed to one or more IIS processes. Finally, you will define the binding port (which is the TCP listening port) you want to use to access the RavenDB virtual directory.

Time for action – running RavenDB from an IIS virtual directory

You will now manually install and run RavenDB from an IIS virtual directory. Then, you will open Management Studio to access RavenDB:

1. Open the Internet Information Services Manager.

 IIS is not enabled by default on Windows operating systems. To use the IIS Manager, you must install or enable IIS on your computer. To learn more about how to install IIS, follow this link: `http://technet. microsoft.com/En-us/library/cc725762.aspx`.

2. Right-click on the **Sites** node and choose **Add Website...**.

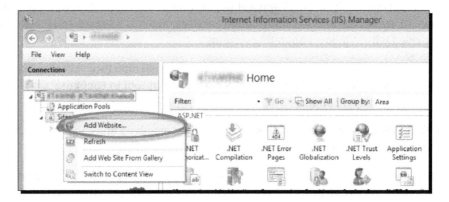

3. Enter `RavenDB` for the **Site** name then click on the **Select** button to select the appropriate **Application pool** (basically ASP**.Net v4.5**):

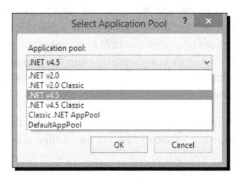

Depending on your operating system version and IIS configuration, you may not have the same application pools listed in this screen capture. Basically, you need to select the **.Net v4.5** application pool.

You may create a new application pool and set it to .NET 4.5 Integrated Pipeline then assign it to the new website. To know more about how to manage and create an IIS application pool, follow this link: `http://technet.microsoft.com/en-us/library/cc753449(v=ws.10).aspx`.

4. Open the **Advanced Settings** of **Applications Pool** and set **Disable Overlapped Recycle** to **True**.

5. Set the **Physical path** of the IIS site to the ~\web directory of the RavenDB installation folder.

6. Set the binding port to 8080 (if available). Finally, your settings should look like the following screenshot:

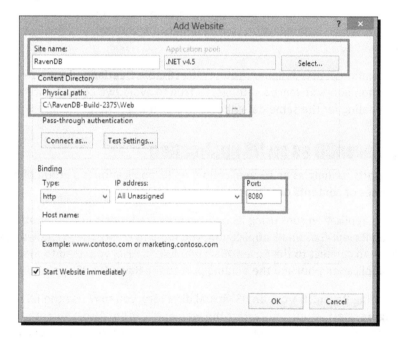

By setting the binding port to 8080, you may get an **HTTP Error 503, The service is unavailable**. This usually occurs when RavenDB has reserved the `http://+:8080/` namespace and IIS is not able to start the site on the same endpoint. In this case, you can resolve this issue by executing the following line of code: `netsh http delete urlacl http://+:8080/`

7. Click on the **OK** button to apply, settings and start the RavenDB website immediately.

8. In the **Browse Website** section of IIS Manager, click on **Browse *:8080 (http)** to open Management Studio. Also, you can open your Internet browser and open it using this URL: `http://localhost:8080/raven/studio.html`.

 Make sure to set an appropriate value to the `Raven/AnonymousAccess` key in the `web.config` file to grant the user the write access to the physical database location.

What just happened?

You just installed and ran a RavenDB server from an IIS virtual directory.

To perform this action, you opened IIS Manager, created a new website, named it RavenDB, and pointed its physical path to the `~\Web` folder of the RavenDB installation folder.

Then, you assigned the appropriate **Application Pool** to the RavenDB website and selected **ASP.Net v4.5** (or similar depending on your system configuration), and finally you set the binding port to `8080`.

Once the application pool is assigned, you set the **Disable Overlapped Recycle** option (in the application pool's advanced settings) to **True** to avoid two concurrent RavenDB instances competing for the same data directory, which will generate failures.

Running RavenDB as an IIS application

RavenDB supports running as an IIS application. An IIS application is a group of files that provides services or contents over protocols, such as HTTP.

Basically, an IIS application runs using its own security credentials and application pool. Before you run RavenDB as an IIS application, you need to create the Windows user account that IIS will use to connect to the RavenDB `~\web` folder. Also, you need to assign the appropriate application pool and the binding port to the RavenDB IIS application.

Similar to running RavenDB from an IIS virtual directory, you may use the IIS management tool to configure, start, stop, and restart the web application. Also, the path that you specify in IIS to map the physical directory on the local or remote server becomes part of the application's URL, and users can request the URL from a browser to access content in the physical directory.

Time for action – running RavenDB as an IIS application

You will, manually install and run RavenDB as an IIS application. This application will use its own application pool and will run in its own security context. Then, you will open Management Studio to access RavenDB:

1. Open your Computer Management Console, add a new user called `RavenDB`, and make it a member of the **IIS_IUSRS** group.

2. Open the Internet Information Services Manager.

3. Right-click on the **Application Pools** node and choose **Add Application Pool...**.

4. Name the new application pool `RavenDBApplicationPool`, select **.NET Framework v4.0.30319**, and click on the **OK** button:

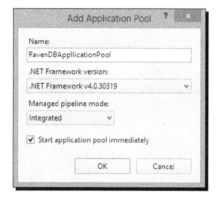

5. Right-click on the **Sites** node then choose **Add Website...** and name it **RavenDBAppli**.

6. Set the **Application pool** to **RavenDBApplicationPool**.

7. Set the **Physical path** of the IIS site to the `~\web` directory of the RavenDB installation folder and the **Binding Port** to `8080` (if available).

8. Click on the **Connect As...** button and set the credentials to the RavenDB account you just created:

9. Click on the **Test Settings** button to validate the user credentials:

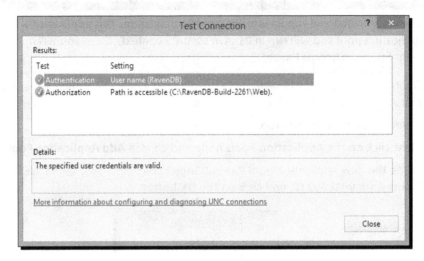

10. Navigate to `http://localhost:8080` or use **Browse *:8080 (http)** in the IIS Manager to open Management Studio.

What just happened?

You just installed and ran RavenDB as an IIS application.

Running RavenDB as an IIS application requires you to create a dedicated user account and application pool. You created the RavenDB user account and made it a member of the **IIS_IUSRS** group (the IIS users group). You also created the `RavenDBApplicationPool` and assigned the **.NET Framework v4.0.30319** Version.

Then, you opened IIS Manager and created the **RavenDBAppli** website and pointed its **Physical path** to the `~\Web` folder of the RavenDB installation folder. You then defined the **Binding Port** to `8080` and assigned the dedicated application pool as **RavenDBApplicationPool**.

To run the **RavenDBAppli** website using custom credentials, you specified to connect using the RavenDB account created earlier and test the connection.

Then, you navigated to Management Studio to verify that the RavenDB server is running.

RavenDB Embedded mode

RavenDB supports embedding into your .NET application. That means your application will contain all necessary files to run RavenDB, which will be part of your application. Running RavenDB in Embedded mode is similar to running it in Console mode (launching the `Raven. Server.exe` file). The main difference is that RavenDB will start automatically in Embedded mode, while you need to start it manually in Console mode. Also, when running RavenDB in Embedded mode, you can interact programmatically with the server instance.

Embedding RavenDB

To run RavenDB in embedded mode, you need to reference the RavenDB Embedded Client in your .NET application. You may add this reference either via the NuGet Package Manager (package name `RavenDB Embedded`) or by taking the files from the `~\EmbeddedClient` folder in the RavenDB distribution package.

After the RavenDB Embedded Client is referenced in your application, you need to create a new instance of the `EmbeddableDocumentStore` object. Then, you can start using the RavenDB embedded storage.

By default, when running RavenDB in Embedded mode, you cannot use the REST API to interact with the server, and you don't have an external access to the RavenDB server. So, it is impossible to use Management Studio to inspect the server databases. For that, we need to provide an access for it.

[　In Embedded mode, other RavenDB features relying on being able to communicate over HTTP (such as replication) will be disabled.]

To allow access to Management Studio while running RavenDB in Embedded mode, you need to set the binary flag `UseEmbeddedHttpServer` to `true`. This will start up Embedded RavenDB with a small HTTP server, which exposes the regular RavenDB functionality. Then, you can use the RavenDB Management Studio to connect to the server databases.

Time for action – running RavenDB in Embedded mode

You will now create a new application, refer the RavenDB Embedded Client, and run RavenDB in Embedded mode. Then, you will open Management Studio to access the embedded RavenDB and create a new database and explore the RavenDB data folder:

1. Open Visual Studio, create a new **Console Application** project, and name it `EmbeddedRavenDB`.

2. Use the NuGet Package Manager to add a reference to the RavenDB Embedded package (it will add two packages automatically, **RavenDB Client** and **RavenDB Database**).

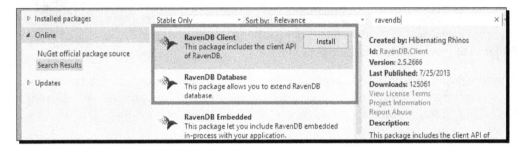

3. Modify the `Program` class to make it look like the following code snippet:

```
12  class Program
13  {
14      static void Main(string[] args)
15      {
16          // ensure that we can open the HTTP server without
17          // requiring administrator privileges.
18          NonAdminHttp.EnsureCanListenToWhenInNonAdminContext(8080);
19
20          // Create a new RavenDB instance
21          using (IDocumentStore instance = new EmbeddableDocumentStore
22              {
23                  DataDirectory = @"C:\RavenDBEmbedded\Database",
24                  UseEmbeddedHttpServer = true // run small HTTP server
25              })
26          {
27              instance.Initialize();
28
29              Console.WriteLine("RavenDB Embedded mode has been initialized");
30              Console.ReadLine();
31          }
32      }
33  }
```

4. Press *F5* to build and run the `EmbeddedRavenDB` project.

5. Open Management Studio, create a new database, and explore the server data directory.

What just happened?

You just created the `EmbeddedRavenDB` Visual Studio project to run RavenDB in Embedded mode.

In order to run RavenDB in Embedded mode, you refer the RavenDB Embedded assemblies using the NuGet Package Manager. Once you add the reference to the package, two other packages will be installed automatically, **RavenDB Client** and **RavenDB Database**.

To run the mini HTTP server, you basically need to run the code using administrator privileges. To open the HTTP server without requiring administrator privileges, you need to run the `NonAdminHttp.EnsureCanListenToWhenInNonAdminContext()` method and specify the RavenDB listening port (line **18**).

Then, you created a new instance of the `EmbeddableDocumentStore` object and specified the `DataDirectory` value, set arbitrary to `C:\RavenDBEmbedded\Database`. To run the mini HTTP server, you set the `UseEmbeddedHttpServer` value to `true` (lines **21** to **26**).

Once you get the new instance, you call the `Initialize()` method to initialize and start up the RavenDB embedded server (line **27**), and any new database will be stored into the `C:\RavenDBEmbedded\Database` folder.

Memory embedded RavenDB

Running RavenDB in-memory is very similar to running "normal" RavenDB Embedded mode. The main difference is that when RavenDB is running in-memory, it will never store files on your disk; all documents and indexes are created in-memory. This is useful for integration testing and useful to create memory database instances which can be created and thrown away quickly.

To run RavenDB in-memory, you will start the same way as when you created the embedded RavenDB and the set the binary flag `RunInMemory` to `true` while creating the instance of the `EmbeddableDocumentStore` object. Then, RavenDB will no longer store any file on your disk.

Time for action – running RavenDB inmemory

You will now modify the EmbeddedRavenDB project to run RavenDB in-memory:

1. Open the EmbeddedRavenDB project in Visual Studio.

2. Modify the Program class to look like the following code snippet:

```
20    // Create a new RavenDB instance
21    using (IDocumentStore instance = new EmbeddableDocumentStore
22        {
23            UseEmbeddedHttpServer = true, // run small HTTP server
24            RunInMemory = true
25        })
26    {
27        instance.Initialize();
28
29        Console.WriteLine("RavenDB Embedded mode has been initialized");
30        Console.ReadLine();
31    }
```

3. Press *F5* to build and run the EmbeddedRavenDB project.

4. Open Management Studio to create a new database and explore the server data directory.

What just happened?

You modified the EmbeddedRavenDB Visual Studio project to run RavenDB in-memory.

In order to run RavenDB in-memory you modified the Program class to set the RunInMemory flag to true while creating the new instance of the EmbeddableDocumentStore object (lines **24**).

The other pieces of code remain the same for now, once you call the Initialize() method, RavenDB will start and run in-memory, and any new created database will no longer be stored on your disk.

Pop quiz – searching the right way

Q1. When you try to create a database on your IIS hosted RavenDB, you get the following error: **The remote server returned an error: (403) Forbidden**. What should you do to allow access?

1. Give current user write access to the ~\RavenDB\Web folder.

2. Give IIS_IUSR write access to the Bin and Data folders of the application.

3. `set configuration key : <add key="""Raven/AnonymousAccess"""` `value="""All"""/>.`

4. `set configuration key : <add key="""Raven/AnonymousAccess"""` `value="""Write"""/>.`

Q2. When you run RavenDB as an IIS application, you get an HTTP Error 503 (**The service is unavailable**). How can you resolve this issue?

1. `netsh http delete cache http://+:8080/.`

2. `netsh http flush cache http://+:8080/.`

3. `netsh http delete urlacl http://+:8080/.`

4. `netsh http flush urlacl http://+:8080/.`

Q3. You want to host your developing and production application on the same machine. What is the preferred deployment mode for RavenDB?

1. Run from an IIS virtual directory.

2. Run as an IIS application.

3. Run as a Windows Service.

4. Run in-memory embedded mode.

Q4. How do you connect RavenDB Management Studio to a memory-embedded RavenDB server?

1. `EnableEmbeddedHttpServer=true.`

2. `EnableEmbeddedHttpServer=true, RunInMemory=true.`

3. `InMemoryEmbeddedHttpServer=true.`

4. `UseEmbeddedHttpServer=true, RunInMemory=true.`

Summary

In this chapter, we learned the different options for deploying RavenDB, and for each option, we covered how to deploy and run RavenDB and the associated benefits. Specifically, we covered RavenDB deployment strategies and how to run RavenDB as a Windows Service as well as how to host RavenDB in an Internet Information Server (IIS).

Also, we covered the Embedded mode and learned how to embed RavenDB inside your application as well as how to embed it in-memory.

In the next chapter, we will talk about RavenDB sharding and how it can help you to scale-out your RavenDB server.

9
Scaling-out RavenDB

As applications grow to support hundreds and thousands of users, database servers must handle more information. To avoid server bottlenecks, we need to scale-out applications and servers to efficiently use more resources in order to do more useful work.

This chapter explains the different options that are available for scaling-out RavenDB, and you will learn how to expand your databases to multiple servers rather than a single, bigger server. Also, in this chapter, we will focus on the expanding factors that go into improving your RavenDB performances.

In this chapter, we will cover:

- RavenDB sharding
- Sharding in blind and smart mode
- Mixing sharding and replication

What is scaling-out?

Scaling-out is a strategy for increasing capacity that involves distributing the load over multiple machines and making multiple servers perform the work of one logical server. A **Web Farm**, which generally involves using multiple machines and distributing the load across them, is an excellent example of scaling-out where each server in the farm is completely independent and hosts an identical copy of the entire website. In such a system, users are load balanced across the servers, and they rarely realize that there is more than one server behind the scenes.

Scaling-out is necessary because individual servers can handle only a finite number of connections. Once a server is processing thousands of requests, adding more RAM, network adapters, or processors may not increase the server's capacity enough to meet the demand, and there is always a performance bottleneck. Do not confuse **scale-out** with **scale-up**. Scale-up typically refers to architectures that use a single fixed resource for all processing. To add capacity, you attach more resources up to the maximum for which the resource is rated.

Scaling can be horizontal (scale-out) or vertical (scale-up). Vertical scaling is when we upgrade a given server to get one very powerful server. It is the easiest approach to deal with high load by adding more hardware: memory, processing power, and disk space. This may make things run faster for a while. Unfortunately, a server has its hardware limitations, and if the loads continues to increase, vertical scaling will no longer suffice and will require a horizontal approach to address the capacity demand. The cost for expansion also increases exponentially. The curve of cost to computational processing is a power law in which the cost begins to increase disproportionally to the increase in processing power provided by larger servers.

In contrast, horizontal scaling is when we add more commodity nodes or machines to the system. The key concept of horizontal scaling is the load distribution. Basically, horizontal scaling is used when we have the ability to run multiple instances on servers simultaneously. Typically, horizontal scaling is much harder to implement than vertical scaling. Also, generally, the total cost incurred by multiple smaller machines is less than the cost of a single larger unit. Therefore, horizontal scaling can be more cost effective when compared to vertical scaling.

Database **sharding** is one of the techniques of horizontal load balancing which is a highly-scalable approach for improving the throughput and overall performance of high-transaction, large database-centric business applications. The term sharding was introduced by Google engineers and popularized through their publication of the **Big Table** (Google's NoSQL database) architecture.

Basically, implementing database sharding means splitting a highly loaded database into several independent chunks. This may denormalize your data, but it allows you to make chunks of your database independent; thus, a single query can hit only one database shard. Also, denormalization may introduce data duplication, as the same information may need to be inserted into several shards to make data consistent.

Database sharding is different from the way most applications are designed initially, and it can be difficult to change an application from a monolithic data store to a sharded architecture.

Another possible way to scale-out is the **functional partitioning** approach. Basically, functional partitioning means dedicating different shards to different tasks.

RavenDB sharding

RavenDB sharding is the way to scale-out RavenDB databases horizontally. The idea is to distribute a single logical database across the RavenDB cluster servers. Unlike replication, where each server contains a complete (replicated) copy of data, RavenDB sharding will distribute data across servers and each server will hold just a portion of the data. RavenDB supports database sharding natively and allows you to split your data across servers in an easy way.

Sharding with RavenDB is as easy as 1-2-3. All you need is a list of connection strings to identify the nodes in the shard cluster. You will also create a shard strategy which is simply a set of instructions that define which node is responsible for what data. Finally, we use the list and the strategy to create a smart client. Let's look at the classes and interfaces that can make this happen.

The `ShardStrategy` object allows you to customize different aspects of the sharding behavior, giving you the option of fine grained control over how RavenDB handles your data. The sharding behavior may be customized using four main elements of the `ShardStrategy` object:

- ◆ `ShardAccessStrategy`: This element allows you to decide how to contact shards and set the shards' access strategy in a sequential or parallel manner. It accepts an instance that implements the `IShardAccessStrategy` interface. There are already two built-in implementations of this interface, `SequentialShardAccessStrategy` and `ParallelShardAccessStrategy`, which you can use to set the access strategy. The default value for this property is `SequentialShardAccessStrategy`.

- ◆ `ShardResolutionStrategy`: This element allows you to set the shards, resolution strategy and decide which shards should be contacted in order to complete a database operation. It accepts an instance that implements the `IShardResolutionStrategy` interface. The default implementation is an instance of the `DefaultShardResolutionStrategy` object.

  For complex sharding environments, you would probably want to implement the `IShardResolutionStrategy` interface which contains three main methods:

  - ❑ `GenerateShardIdFor`: This method defines the shard that should be used in order to store a specific entity

  - ❑ `MetadataShardIdFor`: This method defines which shard should be used in order to store the metadata documents for a specific entity

❑ PotentialShardsFor: This method defines that the shards should be contacted in order to complete a query operation based on available parameters such as the DocumentKey parameter, the EntityType parameter, and the Query parameter

◆ MergeQueryResults: This element is a delegate (.NET type) that lets you decide how to merge query results from shards. The default behavior for this delegate merges the results as they come back and applies minimal sorting.

◆ ModifyDocumentId: This element lets you store the shard ID for a document in the document itself. The default implementation returns an ID based on three parameters: Shard Id, convention.IdentityPartsSeparator, and Document Id.

Those are the main steps required to enable sharding in RavenDB. Once you initialize the **Document Store**, you can do everything you want the same way as in the non-sharded Document Store using the RavenDB API.

Time for action – preparing RavenDB for sharding

To learn how to implement the RavenDB database sharding, we will create a new application (ShardRavenDB) which we will use to create and interact with shards. But before doing that, we need to prepare the shard infrastructure by simulating a RavenDB cluster and running more than one RavenDB server. Then, we will create some empty databases which we will populate when running the application.

Let's say that in our application, we have to handle data from the world's countries. Our choice would be to store countries data on a shard which depends on continents. For example, the countries in Asia will be stored on one shard named AS for Asia, the countries in Europe will be stored on a second shard named EU for Europe, the North American countries would be stored on a third shard named NA for North America, and so on. The next figure illustrates the basic shard infrastructure for the ShardRavenDB application which will communicate with shards using a dedicated TCP port:

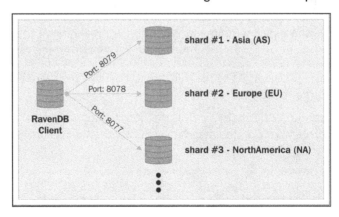

1. In Windows Explorer, create a new folder and name it `RavenShards`.

2. In the `RavenShards` folder, create three folders: `AS`, `EU`, and `NA`.

 In a real-world scenario, you should install each RavenDB shard instance on an independent server and host it in the IIS in order to get the best performance.

3. From the RavenDB package, copy all the contents of the `~\Server` folder and the `Start.cmd` file to each of the three folders: `AS`, `EU`, and `NA`. Each folder should look like the following screenshot:

4. Open each `Raven.Server.exe.config` file and set the `Raven/AnonymousAccess` key to `All`; also, set the `Raven/Port` key for each RavenDB server as follows:

RavenDB Shard Name	Raven/Port
AS	8079
EU	8078
NA	8077

5. Launch the RavenDB server for each shard using the `Start.cmd` command file and create the `Asia`, `Europe`, and `NorthAmerica` databases respectively on the `AS`, `EU`, and `NA` shards.

What just happened?

You just prepared a RavenDB infrastructure to allow database sharding. We aimed to create an application that will handle data of world countries and we wanted to group countries by their respective continent and store each continent group on a different RavenDB shard.

In order to implement the `World` database sharding, we need to launch, at this stage, three RavenDB server instances where each server instance will hold a different shard named `AS` for Asia, `EU` for Europe, and `NA` for North America.

You create a dedicated folder for each shard (`AS`, `EU`, and `NA`) under the `RavenShards` folder and to each folder copy the content of the RavenDB distribution package `~\Server` folder and the `Start.cmd` file.

Then, for each shard, you configure the `Raven/Port` key and assign a dedicated TCP port for the shards and set their values to `8079`, `8078`, and `8077` respectively for the AS, EU, and NA shards. Also, you allow write access to anonymous users by setting the value of the `Raven/AnonymousAccess` key to `All`.

In the last step, you launch each RavenDB shard and create a new database on each instance and you create the `Asia`, `Europe`, and `NorthAmerica` databases respectively on the AS, EU, and NA shards.

RavenDB sharding – the blind mode

Blind mode RavenDB sharding is just for helping you get started with RavenDB sharding and shows you that implementing RavenDB sharding is easy. This mode can be pretty useful for testing and it is not recommended to use it for production.

In blind mode sharding, RavenDB will store documents on the first or the second shard. When querying shards, it needs to "broadcast" all shards to get the query result because it has no way to know where the data is.

In the previous section, we presented you with the required steps to implement RavenDB sharding. Basically, you will use the `ShardStrategy` object to define how to interact with shards. This object contains the `ShardingOn()` method which instructs the sharding strategy to shard specific entity instances based on the **round-robin** strategy. The round-robin strategy is a scheduling algorithm in which processes are activated in a fixed, cyclic order.

The `ShardingOn()` method is an overloaded method with default/optional parameters. If you call this method and do not specify any parameter for it, the `DefaultShardResolutionStrategy` object (used by `ShardStratedy`) will assign all entities within the same session to the same shard.

Time for action – implementing RavenDB sharding (the blind mode)

Now that you have prepared the shard infrastructure for the `ShardRavenDB` application, you are now ready to create it and learn how to create and populate shards. Once the application is created, you will run it and then observe and analyze the RavenDB logs:

1. In Visual Studio, create a new `Console Application` and name it `ShardRavenDB`.

2. Add the `RavenDB Client` reference to the application using the `NuGet` package manager.

3. Add a new class, name it `City`, and complete it using the following code snippet:

```
 8 ⊟     class City
 9   │   {
10   │       public string Id { get; set; }
11   │       public string Name { get; set; }
12   │       public string CountryCode { get; set; }
13   │       public long Population { get; set; }
14   │       public string Province { get; set; }
15   │       public string CountryId { get; set; }
16   │   }
```

4. Add a new class, name it `Country`, and complete it using the following code snippet:

```
 9 ⊟     class Country
10   │   {
11   │       public string Id { get; set; }
12   │       public string Name { get; set; }
13   │       public string Code { get; set; }
14   │       public long Area { get; set; }
15   │       public string Capital { get; set; }
16   │       public string Province { get; set; }
17   │       public string FlagId { get; set; }
18   │       public string ContinentCode { get; set; }
19   │
20   │       [JsonIgnore]
21   │       public List<City> Cities { get; set; }
22   │   }
```

5. Add a new class, name it `Shards`, and complete it using the following code snippet:

```
12 ⊟ class Shards
13   │ {
14   │     public IDocumentStore    ShardStore { get; private set; }
15   │     public IDocumentSession Session { get; private set; }
16   │     public ShardStrategy     ShardStrategy { get; private set; }
17   │
18 ⊟     private void InitializeShardStrategy()
19   │     {
20   │         var shards = new Dictionary<string, IDocumentStore>
21   │         {
22   │             //Shard Name, Shard URL
23   │             {"AS", new DocumentStore {Url = "http://localhost:8079/",
24   │                                       DefaultDatabase = "Asia" }},
25   │             {"EU", new DocumentStore {Url = "http://localhost:8078/",
26   │                                       DefaultDatabase = "Europe"}},
27   │             {"NA", new DocumentStore {Url = "http://localhost:8077/",
28   │                                       DefaultDatabase = "NorthAmerica"}},
29   │         };
30   │
31   │         // Create the new ShardStrategy
32   │         var shardStrategy = new ShardStrategy(shards);
33   │
34   │         // Set Shard access Strategy to Parallel acess
35   │         // Default access strategy is SequentialShardAccessStrategy
36   │         shardStrategy.ShardAccessStrategy = new ParallelShardAccessStrategy();
37   │
38   │         this.ShardStrategy = shardStrategy;
39   │     }
```

6. Add the `Shards` class constructor and destructor then complete them as shown in the following code snippet:

```
40
41   public Shards()
42   {
43       InitializeShardStrategy();
44       this.ShardStore = new ShardedDocumentStore(this.ShardStrategy).Initialize();
45       this.Session = this.ShardStore.OpenSession();
46   }
47   ~Shards()
48   {
49       this.Session.Dispose();
50       this.ShardStore.Dispose();
51   }
52   }// Shards class
```

7. Add a new class, name it `PopulateShards`, and complete it using the following code snippet:

```
12   class PopulateShards
13   {
14       static public Shards Shards {get; private set;}
15
16       static PopulateShards()
17       {
18           PopulateShards.Shards = new Shards();
19       }
```

8. Add the `AddDocumentsToShards()` method to the `PopulateShards` class and complete it using the following code snippet:

```
21   public static void AddDocumentsToShards()
22   {
23       // Add 3 Countries
24       var europian = new Country
25       {
26           Id = "country/1005", Name = "France", Code = "F", Capital = "Paris",
27           Province = "Ile de France", Area = 547030, ContinentCode = "EU"
28       };
29       Shards.Session.Store(europian);
30
31       var middleEastern = new Country
32       {
33           Id = "country/1080", Name = "Lebanon", Code = "RL", Capital = "Beirut",
34           Province = "Beirut", Area = 10400, ContinentCode = "AS"
35       };
36       Shards.Session.Store(middleEastern);
37
38       var american = new Country
39       {
40           Id = "country/1098", Name = "Canada", Code = "CDN", Capital = "Ottawa",
41           Province = "Ontario", Area = 9976140, ContinentCode = "NA"
42       };
43
44       Shards.Session.Store(american);
```

9. Complete the `AddDocumentsToShards()` method using the following code snippet:

```
46          // Add 3 Cities
47          Shards.Session.Store(new City
48          {
49              Id = "city/1012", CountryId = europian.Id, Name = "Paris",
50              CountryCode = "F", Province = "Ile de France", Population = 2152423
51          });
52
53          Shards.Session.Store(new City
54          {
55              Id = "city/3242", CountryId = american.Id, Name = "Montreal",
56              CountryCode = "CDN", Province = "Quebec", Population = 1017666
57          });
58
59          Shards.Session.Store(new City
60          {
61              Id = "city/1068", CountryId = middleEastern.Id, Name = "Beirut",
62              CountryCode = "RL", Province = "Beirut", Population = 702000
63          });
64
65          // store documents in shards
66          Shards.Session.SaveChanges();
67      }
```

10. Add a new class, name it `QueryingShards`, add the `LoadCountry()` method, and complete it using the following code snippet:

```
13  public static Country LoadCountry(IDocumentSession session, string countryId)
14  {
15      var country = session
16          .Include<City>(x => x.CountryId)
17          .Load<Country>(countryId);
18
19      country.Cities = session.Query<City>()
20          .Where(x => x.CountryId.Equals(countryId))
21          .ToList();
22      return country;
23  }
```

11. Modify the `Program` class's `Main()` method to look like the following code snippet:

```
12  static void Main(string[] args)
13  {
14      PopulateShards.AddDocumentsToShards();
15
16      var country = QueryingShards.LoadCountry(PopulateShards.Shards.Session, "EU/country/1005");
17      Console.WriteLine(country.Name);
18      Console.ReadLine();
19  }
```

12. Ensure that the three RavenDB shards instances (AS, EU, and NA created in the previous section) are running, otherwise launch each shard using the respective Start.cmd command file.

13. Save the ShardRavenDB project and press *F5* to build the application and run it.

What just happened?

You just created the ShardRavenDB application to implement RavenDB sharding and interact in the blind mode.

In order to implement RavenDB sharding, you create a new Console Application and add a reference to the RavenDB Client using the NuGet package manager. Then, you add two classes, City and Country, which will be used to handle city and country documents information (Id, Name, Population, and so on) while loading and saving from/to RavenDB shards. The City members (in the Country class) are decorated with the [JsonIgnore] attribute to be ignored by the serialization/deserialization process, and it will not be stored or retrieved by RavenDB (the Country class lines **20-21**).

Then, you add the Shards class which contains two properties (the Shards class lines **14-16**): ShardStore and Session, which will handle the IDocumentStore and IDocumentSession instances which you will use to interact with the RavenDB shards the same way you did with the non-sharded Document Store. The ShardStrategy property will handle the instance of the ShardStrategy object and will define the way to interact with RavenDB shards. All these properties are initialized within the Shards class constructor (the Shards class lines **41-46**).

Within the InitializeShardsStrategy() method, you create a new Dictionary object. The key of this dictionary is the shard name (AS, EU, and NA) and the value is the shard URL which is pointing to a particular database (the Shards class lines **20-29**). Later in this method, you use this Dictionary to create a new instance of the ShardStrategy class (the Shards class line **32**). Also, in this method, once you get the ShardStrategy instance, you set its ShardAccessStrategy member with a new instance of the ParallelShardAccessStrategy object to perform a parallel shard access strategy (the Shards class line **36**). The default behavior is set to perform a sequential shard access strategy.

 A shard's ID dictionary must have at least one value. Otherwise, RavenDB will throw an exception.

The sharded Document Store is initialized within the `Shards` class constructor by calling the `Initialize()` method on the `ShardedDocuemetnStore` object (the `Shards` class line **44**).

To populate shards with some documents, you create the `PopulateShards` class. Within the class constructor, you create a new instance of the `Shards` class and save this instance in the static local field `Shards` (the `PopulateShards` class lines **14-19**).

Then, you add the `AddDocumentsToShards()` method and add necessary code to create three sample `Country` documents stored in three local variables (`europian`, `middleEastern`, and `american`) and three sample `City` documents. You can observe that the `City.CountryId` field of each `City` document is set to the sharded country ID value: `europian.Id`, `middleEastern.Id`, and `american.Id` (the `PopulateShards` class lines **21-67**).

To query the shards, you create the `QueryShards` class and add the `LoadCountry()` method. This method aims to retrieve the `Country` document specified by the calling parameter `countryId` with all its related `City` documents (the `QueryShards` class lines **13-23**).

Within the `Main()` method, you call the `AddDocumentsToShards()` method to populate shards then call the `LoadCountry()` method to query shards and retrieve the `Country` document with the `Id = "EU/country/1005"`.

When running the `ShardRavenDB` application, you can observe that all the documents are stored on a single shard (in our case, the `EU` shard).

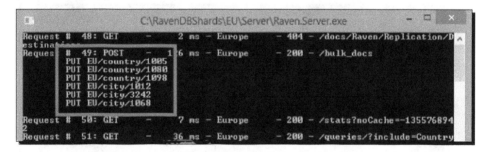

In the blind RavenDB sharding, the `ShardingOn()` method is not used and the `DefaultShardResolutionStrategy` strategy, will assign all entities within the same session to the same shard.

By convention, when you save a document to a given shard, the document ID is modified by RavenDB to store the shard ID. The default implementation returns an ID that will look like `Shard Id/Document Id`. This modified ID should be used when querying a shard to retrieve documents.

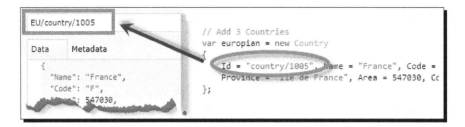

When querying the shards to retrieve the `EU/country/1005` country document (France), you can observe that all the shards are requested (`AS`, `EU`, and `NA`) while we specified the shard ID (`EU`).

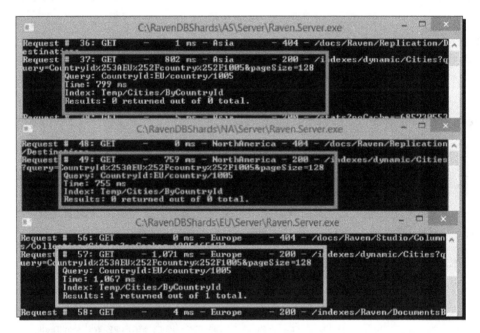

RavenDB sharding – the smart mode

In opposition sharding in blind mode, there is sharding in smart mode which is the mode, you should use in production. In this mode, you will instruct RavenDB on how to shard data and the sharding strategy to apply to shard entity instances.

The sharding database may have a performance impact when finding and retrieving your data which depends on how you sharded your database. Most sharded applications have at least some queries that need to aggregate or join data from multiple shards. When using the sharded Document Store, RavenDB will collect all the query results from different shards and will merge them client side.

In the blind mode, when querying the shards, all shards are requested, while in the smart mode, RavenDB is smart enough to request only one shard to retrieve data.

In the smart mode, you can instruct RavenDB's sharding strategy by calling the `ShardingOn()` method (on the `ShardStrategy` object) and providing the sharding property with an optional translation to the shard ID. When calling the `ShardingOn()` method, the `DefaultShardResolutionStrategy` strategy, implementation will force you to set it up on all entities that are getting stored.

Time for action – implementing RavenDB sharding (the smart mode)

As you can see, blind mode sharding doesn't meet our target of storing country data on independent shards depending on their continents. You will need to modify the `ShardRavenDB` application to interact with shards in a smart way. Then, you will observe and analyze the RavenDB logs:

1. On each RavenDB shard, delete all documents and temporary indexes in the `Asia`, `Europe`, and `NorthAmerican` databases.

2. Open the `ShardRavenDB` project in Visual Studio.

3. Modify the `PopulateShards` class constructor to look like the following code snippet:

```
16    static PopulateShards()
17    {
18        PopulateShards.Shards = new Shards();
19
20        Shards.ShardStrategy
21            // Sharding countries on their continent code
22            .ShardingOn<Country>(x => x.ContinentCode)
23            // Sharding cities on their country id
24            .ShardingOn<City>(x => x.CountryId);
25    }
```

4. Ensure that the three RavenDB shard instances are running.

5. Save the `ShardRavenDB` project and press *F5* to build the application and run it.

What just happened?

You just modified the `ShardRavenDB` application to interact with RavenDB shards in a smart way.

To interact with shards in the smart mode, you call the `ShardingOn()` method on the `ShardStrategy` object and tell RavenDB that you want to use a specific property to shard documents. You modify the `PopulateShards` class to specify the `Country. ContinentCode` field as the sharding property (the `PopulateShards` class line **22**). As the `City` object will also be stored on the shards, RavenDB forces you to define its sharding property, which you specify as the `City.CountryId` field (the `PopulateShards` class line **24**). In this case, the `City` and `Country` documents that have the same `shard Id` will be stored on the same shard.

 RavenDB will search the `CountryId` value in the `Shard Id` list (defined as the dictionary key when shards are initialized), and if it doesn't find a matching value, it will throw an error.

When running the application, it will store three `Country` documents. You can observe that each `Country` document has been stored on the right shard and the `ContinentCode` value matches with the shard name (`AS`, `EU`, and `NA`) where it has been stored. Also, when querying the shards to retrieve the country with `Id = "EU/country/1005"`, RavenDB is smart enough to request only one shard to retrieve data (in our case, the `EU` shard).

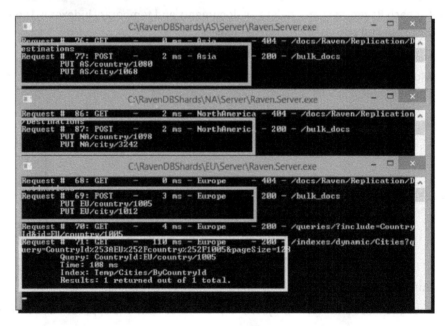

Have a go hero – implementing the Shard ID translator function

By default, RavenDB will throw an exception if it can't find the appropriate shard. You can modify this behavior to have a default shard or to store documents on a particular shard which will catch this exception.

Let's assume that you have a shard named `America` and you have already declared it in the shard's ID dictionary. We want all the `Country` documents whose `ContinentId` is NA or SA to be stored on the `America` shard.

In order to implement this behavior, call the `ShardingOn()` method and specify the translator function to translate the shard ID. The translator function will check for the `ContinentId` value, and when NA or SA is found, it will translate it to `America`.

Mixing sharding and replication

Mixing load balancing and availability is a common and simple way to scale-out your servers and databases. This can be done by distributing your data across several shards and mixing this distribution with replication by replicating every shard. Then, you can use the replicas to read queries. This technique works well for a read-heavy application. RavenDB does this out of the box.

You may choose to shard your database with dedicated failover nodes. In this configuration, each shard is configured as the replication master, and in front of each shard, a dedicated server is configured as the replication slave (for each master). In this case, the replication node numbers are at least the same shard nodes. The advantage is that if one of the primary nodes is failing, RavenDB will automatically switch to the replicated copy.

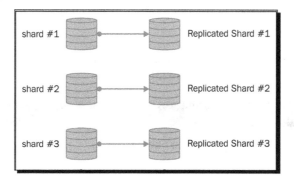

Another option is to use sharding primarily as a means of reducing load on the servers and set up replication between the different nodes without dedicated failover nodes. In this configuration, you will store shard data and replicated data from another shard. This will reduce the number of instances that you use, but it also means the storing capacity of each node will be limited. In a failover case, all the traffic will be directed to a single node which puts the node under higher stress, since it needs to handle both normal and replicated operations. Since a single node may not be able to handle the entire load for the application, this may very well lead to a cascading failure scenario.

This scenario is usually applied when the cost of a server's instances may be considered as high. Also, it may be considered for testing purposes before implementing shards with dedicated failover nodes.

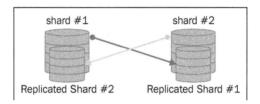

Have a go hero – mixing sharding and replication

In the previous chapter, you learned how to implement a RavenDB replication. In this chapter, you learned how to implement RavenDB sharding. Why not try to create a replicated shard infrastructure?

On each shard, activate the **Replication Bundle** then create three new RavenDB instances. On each instance, create a new database and activate the replication bundle with: `ASReplica` database to replicate the `AS` shard, `EUReplica` to replicate the `EU` shard, and `NAReplica` to replicate the `NA` shard.

Once this is done, the replication node will appear, and now you can create a new (master to slave) replication to replicate shard documents.

Pop Quiz – scaling-out RavenDB

Q1. How does RavenDB allow you to scale databases?

1. Vertically
2. Horizontally
3. Horizontally and Vertically
4. None

Q2. How can you scale-out a RavenDB database?

1. Add more RAM or disk space

2. Implement replication failover

3. Create a shard ID dictionary

4. Split the database on multiple RavenDB shards

Q3. Why do you need to call the `ShardingOn()` method on the `ShardStrategy` object?

1. It is good for shard testing

2. It takes less resources to retrieve documents from the server

3. It lets you interact with shards in blind mode

4. To interact with RavenDB shards in smart mode

Q4. By default, RavenDB throws an exception if it can't find an appropriate shard. How can you catch this exception and redirect it to the "Default" shard?

1. This is not possible to do

2. Rewrite the `ShardingStrategy` class

3. Rewrite the `ShardingOn()` method

4. Provide a translator function when calling the `ShardingOn()` method

Summary

In this chapter, we learned how to scale-out RavenDB and how it is easy to implement sharding in RavenDB which is supported natively. We covered RavenDB sharding modes and database sharding techniques. Also, we learned how to initialize, populate, and query a sharded Document Store. Specifically, we covered RavenDB sharding in blind mode and smart mode, including when and how to use each of these sharding modes.

We learned how to mix RavenDB sharding and replication in order to improve the server performance and availability.

In the next chapter, we will talk about RavenDB profiling and how it can help you to improve your RavenDB server performances. Keep reading!

10
RavenDB Profiling

How do you know if a server is doing its work optimally? One of the most common performance-related requests we receive in our consulting practice is to find out why a specific query is not executing quickly enough and to troubleshoot mysterious intermittent bottlenecks.

This chapter discusses the RavenDB profiling and stress tools. You will learn how to enable and use these tools which may help you to speed up your server's overall workload, speed up a single query, or troubleshoot and solve a problem when it's hard to observe and you don't know what causes it or even how it manifests.

In this chapter, we will cover:

- ◆ The RavenDB profiler
- ◆ Using the profiler information
- ◆ RavenDB visual host, workload simulator, and stress tests

What is profiling?

Talking about profiling and performance optimization is out of the scope of this book. In easy words, the profiling process consists of multiple analyses that investigate the structure and the content of the data, the processing time, and also make inferences about this information. After the analysis is complete, we can review the results and accept or reject the inferences. Basically, we use the profiling process to evaluate the quality of the data and the time taken to process this data. So, we can say that profiling is the primary means of measuring and analyzing where time is consumed.

When analyzing a profiling result, we aim to understand why a given server requires a certain amount of time to respond to a query and try to reduce or eliminate whatever unnecessary work it's doing to achieve the result. This is called **optimization**. In other words, we need to measure where the time goes in order to optimize it. The following figure illustrates the profiling process cycle:

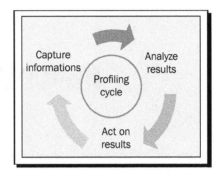

RavenDB profiler

The **RavenDB profiler** is an integrated feature implemented as an external .NET assembly named `Raven.Client.MvcIntegration.dll` which can be found in the `~\Client` folder of the distribution package. It is designed to be integrated in an ASP.NET MVC 3+ web application in a very easy way.

The RavenDB profiler allows you to track specific actions performed against RavenDB server databases. It provides valuable information about the processing time of queries, indexes, and data in order to tune database performance or troubleshoot database issues.

This profiling tool enables you to monitor data exchanges between your RavenDB server and your RavenDB application client. It provides a real-time view of submitted actions to the server and the response time that those actions took to process. Also, it allows you to see how long a query takes to execute, how many logical reads occur during execution, and so on.

A RavenDB instance's performance is measured by query response time, and the unit of measurement is time in milliseconds. After a RavenDB operation is complete, you can open the RavenDB profiler to view and analyze the results. The profiling results contain a variety of analytical and statistical information about the profiled operation and data. You can immediately drill down into query details and view the data that has been exchanged with the server. Then, you can analyze results to determine if something needs to be corrected or optimized.

The output report of the profiler consists of a table of tasks, one line per task. Each line shows the duration, the status, the HTTP result, the HTTP method, the URL, the query, and the actions that were performed by the server.

While initializing the RavenDB profiler, it accepts an optional filter which allows you to exclude some data from the profiling information. This is particularly useful when your database contains some sensitive information such as passwords which you don't want to be revealed to others.

It is easy to implement the RavenDB profiler in your ASP .NET MVC application. You just need to initialize it within the `Application_Start()` method or anywhere else where you initialize the `DocumentStore` object; just make sure that the `InitializeFor()` method on the `RavenProfiler` object is called once. Then, you may get the profiling results by calling the `CurrentRequestSessions()` method on the `RavenProfiler` object within the layout file for your application (`_layout.cshtml` is the default layout file in ASP .NET MVC 3+) or any MVC view in your application.

When the RavenDB profiler is launched, you might notice a small orange rectangle in the upper-left corner of the page. When you click on it, you'll see information about how long the RavenDB session has been opened for, how many requests were made, which resource was freshly fetched, which was cached, what the path of the request made to RavenDB was, and information about the query.

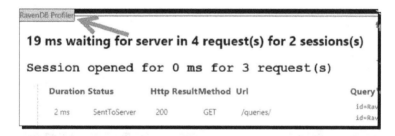

Time for action – enabling the RavenDB profiler

To learn more about the RavenDB profiler's capabilities, you will now create the ASP.NET MVC application `RavenDBProfiling`, which implements the profiler. You will implement only the necessary code to enable the profiler to monitor the application which will connect to the `World` database (created in the previous chapters) and retrieve documents from the `Countries` collection. Then, you will view and analyze the profiler's information report:

1. Open Visual Studio, create a new **ASP.NET MVC 4 Web Application**, and name it `RavenDBProfiling`.

2. Use the `NuGet` package manager to add the `RavenDB Client MVC` integration package. While it installs the package, it will automatically add the `RavenDB Client` package.

3. In the **Solution Explorer**, select the `Models` folder, right-click on it to add a new class, and name it `Country` (the class definition that we used in the previous chapters).

```
 9    public class Country
10    {
11        public string Id { get; set; }
12        public string Name { get; set; }
13        public string Code { get; set; }
14        public long Area { get; set; }
15        public string Capital { get; set; }
16        public string Province { get; set; }
17        public string FlagId { get; set; }
18        public string ContinentCode { get; set; }
19    }
```

4. Add the static `IDocumentStore` field and the `InitializeRavenProfiler()` method to the `Global.asax.cs` file.

```
17    public class MvcApplication : System.Web.HttpApplication
18    {
19        public static IDocumentStore Store { get; set; }
20
21        private void InitializeRavenProfiler()
22        {
23            Raven.Client.MvcIntegration.RavenProfiler.InitializeFor(Store);
24        }
25
26        protected void Application_Start()
```

5. In the `Global.asax.cs` file, modify the `Application_Start()` method, and as in the following existing code, add the `DocumentStore` object and the RavenDB profiler initialization.

```
26    protected void Application_Start()
27    {
34        // Code removed for clarity //
35
36        // Initialize RavenDB DocumentStore
37        Store = new DocumentStore
38        {
39            Url = "http://localhost:8080/", DefaultDatabase ="World"
40        }.Initialize();
41
42        // Initialize RavenDB Profiler
43        InitializeRavenProfiler();
44    }
```

6. In the **Solution Explorer**, select the `Controllers` folder, right-click on it to add a new controller, and name it `HomeController`. While creating the controller, ensure that you selected the **MVC** controller with the empty read/write actions template.

7. Modify the `Index()` method of `HomeController` to load the `Countries` list.

```
13    // GET: /Home/
14
15    public ActionResult Index()
16    {
17        using (var session = MvcApplication.Store.OpenSession())
18        {
19            var countries = session.Query<Country>().ToList();
20            return View("Index", countries);
21        }
22    }
```

As we don't paginate the query result, only the first 128 elements are returned to the client application.

8. Build the `RavenDBProfiling` solution.

You should always build your solutions before adding views to ensure that your class models are listed in the **Model Class** list.

9. Right-click on the `Index()` method and create the `Index` view. Ensure that you check the **Create a strongly typed-view** and choose the `Country` (`RavenDBProfiling.Models`) class model. Then, check **Use a layout or master page** and select the `~/Views/Shared/_Layout.cshtml` layout.

10. Add the following line to the `_Layout.cshtml` file:

```
<body>
    @Raven.Client.MvcIntegration.RavenProfiler.CurrentRequestSessions()
    @RenderBody()

    @Scripts.Render("~/bundles/jquery")
```

11. Ensure that the RavenDB server is launched and is listening on port `8080`.

12. Save the `RavenDBProfiling` project and press *F5* to build and run the web application.

13. Once the application's default page is loaded, click on the small orange rectangle in the upper-left corner to view the RavenDB profiler information report.

What just happened?

You just created the ASP .NET MVC web application `RavenDBProfiling`, which implements the RavenDB profiler. This application will connect to the `World` database to retrieve the `Countries` collection and displays it while the RavenDB profiler records all requests and display the profiling information.

To enable the RavenDB profiler, you add a reference to the `RavenDB Client MVC` integration package using the NuGet package manager. As this package depends on the `RavenDB Client` package, this is automatically installed.

 As an alternative to the NuGet package manager, you can reference `RavenDB.Client.MVCIntegration.dll` manually from the `~\Client` folder of the RavenDB distribution package.

As the `DocumentStore` and `RavenProfiler` objects should be initialized only once, you modify the `Global.asax.cs` file in order to call the initialization code (lines **37-43**). The static field `Store` holds the instance of the `DocumentStore` object which will be used to create a new RavenDB session (line **19**).

In the `InitializeRavenProfiler()` method, you initialize the profiler and tell it to enable profiling against the `DocumentStore` object you just created. This line is essentially sniffing for the requests coming in, recording these requests, and then sending them to the layout.

 It is good practice to dedicate a method to initializing the profiler. This will allow you to enable profiling only in `Debug` mode by decorating this method with the conditional attribute `[Conditional("DEBUG")]`.

You may filter fields out while the profiler initialization is taking place. Just pass an array of string fields that you want to filter and pass it as a second parameter of the `RavenProfiler.InitializerFor()` method.

To retrieve the `Countries` collection and display it within the `Index()` method in the `HomeController` class, you open a RavenDB session and call the `Query()` method then transmit the query response to the `Index` view in order to display it. As we didn't paginate the query result, only the first 128 elements are returned by the server (lines **15-22**).

To display the profiling result, you call the `CurrentRequestSessions()` method on the `RavenProfiler` object. You add this call to the `_Layout.chtml` layout which represents the layout of each page in the application. It is located in the `\Shared` folder inside the `\Views` folder.

The CurrentRequestSessions() method returns an HtmlString type which represents an HTML-encoded string and allows the execution of HTML tags.

When launching the application, the RavenDB profiler is enabled and a small orange rectangle appears in the upper-left corner of the page. By clicking on this button, you can display the profiling report and various information can be pulled, starting from request duration, HTTP method, URL, and so on.

In our case, the profiler reports that a GET method is sent to the server to retrieve the Countries collection and that this operation took 23 milliseconds to execute.

To display the request details, you may click on the **Request Details** link. This will open a new view with the exact request response results.

Using the profiler information

Slow-running queries are ones that take too long to run. So, the first question to answer is how long is too long? That is a decision you have to make. One of your first steps is to determine what you think a long-running query is, and then use this as your standard during the performance audit.

There are several ways to define an execution time reference. You may profile your server in normal running condition several times and get an average execution time. Also, you may define a cutoff time such as 5 seconds then consider that any query running 5 seconds or less is generally fast enough, while queries that take longer than 5 seconds to run are long-running.

The following non-exhaustive steps set out some of our preferred ways of performing an analysis on slow-running queries. These practices have come about from rigorous testing, years of experience, and ongoing efforts at dealing with performance issues:

- After you have completed the capture, scroll through the events to get a feeling for the results you got back.

- Review each event in the capture; look at which are the slowest-running events that took the most time to execute.

- Identify long-running queries and also those queries that execute most often. It is important to identify both. For example, which is worse, a query that runs once an hour and takes 30 seconds to run, or a query that runs 100 times a second that takes 1 second to run? I think you would agree that the shorter query would probably have more effect on the overall performance of the system than the longer one.

- Once you have identified a specific query, start analyzing it so that you can identify what is the cause of its slowness, with the presumption that it will enable you to fix the problem.

- Does the query run slowly every time?

Once you identify the bad queries, you need to work on those individual queries to address the problems.

Have a go hero – profiling the RavenDB shards

In the previous chapter, you learned how to implement RavenDB shards. This scenario is very close to real-world scenarios, so why not try to profile RavenDB shards? As in real-world scenarios, we often need to profile distributed database servers.

Enabling the RavenDB profiler is pretty easy, as you learned in the previous section, but first you need to create an ASP.NET MVC application to interact with the RavenDB shards and then use the RavenDB profiler in order to measure its request time.

RavenDB visual host

The RavenDB package provides another tool named `RavenDB Visual Host`, which may help you to profile and simulate the RavenDB server instances. This tool is provided as a code source and it can be found in the `~\Samples` folder of the distribution package. So, before you can use this tool, you need to build its binary file.

The RavenDB visual host's graphical user interface has three main areas:

- The first area lets you specify the number of server instances you want to create and start. The default number of server instances is set to `1`.

◆ The second area displays each RavenDB instance you start in a dedicated tab. Each tab will show the server request number and display the HTTP method, HTTP status, and the URL invoked by the request.

◆ The third area is a tabbed area and contains two tabs. Each tab will show request and response details for each server instance.

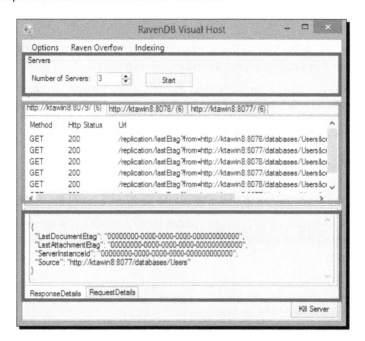

When you start the RavenDB visual host, it waits until you click on the **Start** button. Then, it will create the number of RavenDB instances you specified and allocate to each instance a specific free TCP port going down from port `8080`. Once instances are created and ready, the visual host starts monitoring server requests and display results in real-time.

 The RavenDB visual host runs in the `Memory Embedded` mode and database instances are created in memory and are thrown away when exiting the visual host.

The RavenDB visual host may be very useful for testing and simulating replication relations and RavenDB shards. For example, to test RavenDB sharding, all you need is to create some RavenDB instances using the visual host. Then, add each instance connection string to a list of connection strings and use this list to initialize the `ShardedDocumentStore` object.

Time for action – running the RavenDB visual host

You will now modify the RavenDBProfiling application to address the RavenDB visual host. You will add the Create Country view to the RavenDBProfiling application in order to enter some document data in an easy way and store these documents in the visual host instances. Then, you will observe and analyze request and response details in the visual host:

1. In Windows Explorer, go to the ~\Sample folder of the RavenDB installation package and open the Raven.Samples.sln solution.

2. Set the Raven VisualHost project as the startup project. Then, press *F5* to build and run the Visual Host (or run the Raven.VisualHost.exe file).

 You may need the administrator privileges in order to run the RavenDB visual host.

3. Click on the **Start** button in order to create and run 1 (one) RavenDB instance.

4. Open the RavenDBProfiling application and modify the DocumentStore object initialization code in the Global.asax.cs file to look like the following code snippet:

```
35        // Initialize RavenDB DocumentStore
36        Store = new DocumentStore
37        {
38            // RavenDB Visual Host listening TCP port
39            Url = "http://localhost:8079/"
40
41        }.Initialize();
```

 The port number should be the same port allocated by the visual host to the instance it runs.

5. Open HomeController.cs and modify the [HttpPost] Create() method to look like the following code snippet:

```
40  □   //
41      // POST: /Home/Create
42
43      [HttpPost]
44  □   public ActionResult Create(Country country)
45      {
46          if (!ModelState.IsValid)
47              return View();
48
49          using (var session = MvcApplication.Store.OpenSession())
50          {
51              session.Store(country);
52              session.SaveChanges();
53
54              return RedirectToAction("Index");
55          }
56      }
```

6. Right-click on the `Create()` method and create the `Create` view. Ensure that you check the **Create a strongly typed-view** and choose the `Country (RavenDBProfiling.Models)` class model. Then, check **Use a layout or master page** and select the `~/Views/Shared/_Layout.cshtml` layout.

7. Save the `RavenDBProfiling` project and press *F5* to build and run the application.

8. Add a new `Country` (with the details as `France, F, Paris, "Ile de France", 547030, EU`).

9. Switch to the RavenDB visual host and click on each log entry to display the response/request details.

What just happened?

You just modified the `RavenDBProfiling` application and created the `Create Country` view in order to store documents and interact with the RavenDB visual host.

As the RavenDB visual host is provided as a source code (located in the `~\Sample` folder of the RavenDB package distribution), you need to build the binary files before you can use it. Once you have built the binary files, you run it and you click on the **Start** button to run a new RavenDB server instance (instances run embedded in memory), which basically will run on the first free port going down from `8080`.

Then, you open the `RavenDBProfiling` application and modify the `Global.asax.cs` file in order to address the visual host instance which is running on port `8079` (line **39**).

The next step was to create the Create Country view. To do that, you first implement the [HttpPost] Create() method code which opens a RavenDB session and store the Country object sent by the web page form. Then, you add the Create Country view using the Visual Studio wizard and set the Model class to Country and use the _Layout. chtml page.

When you run the RavenDBProfiling application, you add a new Country and switch to the RavenDB visual host.

In the visual host, you can observe the POST HTTP method performed in order to store the Country document on the server and the RequestDetails tab shows the document content submitted to the server.

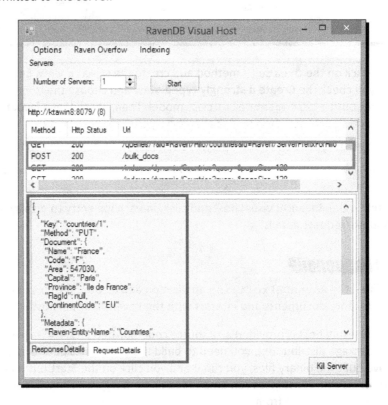

RavenDB workload simulator/stress tests

A **workload** is the amount of work a system has to perform in a given time. In the performance field, a workload usually refers to the combined load placed on an application by the set of clients it services. A database workload can be defined as a set of statements that you execute against a database server that you want to tune.

Basically, a workload simulator aims to help in performance analysis, and it is important that it reproduces repeatable results. If the workload is run several times in an identical fashion, it should produce results that are almost identical.

Stress testing is a part of the process of performance testing which tries to identify the breaking point in a system under test by overwhelming its resources or by taking resources away from it. The main purpose of a stress test is to find the infrastructure problems within an installation. It can also be used for hardware sizing, system tuning, or benchmarking.

RavenDB provides two external tools: a workload simulator (`Raven.SimulatedWorkLoad`) and a stress test tool (`Raven.StessTests`), which you can use to tune your RavenDB server infrastructure. These tools are part of the RavenDB source package. They are provided as source code and you need to build them before you can use them. You may download the source code package directly from the RavenDB official website at `http://github.com/ravendb/ravendb/`.

`Raven.SimulatedWorkLoad` writes more than 250,000 documents and launches a process that creates the indexes, queries the database, and retrieves and stores the documents. Basically, when the simulator is running, your machine will be very busy and may not be able to perform other tasks.

`Raven.StessTests` is similar to `Raven.SimulatedWorkLoad`. It loads a big data file and launches a multisession process that should run under 30 minutes.

In a real-world scenario, these tools may be helpful to tune a server's capacities in order to ensure that they are capable of doing the work they are asked to do.

Summary

In this chapter, we learned about RavenDB profiling and stress tools. We covered how to enable and use these tools in order to optimize and tune a RavenDB server. Specifically, we covered the RavenDB profiler and how to install it and analyze its output information.

We learned about the RavenDB visual host and how it may help you to profile and simulate the RavenDB server instances.

We also took a look at two RavenDB externals tools: the RavenDB simulated workload and the RavenDB stress test tools which you can build and use to tune your RavenDB server performance.

Now we've learned a lot about RavenDB, we're ready to learn how to connect to the RavenDB server using the REST protocol rather than the Microsoft .NET framework—which is the topic of the next chapter.

11
RavenDB HTTP API

RavenDB allows interactions over the HTTP protocol and is exposing itself as a RESTful web service.

In this chapter, you will learn how to access the RavenDB server using technologies other than .NET and without using the Management Studio. The RavenDB HTTP API allows communicating with it using the HTTP protocol.

You will learn about the REST main verbs and how to use them to retrieve documents from RavenDB or add documents to the database. To simplify the REST requests composition, you will use an HTTP tool to do some interaction with RavenDB through the RavenDB RESTful API.

In this chapter we will cover:

- The RavenDB HTTP API
- Performing requests using the main REST verbs (`GET`, `PUT`, `POST`, `PATCH`, and `DELETE`)
- Retrieving multiple documents
- Querying Indexes

The RavenDB HTTP API

RavenDB fully supports an API based on HTTP that basically permits to interact with the database engine with simple HTTP requests. This means that if you have an application or environment that can talk HTTP, you can communicate through the RavenDB HTTP API. This HTTP API follows commonly understood RESTful principles and the interactions are entirely based around the HTTP protocol. When using the HTTP protocol to access RESTful resources, the resource identifier is the URL of the resource and the standard operation to be performed on that resource is one of the HTTP methods such as GET, PUT, DELETE, POST, or HEAD. RavenDB is exposing itself as the RESTful web service. Utilizing a RESTful HTTP API allows an application functionality to be consistently used across different platforms. It's possible to write a fully functioning RavenDB application just using JavaScript, HTML, and the HTTP API.

Understanding REST

REST is an architectural paradigm and RESTful is used as an adjective describing something that respects the REST constraints. REST stands for REpresentational State Transfer. It is a way of interacting with resources on the web via plain human-readable URLs.

Any interaction of a RESTful API is an interaction with a resource. In fact, the API can be considered simply as mapping and endpoint—or resource identifier (URL)—to a resource. Resources are sources of information, typically documents or services. An HTTP-based REST API makes communicating with the database easier, because so many modern environments are capable of talking HTTP. The simple structure of HTTP resources and methods is easy to understand and develop with.

The REST interface defines four commonly used HTTP main verbs: GET, POST, PUT, and DELETE, and others that are not used as often such as HEAD, OPTIONS, and so on. Each verb has certain characteristics and it is critical to choose the right verb.

The GET verb tells the service that the client wishes to get a read-only representation of a resource. POST indicates the desire to create a new resource. PUT is typically used for modifying an existing resource also for resource creation. And DELETE indicates that a client wishes to delete a resource.

Both `PUT` and `POST`, can be used to create resources, so which one should you use? Using the right verb will depend on what object you are referencing in the request.

- ◆ `PUT` means "insert or replace if already exists" and here is the data for the object
- ◆ `PUT` is idempotent, so if you `PUT` an object twice, it has no effect
- ◆ `POST` means "create new" and here is the input for creating the object, create it for me
- ◆ With `POST` you can have more than one request coming in at the same time making modifications to the same object and they may update different parts of the object

To learn more about RESTful, a good starting point would be this URL: `http://en.wikipedia.org/wiki/Representational_state_transfer`

Anatomy of the RavenDB REST request URL

REST requests are URL-based. In order to get or put any document in RavenDB, we will basically create a request and use a RavenDB target structure. Then we will specify what type of entity it is and the document ID or the data to be sent to the server within the URL. To create the RavenDB REST request, we will make a request to a specific URL that will look like:

`http://url:port/databases/databaseName/target/RequestData`

- ◆ `url`: This represents the URL where RavenDB is running.
- ◆ `port`: This is the TCP port number, by default the port number is `8080`.
- ◆ `databaseName`: This is the name of the database where the documents are stored.
- ◆ `target`: This represents the target structure in RavenDB we want to deal with. This might be the `docs` structure, the `indexes` structure, the `queries` structure, and so on.
- ◆ `RequestData`: This represents the data resources for the request. It might be the document ID on which the action is performed (create, retrieve, update, or delete) or all other data needed to perform the action.

The RESTClient tool

To experiment and interact with the RavenDB HTTP API, we need to use a REST client tool to create HTTP requests and display HTTP responses easily. We will use the **RESTClient** tool, which is an open source Java application for composing and submitting the HTTP REST requests to the RavenDB server and for viewing and analyzing the RavenDB server responses.

The RESTClient graphic interface is divided into two main sections:

1. The **HTTP Request** screen section: This screen section has several tabs to view and manage the parameters of the generated request that will be sent to the server. We can choose the HTTP action method to perform on the server, change the request header if we need to, and to do all the things we need to do to interact with the RavenDB web service.

2. The **HTTP Response** screen section: This screen section has many tabs that shows the metadata included in the header of the server response and the document body data in colored plain text format.

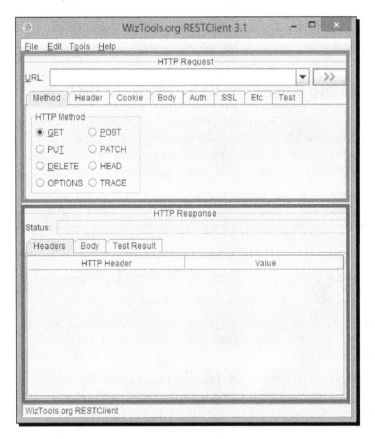

Time for action – downloading and launching the RESTClient tool

Let us start by downloading the RESTClient tool to begin using the RavenDB HTTP API:

1. Open your web browser and go to this URL: `http://www.wiztools.org/`.

2. In the projects list click on the **RESTClient** link.

3. Download the **RESTClient 3.1 GUI Executable Jar** file.

> At the time of writing, RESTClient v3.1 GUI was the latest version. If a newer stable release is available, you should download that version instead.

4. Once downloaded, double-click on the JAR file to launch the RESTClient tool.

> RESTClient requires a Java Runtime Environment (JRE) to run, which might be already installed on your system. If the JRE is not present on your system, please install the latest JRE from `http://www.java.com` before installing and launching RESTClient.

What just happened?

We just downloaded the latest version of the open source Java application RESTClient to compose REST requests easily.

We will use this third party tool to create the HTTP requests that we will send to the RavenDB server. Once the requests are sent to the RavenDB server, we will use this tool to view the RavenDB server HTTP responses.

To launch the RESTClient tool, you double-click on the downloaded JAR file which requires the Java Runtime Environment to be installed on the computer where RESTClient is running.

The GET request

The GET verb is used for read-only operations. There are no side effects for which the client is responsible. So GET should not be used to update or delete a resource or to make a new resource. Every system that understands the HTTP protocol assumes that a GET request will *not* change the state of the system and hence will make assumptions based on that.

In order to get any document in RavenDB, we will basically create a GET request and use the RavenDB docs structure. Then we will specify the type of entity which will hold the document data and the document ID we want to retrieve from the server.

Once the GET request is sent to RavenDB in order to retrieve a given document, it will respond with the contents of that document and an HTTP response code:

HTTP Method	On Success	On Error
GET	HTTP/1.1 200 OK	HTTP/1.1 404 Not Found
	HTTP/ 1.1 304 Not Modified	

Time for action – performing a GET request

You will learn to create a GET request using the RESTClient tool we have downloaded in the previous section to retrieve the document with the ID = Orders/A655302 from the Orders database and view it. (We created the Orders database in *Chapter 2, RavenDB Management Studio.*)

1. If it is not already open, double-click on the RESTClient tool's JAR file in order to launch it.

2. Click on the **Method** tab and select the **GET** HTTP method.

3. In the **HTTP Request** section, enter this URL: http://localhost:8080/databases/orders/docs/orders/a655302.

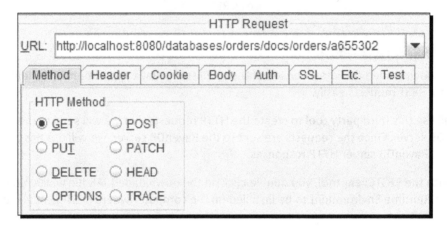

 To perform this GET request, we don't need to change any of the **Header** or the **Body**, or other parameters.

4. Click on the green **Go!** button to send your first request to the server.

What just happened?

You just created your first GET request to retrieve the order document with the ID Orders/A655302 from the Orders database directly by using the RavenDB HTTP API.

Let's have a look at the server response and analyze it. The first thing that we need to check when we receive an HTTP response from the server is the status code. In case of a `GET` request, receiving an `HTTP/1.1 200 OK` code indicates that the request has succeeded. Otherwise there is an error and the server has not received, understood, or has not accepted the request.

HTTP Header	Value
HTTP Response	
Status: HTTP/1.1 200 OK	
Headers Body Test Result	
HTTP Header	Value
Transfer-Encoding	chunked
Content-Type	application/json; charset=utf-8
Expires	Sat, 01 Jan 2000 00:00:00 GMT
Last-Modified	Thu, 21 Feb 2013 20:25:39 GMT
ETag	00000001-0000-0c00-0000-000000000...
Server	Microsoft-HTTPAPI/2.0
Raven-Server-Build	2261
Raven-Entity-Name	Orders
Non-Authoritative-Information	false
Raven-Last-Modified	2013-02-21T20:25:39.0055429Z
__document_id	Orders/A655302
Temp-Request-Time	1
Date	Thu, 28 Feb 2013 05:00:16 GMT

Select the **Headers** tab in the **HTTP Response** section and look to the header's data which came with the server response. We can see the RavenDB metadata **Raven-Entity-Name** from which the document has been retrieved.

Click on the **Body** tab to show the response body and you will see what the server sent back is a JSON document which is the actual JSON data document stored on the RavenDB server (which you can see using the Management Studio).

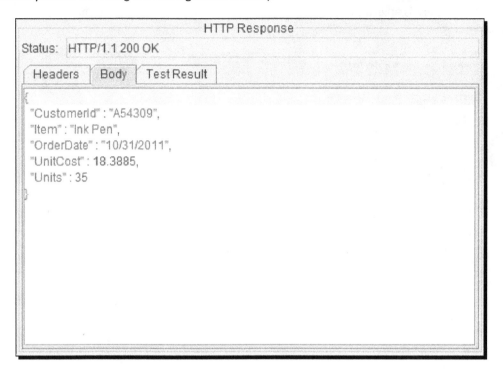

You see how simple it was to get a document from RavenDB server using the HTTP API. We can basically get any document from the RavenDB server using the same approach.

Have a go hero – retrieving the databases list

You now know how to get any document from the RavenDB server using the HTTP API. Open the RESTClient tool and by using a GET HTTP method retrieve the databases' list from the server and compare it with the list you see when you open the Management Studio.

Need a hint? Use the RavenDB regular URL and the databases endpoint.

The PUT request

The PUT verb is an HTTP method that can be used to create a resource, with the information in the request, for the URL specified by the client. It is important to note that a PUT verb in RavenDB will always create the specified document at the requested URL. If the resource already exists, PUT simply replaces what existed with the new information.

In order to put any document into RavenDB, we will create a PUT request and use the docs structure. We have to specify the document ID and the document data in JSON format. Also, we need to specify the name of the collection to which the document will belong. The PUT request URL is similar to the GET request URL we created in the previous section.

In case that a PUT request is sent to the RavenDB's docs structure without specifying the document ID in the request URL, this request is considered as invalid and RavenDB will return an HTTP error response code.

Once the request is sent to RavenDB, it will respond with the ID of the document it generated and an HTTP response code:

HTTP Method	On Success	On Error
PUT	HTTP/1.1 201 Created	HTTP 400 Bad Request

By default, anonymous users in RavenDB can get any documents they want, but they are not able to modify or add any documents or indexes to the server. This behavior is defined by the Raven/AnonymousAccess configuration key option that can be found in the Raven.Server.exe.config file located in the Server folder. This option is set by default to Get.

Setting this value to All will grant anonymous users all privileges on the database, and None will grant no access at all. To grant all actions, including administrative actions, you need to set this value to Admin.

In order to make changes take effect, you need to restart the RavenDB server.

Time for action – granting access to perform a PUT request

Performing a PUT request needs writing privileges on the server. By default, RavenDB grants a read-only access to anonymous users. You will change the Raven/AnonymousAccess key value which is Get by default and set it to All which will allow you to add new documents to the RavenDB server:

1. Shutdown the RavenDB server and close the Management Studio.

2. Open the Raven.Server.exe.config file located in the \Server folder of the RavenDB installation folder.

3. Change the Raven/AnonymousAccess key value and set it to All.

4. Save the `Raven.Server.exe.config` file and launch the RavenDB server using the `Start.cmd` file.

```
3    <appSettings>
4      <add key="Raven/Port" value="*"/>
5      <add key="Raven/DataDir" value="~\Database\System"/>
6      <add key="Raven/AnonymousAccess" value="All"/>
7    </appSettings>
```

What just happened?

By default, RavenDB grants the read-only permission for anonymous users.

In order to allow write operation and grant anonymous users permission to add a new document to the RavenDB server, we change the `Raven/AnonymousAccess` key's value and set it to `All`.

Time for action – performing a PUT request

We will add a new document to the `Orders` database by creating a `PUT` request using the RESTClient tool. The new document will have the ID = `Orders/C676332` and will be added to the `Orders` collections which belongs to the `Orders` database.

Once the document is added to the server, we will take a look at the server response. Then, we will open the Management Studio and verify that the document has been correctly added to the server:

1. Launch the RESTClient tool.

2. Click on the **Method** tab and select the **PUT** HTTP method.

3. In the **HTTP Request** section, enter this URL: `http://localhost:8080/databases/orders/docs/Orders/C676332`.

4. Click on the **Body** tab and select **String body** from the drop-down list and enter the following JSON snippet:

```json
{
    "CustomerId": "A55689",
    "Item": "Mouse Pad",
    "OrderDate": "11/3/2011",
    "UnitCost": 8.5,
    "Units": 10
}
```

5. Click on the **Header** tab and enter `Raven-Entity-Name` in the **Key** textbox and `Orders` in the **Value** textbox and then click on the green plus sign to add this metadata key to the header of the request which will be sent to the server.

6. Click on the green **Go!** button to send the `PUT` request to the server.

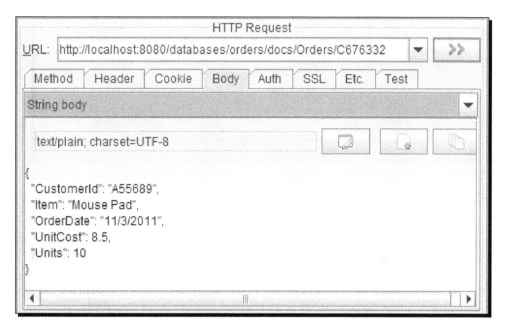

7. Open the Management Studio and select the `Orders` database.

8. Click on the **Documents** tab and verify that a new document with the ID = `Orders/C676332` has been added to the `Orders` database.

What just happened?

We add a new `Order` document with the ID = `Orders/C676332` to the `Orders` database using a `PUT` request using the RavenDB HTTP API.

 If the `Raven-Entity-Name` metadata is not sent to the server as part of the request header, the new document will not be classified as we expect in the `Orders` collection.

Let's have a look at the server response and check the HTTP server status code.
In case of a success PUT request, the status code returned by the server will be
HTTP/1.1 201 Created which indicates that the request has succeeded. Otherwise, there
is an error and the server has not received, understood, or has not accepted the request.

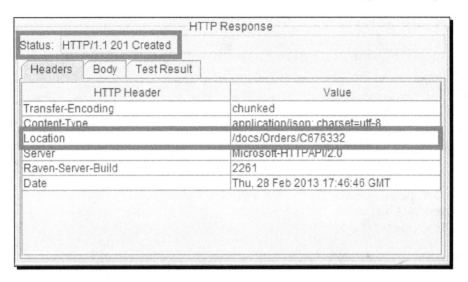

You can see the RavenDB metadata **Location** which indicates the location path for the new
document and the new document has been inserted into the docs structure.

Click on the **Body** tab to visualize the response body and you will see that the server sent
back is a JSON document that contains two fields: Key which contains the ID of the new
document and the ETag (entity tag), which is used by RavenDB to handle concurrent
requests and is updated by RavenDB every time the document is changed.

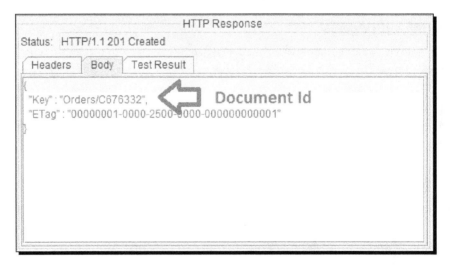

The POST request

The POST verb can be used to either create a resource or update an existing resource. All HTTP aware components assume that POST will make a change to the state of the system and will not repeat a POST request in case of an error.

When we perform a POST request to the RavenDB's docs structure, it will create the specified document and allow RavenDB to assign a unique ID to it. We have to specify the document data in JSON format and will not specify the document ID. It is important to note that a repeated POST request for the same document will create that document with a new ID each time.

The POST request URL is very similar to the PUT request URL with the difference that we do not specify the document ID in the URL.

A POST request to a document URL is considered as an invalid request and RavenDB will return error status code. Otherwise, if the POST request succeeded, the server response will contain the generated ID for the document and an HTTP response code:

HTTP Method	On Success	On Error
POST	HTTP/1.1 201 Created	HTTP 400 Bad Request

Time for action – performing a POST request

You will add a new document to the Orders database by creating a POST request using the RESTClient tool. As RavenDB will generate the ID for the new document, we will not specify any ID for the document. Once the document is added to the database on the server, we will open the Management Studio and verify that the document has been correctly inserted into the database and we will analyze the server response:

1. Launch the RESTClient tool.

2. Click on the **Method** tab and select the **POST** HTTP method.

3. In the **HTTP Request** section, enter this URL: http://localhost:8080/ databases/orders/docs.

4. Click on the **Body** tab and select **String body** from the drop-down list and enter the following JSON snippet:

```
{
  "CustomerId": "B66689",
  "Item": "USB Key",
  "OrderDate": "1/7/2012",
  "UnitCost": 28.5,
  "Units": 5
}
```

5. Click on the **Header** tab and enter `Raven-Entity-Name` in the **Key** textbox and `Orders` in the **Value** textbox and then click on the green plus sign to add this metadata key to the header.

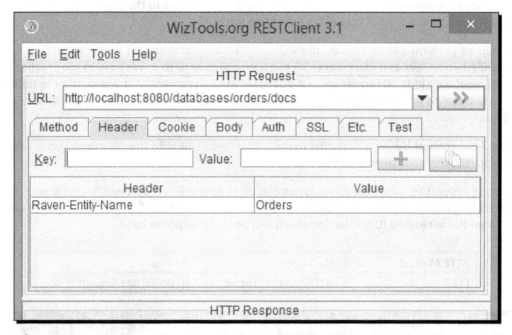

6. Click on the green **Go!** button to send the `POST` request to the server.

7. Open the Management Studio and select the `Orders` database.

8. Click on the **Documents** tab and verify that a new document with a `Guid` ID has been added to the `Orders` database.

What just happened?

We add a new `Order` document to the `Orders` database using a `POST` request which allows RavenDB to generate an ID for the new document. Then, we open the Management Studio to verify that the new document is in the database.

To ensure that the new document will belong to the `Orders` collection, you set the metadata `Raven-Entity-Name` key with the `Orders` value.

Once the POST request is performed, the server returns the status code and sends back a JSON document that contains the generated Guid for the new document and its ETag (entity tag).

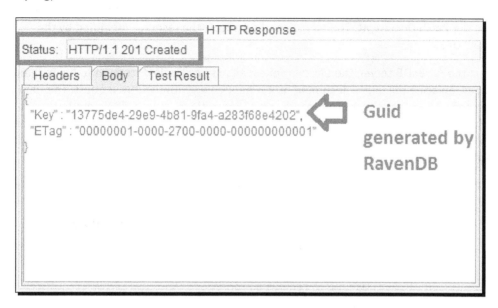

GUIDs are supposed to be unique. So, the GUID generated for you by RavenDB when you add the document to the database will certainly be different from the Guid generated and shown in the preceding screen capture.

Have a go hero – retrieving the inserted document

You just added a new document to RavenDB server using a POST request. Open the RESTClient tool and try to retrieve this document from the database. Then open the Management Studio and load the document you just added in the edit screen mode and compare its data and metadata to those you have retrieved using the RESTCllient tool.

The PATCH request

The PATCH method requests that a set of changes described in the request entity be applied to the resource identified by the request URL. The set of changes is represented in a format called the **Patch Document**. The PATCH method affects the resource identified by the request URL.

Within the RavenDB server, the PATCH request allows any single document to be updated without replacing the entire document as it is happening with the PUT request. The PATCH command accepts an array of commands, so it is possible to issue multiple modifications for the same document. The PATCH command keys are case sensitive and they have to be specified with the correct **Pascal Casing**. The six different command keys which you need to specify are listed as follows:

1. Type: This represents the operation type. RavenDB supports the following patch operations:

   ❑ Set: It is a property to a new value. (Optionally, creating the property).

   ❑ Inc: Use this to increment a property value by a given value. (Optionally, creating the property).

   ❑ Unset: Use this to remove a property.

   ❑ Add: Use this to add a value to an existing array.

   ❑ Insert: Use this to insert a value to an existing array at the specified position.

   ❑ Remove: Use this to remove a value from an existing array at a specified position.

   ❑ Modify: Use this to apply nested patch operation to an existing property value.

   ❑ Copy: Use this to copy a property value to a new property.

   ❑ Rename: Use this to rename a property.

2. Name: This is used to identify a property by its name.

3. Position: This is used to specify the position (index) in an array field.

4. Value: This represents the new value for a property.

5. PrevVal: This is the old property value.

6. Nested: This indicates that there are more (nested) patch operations.

Once the PATCH request is performed by the RavenDB server, it will return a short JSON acknowledgment with { "patched":true }and a status code:

HTTP Method	On Success	On Error
PATCH	HTTP/1.1 200 OK	HTTP/1.1 500 Internal Server Error

Time for action – performing a Patch request

You will open the document you just added to the Orders database using the Management Studio in order to copy its ID. Then, you will patch this document using the PATCH request. The patch request will add two new fields to the document: Colour and Discount. After that, you will view the modified document in the Management Studio:

1. Open the Management Studio and select the Orders database.

2. Click on the **Documents** tab and open the document which has a Guid as ID.

3. Copy the document ID to the clipboard.

4. Launch the RESTClient tool.

5. Click on the **Method** tab and select the **PATCH** HTTP method.

6. In the **HTTP Request** section, enter this URL and complete it by the document Guid you stored on the clipboard: http://localhost:8080/databases/orders/docs/{your Guid}.

7. Click on the **Header** tab and ensure that the Raven-Entity-Name metadata key is sent to the RavenDB server with the Value = Orders.

8. Click on the **Body** tab and select **String Body** in the drop-down list.

9. Enter the following code snippet:

```
[
   { Type: 'Set', Name: 'Colour', Value: "Black"},
   { Type: 'Inc', Name: 'discount', Value: 2},
]
```

10. Click on the green **Go!** button to send the PATCH request to the server.

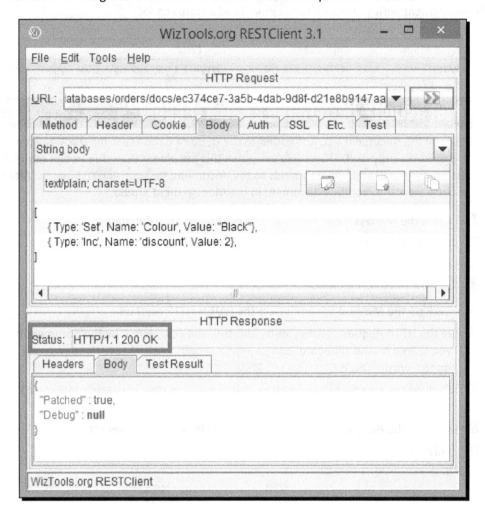

11. In the Management Studio, click on the **Documents** tab and verify that the document has been modified and contains the two new fields.

What just happened?

We used a PATCH request to add two new properties (Colour and discount) to a document from the Orders database.

We used two operation types in the patch script.

In the first line of the patch script code snippet, the Set operation is used to create a new property named Colour and will give it Black as Value.

In the second line, the Inc operation is used to increment an existing property value, but this property named discount doesn't exist; a new one will be created and the patch request assumes that its Value equals 2.

Then we open the document in the Management Studio to view the new modifications.

 Note that a much better approach is the scripted patching, exposed via the EVAL method.

Have a go hero – removing the document properties with a PATCH request

You just added two new properties using a PATCH request to a document from the Orders database. Open the RESTClient tool and try to remove these properties.

Then open the Management Studio and load the document you just patched in the edit screen mode and ensure that the document properties have been removed.

Do you need a hint? You might use the Unset operation which it is used to remove a property from a document.

The DELETE request

The DELETE verb asks the server to delete the resources. This will instruct RavenDB to delete the JSON document specified by the URL. It is important to note that deleting a document through the HTTP API is not reversible and has to be considered as a "hard" delete.

To avoid potential data loss, you can use a *soft* delete and there are multiple ways to do that. You may choose to move the existing documents to another database, or to mark a document with a deleted flag and then ignore documents like this in your business logic.

If the document we want to delete exists on the server or it doesn't exist, a DELETE request will still respond with a successful status code.

HTTP Method	On Success
DELETE	HTTP/1.1 204 No Content

Time for action – performing a Delete request

You will delete the document just added to the Orders database using a DELETE request. You will specify the document Guid in the request URL and perform the request on the server to delete the document. Then, you will verify in the Management Studio that the document has been removed and you will take a look to the server response:

1. Open the Management Studio and select the Orders database.
2. Click on the **Documents** tab and open the document which has a Guid as the ID.
3. Copy the document ID to the clipboard.
4. Launch the RESTClient tool.
5. Click on the **Method** tab and select the **DELETE** HTTP method.

6. In the **HTTP Request** section, enter this URL and complete it by the document `Guid` you stored on the clipboard: `http://localhost:8080/databases/orders/docs/{your guid}`.

7. Click on the green **Go!** button to send the `DELETE` request to the server.

8. In the Management Studio, click on the **Documents** tab and verify that the document has been deleted from the `Orders` database.

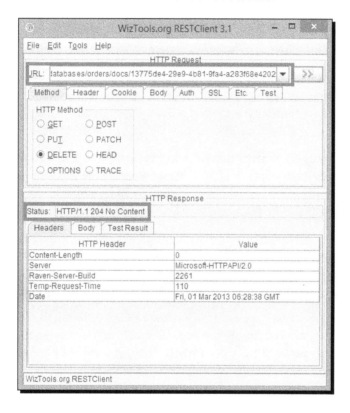

What just happened?

We used a `DELETE` request to delete a document from the `Orders` database.

The document we deleted has a generated `Guid` as ID which we specified in the request URL. Once the server has deleted the document, it sends back the HTTP status code which it is displayed in the **HTTP Response** screen section.

Also, you verified in the Management Studio that the document has been permanently deleted from the server.

Getting multiple documents with a single request

You may need, in your application, to get back multiple documents from RavenDB directly. In order to avoid sending to the server multiple queries, RavenDB supports the ability to get multiple documents in a single call. The way to do this is to create a POST request that we will post to a special URL.

 Getting multiple documents via one single call is also exposed via a GET method.

Instead of posting to the docs area structure, we will address the queries area and in the body of our POST request, we will specify a JSON array of all IDs we want to get back from RavenDB. The response for such a request is a JSON object that consists of two arrays of documents: Results and Includes. Each document also includes the metadata.

The Results array has documents that we asked for, while the Includes array contains optionally referenced documents. To determine what reference you want to retrieve together with a document an include parameter has to be added to the query string (http://localhost:8080/databases/{databaseName}/queries?include= CollectionName).

Time for action – getting multiple documents within a single request

You will learn to retrieve two documents in a single remote call from the Orders database using a POST request. You will specify the documents IDs in the request body and perform the request on the server to retrieve documents. Then, you will view the server response in the RESTClient tool:

1. Launch the RESTClient tool.
2. Click on the **Method** tab and select the **POST** HTTP method.
3. In the **HTTP Request** section, enter this URL: http://localhost:8080/ databases/orders/queries/.
4. Click on the **Body** tab and select **String Body** in the drop-down list and enter the following code snippet:

   ```
   [ 'Orders/C676332','Orders/A179854' ]
   ```

 We have to arbitrarily choose two document IDs from the Orders database.

5. Click on the green **Go!** button to send the POST request to the server.

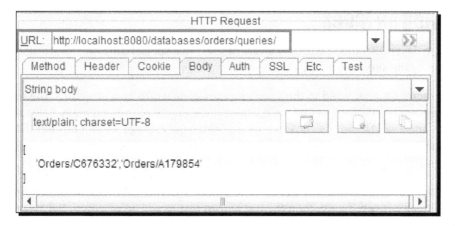

What just happened?

We retrieved two documents from the `Orders` database using a single `POST` request addressed to the `queries` structure.

In the request body, we specify a JSON array with all the IDs we want to retrieve. The server response is a JSON object that contains two arrays: `Results` which contains the retrieved two documents and `Includes` which is empty because we did not specify any related documents to include.

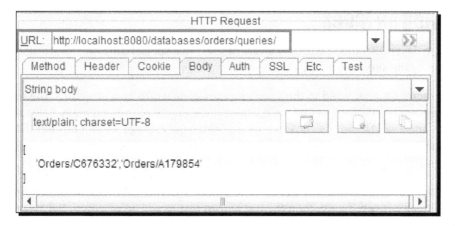

Querying an Index

Querying a RavenDB Index is basically a GET request to a special URL. An index may be generated by the server as a result of the query.

The GET request is addressed to the indexes special RavenDB area structure. The result for this request is a JSON object which contains the array Results and many fields such as IsStale and TotalResults. IsStale is a boolean indicator of whether or not this index (and results) are up to date, and TotalResults is the count of the matching records.

When an index is first created or when new documents are added that could be part of the index, RavenDB runs a background process to update the index. If this process is running while an index query is issued, then the last known results will be returned, but clearly marked as stale with IsStale set to true.

Time for action – querying an Index

We will query the TotalOrdersPerCustomer index from the Orders database which we created in the previous chapter. You will use the RESTClient tool to send the request to RavenDB and view the server response and analyze it:

1. Launch the RESTClient tool.

2. Click on the **Method** tab and select the **GET** HTTP method.

3. In the **HTTP Request** section, enter this URL: http://localhost:8080/ databases/orders/indexes/TotalOrdersPerCustomer.

4. Click on the green **Go!** button to send the GET request to the server.

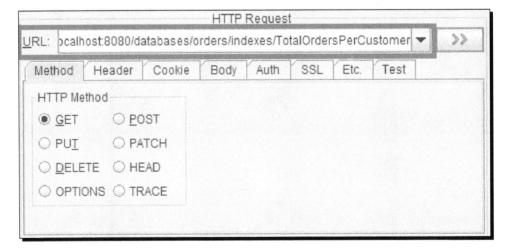

What just happened?

We queried the `TotalOrdersPerCustomer` index from the `Orders` database using a `GET` request addressed to the `indexes` structure.

The server response is a JSON object that contains the arrays: `Results` which contains all returned documents by the index and `Includes`. Also, in the server response, we have two fields: `IsStale` the value of which is `false` and the `TotalResults` the value of which is set to `4` which is the documents count that have been returned by the index.

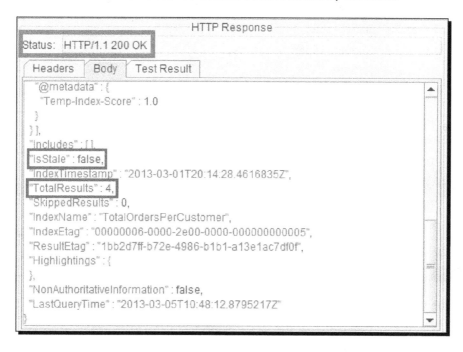

The `TotalResults` property tells us how many results are returned from the query itself. This can be used for paging the query results if the queries returned are more than 128 documents. There is a second useful property for paging, `SkippedResults`, which is needed in some cases where RavenDB will filter out duplicate results.

Pop Quiz – deep into RavenDB

Q1. What is RavenDB HTTP API for?

1. RavenDB internal HTTP web server.

2. Creating RESTful web services.

3. Interacting with the server using HTTP.

4. Sending REST requests to the server.

Q2. You want to replace an existing object on the RavenDB server, which REST verb you should use?

1. REPLACE.

2. UPDATE.

3. POST.

4. PUT.

Q3. What does { Type: 'UnSet', Name: 'Colour', Value: "Black"} mean?

1. Delete the "Black" value.

2. Delete the "Colour" property.

3. Replace "Black" with empty string.

4. Replace "Colour" with empty string.

Q4. You want to create a new document using the RavenDB HTTP API and provide the object data, which REST verb should you use?

1. PUT.

2. POST.

3. CREATE.

4. INSERT.

Summary

We learned a lot in this chapter about RavenDB's RESTful API and the main REST verbs that you can use to interact with RavenDB over HTTP.

Specifically, we covered the RavenDB HTTP API REST requests basics and anatomy and introduce a third party tool, the RESTClient which we used to compose and send requests to the RavenDB server.

We learned about the main REST verbs used to address the RavenDB server over HTTP and talked about GET, PUT, POST, PATCH and DELETE requests.

Also we learned how to get multiple documents in one single remote call and how to query an index using the RavenDB HTTP API.

There are more advanced commands but we covered what will give us a good understanding if we want to query RavenDB directly from our web page or other technologies that do not use the .NET Client.

In the next chapter, we will present the basics of building an ASP.NET MVC 4 web application that uses and interacts with RavenDB. Keep reading!

12
Putting It All Together

Well this is the grand finale! We have learned how to use RavenDB and we have spent the bulk of this book so far laying down important fundamentals. It's almost time to start writing a web application that uses RavenDB for storage.

In this chapter, we shall see how we can build an ASP.NET MVC Internet application that interacts with RavenDB and which you can use as a base for your future developments. We will not go deep into how the ASP.NET MVC framework works but we will focus on how to get connected to RavenDB and we will take things a step at a time, so you can see how the application is constructed.

In this chapter we will cover:

- ◆ Creating the ASP.NET MVC 4 World application
- ◆ Adding models, views, and controllers
- ◆ Creating Indexes automatically
- ◆ Paging the queries results
- ◆ Creating the Master/Details view
- ◆ Creating the Search view

A word about ASP.NET MVC

ASP.NET MVC is a very large concept and its complete coverage is out of the scope of this book. ASP.NET MVC is a framework for building scalable web applications from Microsoft. It emphasizes on clean architecture, design patterns, and testability, and it doesn't try to conceal how the web works.

It combines the effectiveness and tidiness of the **Model-View-Controller** (**MVC**) architecture. The Model-View-Controller pattern is an architectural pattern that encourages strict isolation between the individual parts of an application. This isolation is better known as **Separation of Concerns**, or in more general terms, **loose coupling**.

The MVC pattern is a complete alternative to traditional ASP.NET web forms. It involves the most up-to-date ideas and techniques from agile development, and the best parts of the existing ASP.NET platform, delivering considerable advantages for all the web development projects.

In the MVC pattern, the **Model** represents the core business logic and data. Models encapsulate the properties and behavior of a domain entity and expose properties that describe the entity.

The **View** is responsible for transforming a Model into a visual representation which can manifest in many forms. The same Model might be visualized in a different format as HTML, PDF, XML, and so on. Views should not contain any business logic and should concentrate only on displaying data. Business logic stays in the Model, which should provide the View with everything it needs.

The **Controller** controls the application logic and acts as the coordinator between the View and the Model. Controllers receive input from users via the View, then work with the Model to perform specific actions, passing the results back to the View. The next figure shows how these three components are related:

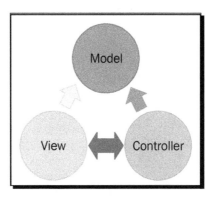

The current version of ASP.NET MVC is 4 which was released on 15th August 2012. It is packaged with Visual Studio 2012 and includes all you need to create the `World` application.

Further details about ASP.NET MVC can be found on the official Internet ASP.NET website at `http://www.asp.net/mvc`.

ASP.NET MVC is open source! The entire source code is available to browse and download on *CodePlex* website at `http://aspnetwebstack.codeplex.com/`.

Application architecture key concepts

The application architecture is the process of defining a structured solution that meets all of the technical and operational requirements while optimizing common quality attributes such as performance, security, and manageability. It involves a series of decisions based on a wide range of factors and each of these decisions can have considerable impact on the quality, performance, maintainability, and overall success of the application.

When designing your application keep in mind the key principles that will help you to create an architecture that adheres to proven principles, minimizes costs and maintenance requirements, and promotes usability and extendibility. Here are some key principles to observe:

- **Separation of concerns**: Divide your application into distinct features with as little overlap in functionality as possible. Your design should allow clear and defined layers. The important factor is minimization of interaction points to achieve high cohesion and low coupling.

- **Single responsibility principle**: Each component or module should be responsible for only a specific feature or functionality or aggregation of cohesive functionality.

- **Principle of least knowledge**: A component or object should not know about the internal details of other components or objects.

- **Don't repeat yourself (DRY)**: You only need to specify intent in one place. Specific functionality should be implemented in only one component and should not be duplicated in any other component.

- **Re-usability**: This is one of the main factors to decrease the total cost of ownership.

- **Adaptability**: An application should be easily adapted with new technical features, such as different frontends. This should be easy to achieve as your software architecture creates a clear separation of concerns.

- **Productivity**: It should be easy to add new features to application.

If you want to learn more about software architecture and application design, you may find more detailed information about the **SOLID** principles by browsing this link: `http://en.wikipedia.org/wiki/SOLID_(object-oriented_design)`.

Creating an ASP.NET MVC 4 project with RavenDB

In this section, we'll introduce the `World` application that will be our example for the rest of this chapter. The `World` application is a simple application which allows users to display country and city information. Although the concept of the `World` application is simple, we'll use it to explore steps to create an ASP.NET MVC application which uses RavenDB as a backing store.

Before you begin creating the `World` application, you need to ensure that your development environment is properly configured. To begin, you'll need to have Visual Studio 2012 installed.

 Microsoft's Web Platform Installer includes IIS Express, SQL Server Express, SQL Server Compact, MVC, and Visual Web Developer Express. You may get more information about this tool on its official web page: `http://www.microsoft.com/web/downloads/platform.aspx`.

Getting connected to RavenDB

The primary goal of this step is to wrap the `World` application to the RavenDB instance in order to provide access to the RavenDB server. This access will allow the application to access the data and perform persistence operations against the database. Also, this step is responsible to maintain the RavenDB sessions and connections.

Time for action – creating the World ASP.NET MVC application

You will create a new Visual Studio solution using one of the default templates and then expand it to connect to RavenDB.

1. Open Visual Studio, create a new **ASP.NET MVC 4 Web Application** project and name it `World`.

2. Select the **Basic** template and keep the **Razor** view engine selected (the **Razor** engine is selected by default).

3. Use the **NuGet Package Manager** to add the `RavenDB Client` package.

 Please ensure that you are using the same versions of the RavenDB server and the RavenDB client in order to avoid version incompatibilities.

4. Open the `Web.config` file and add a new connection string for `RavenDB`.

```
11   <connectionStrings>
12     <add name="RavenDB" connectionString="Url=http://localhost:8080/" />
13   </connectionStrings>
```

5. Add a new **Folder** to the `World` application and name it `DAL`.

6. Add a new class to `World.DAL` and name it `RavenStore`. Then complete it so that it looks like the following code snippet:

```
14   public class RavenStore
15   {
16       public const string DefautlDatabase = "World";
17
18       public static IDocumentStore Initialize()
19       {
20           // Use RavenDB Conection string Parser
21           var parser = ConnectionStringParser<RavenConnectionStringOptions>
22                       .FromConnectionStringName("RavenDB");
23
24           parser.Parse();
25
26           IDocumentStore Store = new DocumentStore
27           {
28               Url = parser.ConnectionStringOptions.Url,
29               DefaultDatabase = DefautlDatabase,
30           };
31
32           Store.Initialize();
33
34           return Store;
35       }
36   }
```

 To initialize a RavenDB Embedded instance or create the RavenDB shards, you just need to replace the initializing code.

7. Modify the `MvcApplication` class in the `Global.asax` file as follows:

```
16  public class MvcApplication : System.Web.HttpApplication
17  {
18      public static IDocumentStore Store { get; private set; }
19
20      protected void Application_Start()
21      {
22          AreaRegistration.RegisterAllAreas();
23
24          WebApiConfig.Register(GlobalConfiguration.Configuration);
25          FilterConfig.RegisterGlobalFilters(GlobalFilters.Filters);
26          RouteConfig.RegisterRoutes(RouteTable.Routes);
27          BundleConfig.RegisterBundles(BundleTable.Bundles);
28
29 ➤        Store = World.DAL.RavenStore.Initialize();
30      }
31  }
```

8. Save the `World` application and build it to ensure that it builds successfully.

What just happened?

You just created the `World` application, an ASP .NET MVC web application which implements the necessary code to get connected to the RavenDB server.

The first major step of developing our `World` web application is to create the data layer for handling the RavenDB database connections. You begin by creating an ASP.NET MVC 4 project based on the **Basic** template and name it `World`.

We choose the **Basic** template for simplicity. You may select other template which meets your needs. Following is a little description for each available template:

This should be formatted as a note, including all the following bullets. Please include all necessary note page formatting

- ◆ The **Empty** template provides a very simple empty project structure.
- ◆ The **Internet Application** template comes with some basic layout and authentication features.
- ◆ The **Intranet Application** template is similar to the **Internet Application** template, but it uses Windows authentication rather than the ASP.NET forms authentication.
- ◆ The **Mobile Application** template is optimized for mobile devices and includes the jQuery Mobile JavaScript framework and views that apply the HTML which works best with jQuery Mobile.

◆ The **Web API** template makes it easy to build the HTTP services that reach a broad range of clients, including browsers and mobile devices. It is an ideal platform for building RESTful applications on the .NET framework.

To connect to RavenDB, you specify its access URL in the `web.config` file. This URL includes the listening TCP port `8080` (which is the default port).

 It is good practice to store the connection string for your application in the `web.config` file rather than as a hardcoded string in your code.

In order to respect the Separation of Concern design principle, we need to separate data access code from the web application. So you add a new **Folder** and name it `DAL`.

Then you add the `RavenStore` class to the `World.DAL` folder. This class is responsible to initialize the RavenDB `DocumentStore` object. This class contains the database instance name (`World`) and the `Initialize()` method which will be used to initialize the RavenDB Document Store.

In order to retrieve the server URL, which you provided in the `web.config` file in step 4, you call within the `Initialize()` method the `FromConnectionStringName()` method on the `ConnectionStringParser` class (the `RavenStore` class, lines **17-27**).

 The '/' (slash) character may create problems in the ASP.NET MVC framework when attempting to parse the URL route parts, which would appear as separate controllers/actions. You can resolve this by converting the '/' (slash) to a '-' (dash) during the initialization process. To set the RavenDB identity separator character to be the '-' (dash) character, you set the `Store.Conventions.IdentityPartsSeparator = "-"`, which will instruct RavenDB to use the '-' (dash), rather than the default '/' (slash) character.

This property is used by RavenDB when auto-generating the identity keys for the database documents.

Then you modify the `MvcApplication` class in the `Global.asax` file. You add the `Store` property to hold the Document Store instance (the `MvcApplication` class, line **18**) and add a call to the `RavenStore.Initalize()` method (class you add to the `World.DAL` folder) in order to initialize the RavenDB Document Store (the `MvcApplication` class, line **29**). This is the ideal place to call the `Initialize()` method because the Document Store initialization must be done only once.

Adding Models

A Model represent the data that users work with and is the representation of the real-world entities, processes, and rules. It encapsulates the properties and behavior of a domain entity and expose properties that describe the entity.

 In ASP.NET MVC, the **M** stands for **Model**. It is a very important part of the application.

This step aims to provide entity descriptions which will hold the RavenDB document data.

Time for action – adding the World application's Models

You will add a new class library to the `World` application. Then you will add two container classes to the library which will represent the `Country` and `City` documents retrieved from RavenDB.

1. Open the `World` application.

2. Add a new class to the `World.Models` folder and name it `City`. Then complete it as follows:

```
 8      class City
 9      {
10          public string Id { get; set; }
11          public string Name { get; set; }
12          public string CountryCode { get; set; }
13          public long Population { get; set; }
14          public string Province { get; set; }
15          public string CountryId { get; set; }
16      }
```

3. Add a new class to the `World.Models` folder and name it `Country`. Then complete it as follows:

```
9      class Country
10     {
11         public string Id { get; set; }
12         public string Name { get; set; }
13         public string Code { get; set; }
14         public long Area { get; set; }
15         public string Capital { get; set; }
16         public string Province { get; set; }
17         public string FlagId { get; set; }
18         public string ContinentCode { get; set; }
19
20         [JsonIgnore]
21         public List<City> Cities { get; set; }
22     }
```

4. Save the `World` application and build it to ensure that it builds successfully.

What just happened?

You just added two classes to the `World.Models` folder of the `World` application in order to implement all the Models needed to define the `World` database entities.

The two classes you added, `Country` and `City`, are the same classes you used in previous chapters. Each class is used to represent an entity in the RavenDB database, each instance of the `City` or `Country` objects will correspond to a document within the database, and each property of the `Country` or `City` classes will map to a field in the `Country` or `City` RavenDB documents.

Adding Controllers

Controllers control the flow of the application and are responsible for processing incoming requests, performing operations on the domain Model, and selecting Views to render to the user. They expose public methods as `Actions` which return different result types.

 In ASP.NET MVC, the **C** stands for **Controller**. They handle end user interaction, manipulate the Model, and ultimately choose a View to render to display UI.

Action methods are exposed on a different URL and are invoked with parameters extracted from the incoming request. They typically map with user interaction. When user requests a URL, the ASP.NET MVC framework uses the route to determine the controllers and the action methods to handle the request. Most action methods return an instance of the `ActionResult` object.

To interact with RavenDB, our approach is to implement a base controller which is responsible for handling and managing RavenDB session. This controller will be the base class for all other controllers that need to interact with RavenDB.

Technically, the base controller inherits from the `Controller` class part of the `System. Web.Mvc` namespace. Also, the base controller overrides the `OnActionExecuting()` and `OnActionExecuted()` methods in order to manage the RavenDB session. It will open the RavenDB sessions before an action method is invoked and then potentially saves the changes to the database when the work is finished. The `Dispose()` method of the controller is the last invoked method, which is used when the work is over.

 There are several ways to interact with RavenDB and they all have their benefits and drawbacks. For example, it is possible to:

- Use a custom Controller factory (versus the default one)
- Use action filters to open and close the sessions
- Add application-level event handlers to the begin request and end request application events as it is done in the RaccoonBlog application (https://github.com/ayende/ RaccoonBlog/blob/master/RaccoonBlog.Web/ Global.asax.cs)

Time for action – adding the Controllers

You will add the `RavenBaseController` class to the `World` application to handle and manage a RavenDB session for the `World` application. Then you will add the `CountryController` class to handle incoming requests for the `Country` entity.

1. In the `World` project, right-click on the `Controllers` folder, add a new class, and name it `RavenBaseController`. Then complete it with the following code:

 In ASP.NET MVC applications, all the Controller classes must be named by using the *Controller* suffix.

```
10  public abstract class RavenBaseController : Controller
11  {
12      public IDocumentSession RavenSession { get; protected set; }
13
14      public static IDocumentStore RavenStore
15      {
16          get { return MvcApplication.Store; }
17      }
18
19      protected override void OnActionExecuting(ActionExecutingContext filterContext)
20      {
21          RavenSession = MvcApplication.Store.OpenSession();
22      }
23
24      protected override void OnActionExecuted(ActionExecutedContext filterContext)
25      {
26          if (filterContext.IsChildAction)
27              return;
28
29          using (RavenSession)
30          {
31              if (filterContext.Exception != null)
32                  return;
33
34              if (RavenSession != null)
35                  RavenSession.SaveChanges();
36          }
37          base.OnActionExecuted(filterContext);
38      }
39
40      protected override void Dispose(bool disposing)
41      {
42          base.Dispose(disposing);
43          using (RavenSession)
44          {
45              if (RavenSession != null)
46                  RavenSession.SaveChanges();
47          }
48      }
49  }
```

3. In the **Solution Explorer**, right-click on the `Controllers` folder, add a new Controller, and name it `CountryController`. While creating the Controller ensure that you select the **MVC Controller with empty read/write actions template.**

4. Modify the `CountryController` class to inherit from the `RavenBaseController` class instead of the `Controller` class (by default).

5. Modify the `Index()` method of the `CountryController` class to make it look like the following:

```
12      //
13      // GET: /Country/
14
15      public ActionResult Index()
16      {
17          var countries = RavenSession.Query<Country>().ToList();
18          return View("Index", countries);
19      }
```

6. Modify the `Details()` method of the `CountryController` class as follows:

```
21      //
22      // GET: /Country/Details/5
23
24      public ActionResult Details(string id)
25      {
26          var country = RavenSession.Load<Country>(id);
27          return View(country);
28      }
```

7. Modify the `Create()` method of the `CountryController` class as follows:

```
30    //
31    // GET: /Country/Create
32
33    public ActionResult Create()
34    {
35        var country = new Country();
36        return View(country);
37    }
38
39    //
40    // POST: /Country/Create
41
42    [HttpPost]
43    public ActionResult Create(Country country)
44    {
45        RavenSession.Store(country);
46        return RedirectToAction("Index");
47    }
```

8. Modify the `Edit()` method of the `CountryController` class as follows:

```
49    //
50    // GET: /Country/Edit/5
51
52    public ActionResult Edit(string id)
53    {
54        var country = RavenSession.Load<Country>(id);
55        return View(country);
56    }
57
58    //
59    // POST: /Country/Edit/5
60
61    [HttpPost]
62    public ActionResult Edit(string id, Country country)
63    {
64        RavenSession.Store(country);
65        return RedirectToAction("Index");
66    }
```

9. Modify the `Delete()` method of the `CountryController` class as follows:

```
68   //
69   // GET: /Country/Delete/5
70
71   public ActionResult Delete(string id)
72   {
73       var country = RavenSession.Load<Country>(id);
74       return RedirectToAction("Index");
75   }
76
77   //
78   // POST: /Country/Delete/5
79
80   [HttpPost]
81   public ActionResult Delete(string id, Country country)
82   {
83       this.RavenSession.Advanced.DocumentStore
84           .DatabaseCommands.Delete(id, null);
85       return RedirectToAction("Index");
86   }
87
```

10. Save the `World` application and build it to ensure that it builds successfully.

What just happened?

You created the `RavenBaseController` class in order to manage and handle the RavenDB session and the `CountryController` class in order to handle requests for the `Country` entity.

The `RavenBaseController` class is an abstract class that inherits from the `Controller` class and is responsible to manage the RavenDB session. This Controller will be the base class of all your Controllers that will need to access RavenDB. It contains two public fields, `RavenSession` and `RavenStore`, to hold an instance of the RavenDB Document Store and the RavenDB Session. These fields cannot be set from outside the `RavenBaseController` class (the `RavenBaseController` class, lines **12-17**).

Then you override two methods, (inherited from the `Controller` class) the `OnActionExecuting()` method, which is called just before the action begins execution, and the `OnActionExecuted()` method which is called once the action is executed.

In the first method, you call the `OpenSession()` method to open a new connection to the RavenDB store just before the Controller method's action execution starts. This is to ensure that a valid RavenDB session is opened before an ASP.NET MVC action is performed.

In the second method, and once the action is executed, you check if there is an error; if not, the document session is saved by calling to the `SaveChanges()` method. This saves whatever entities you put in the RavenDB's document Session (the `RavenBaseController` class, lines **19-38**).

The `Dispose()` method of the Controller is called when the work is over implicitly upon leaving the using block, and if there are valid opened sessions, you call the `SaveChanges()` method to persist all waiting changes (the `RavenBaseController` class, lines **40-48**).

> This is a simple way to persist object without having to call the `SaveChanges()` method, explicitly in any of your Controllers. All changes on any document in the session will be persisted once the action completes. On the flip side, this couples data persistence to the View layer. So use it with caution.

After that you create the `CountryController` class. This Controller inherits from `RavenBaseController` class instead of the `Controller` class (by default). It targets to process requests on the `Country` entity and contains several methods (generated by the **Add Controller** wizard): `Index`, `Create`, `Edit`, `Details`, and `Delete`.

> When the user requests a URL, the ASP.NET MVC framework uses the route to determine the Controller and the action method to handle the request.

Then you implement each of the `CountryController` class's methods:

- In the `Index()` method, you return the complete list of the `Country` documents in the RavenDB database (the `CountryController` class, lines **15-18**). (Note that the RavenDB Client limits the result to the first `128` elements.)

- In the `Details()` method, you load a single `Country` document with the given `Id` (the `CountryController` class, lines **24-28**).

- The `Edit()` and `Delete()` methods are used to update a `Country` entity. In each method, you load the existing `Country` from the RavenDB store using the current ID of the `Country`. Once the `OnActionExecuted()` method (in `RavenBaseController`) is called, it calls the `SaveChanges()` method to persist changes to the database (the `CountryController` class, lines **52-87**).

- The `Create()` method is used to add a new `Country` document to the database (the `CountryController` class, lines **33-36**).

Have a go hero – adding the CityController class

You just learned how to create the `CountryController` class which is used to manage the RavenDB session and save changes after an action method is called. You can follow the same steps to create a new controller that handle request for the `City` entity, the `CityController` class.

Don't forget to make the `CityController` class inherit from `RavenBaseController`.

Adding Views

The View is responsible for providing the user interface (UI) to the user. It creates the HTML response or any responses, such as PDFs or spreadsheets, back to the browser.

In ASP.NET MVC, the **V** stands for **View**. It is responsible for transforming a Model (or Models) into a visual representation.

Views are associated with the Controller action method. By convention, the `Views` directory in an ASP.NET MVC project contains a folder per Controller, with the same name as the Controller, but without the `Controller` suffix. Within this Controller folder, there's a View file for each action method, named the same as the action method.

Adding a View is pretty easy. You could certainly create a file by hand and add it to your `Views` directory, but the ASP.NET MVC tooling for Visual Studio makes it very easy to add a View using the **Add View** dialog.

Time for action – adding the Views

You will add a View for each action method in the `CountryController` class.

1. In the `World.Web` project, open the `CountryController` class.
2. Right-click on the `Index()` method, select **Add View...** to create the `Index` View as follows:
   1. In the **Add View** Dialog, check the **Create a strongly typed-view option**.
   2. Choose the `Country` (`World.Models`) class model.
   3. Select `List` as **Scaffold Template**.

4. Check **Use a layout or master page** and select the
   `~/Views/Shared/_Layout.cshtml` layout.

 You should always build your solutions before adding Views to ensure
that your class Models are listed in the **Model Class** list.

3. Repeat step 2 to create Views for `Edit`, `Create`, `Details`, and `Delete` actions
   methods; you may use this table to specify **Scaffold Template** for each view:

Action method	View Scaffold Template
Details	Details
Edit	Edit
Create	Create
Delete	Delete

4. Save the `World` application and build it to ensure that it builds successfully.

What just happened?

You just created a standard MVC strongly-typed View for each action method of the
`CountryController` class in order to display entity data on the browser and handle
the input data and requests.

To assign a View to each action method, you use the **Add View...** dialog provided by the
Visual Studio tooling.

While creating Views, you choose to **Create a strongly typed-view** and select the `Country`
(`World.Models`) class as a base Model. Strongly-typed Views are used for rendering
specific types of Model objects instead of using a general data structure.

 By specifying the type of data for a View, you get access to the Visual Studio
IntelliSense for the Model class.

In Visual Studio 2012, in the Solution Explorer, right-click on any CSHTML's
View file and select **View** in the Page Inspector. The Page Inspector is a web
development tool with an integrated browser that lets you quickly locate and
edit markup and CSS within your web project. You may get more information
about this tool on its official web page: `http://www.asp.net/mvc/`
`tutorials/mvc-4/using-page-inspector-in-aspnet-mvc`.

Now you have created the `CityController` class, you are ready to create a View for each action method in this controller.

To create the `CityController` Views, you can repeat the same steps you performed to create the `ContryController` Views.

Launching the World application

Now our basic RavenDB ASP.NET MVC application is ready. It is time to launch it and verify that it interacts correctly with RavenDB.

Before you can run the `World` application, we need to make some little changes to it. You need to define the home controller route for the application in order to make it work.

1. In the `World.Web` project, open the `RouteConfig.cs` file (located in the `App_Start` folder).

2. Modify the `Default MapRoute` to make it look as follows:

```
12 □  public static void RegisterRoutes(RouteCollection routes)
13     {
14         routes.IgnoreRoute("{resource}.axd/{*pathInfo}");
15
16         routes.MapRoute(
17             name: "Default",
18             url: "{controller}/{action}/{*id}",
19             defaults: new { controller = "Country",
20                             action = "Index",
21                             id = UrlParameter.Optional
22                           }
23         );
```

3. Save the `World` application and press *F5* to build it and run it.

What just happened?

You just prepared and launched the `World` application.

The `Basic ASP.NET MVC` template we used to create the `World` application doesn't have a single controller or view defined. So we need to define the controller manually. For that, you replace in the `RouteConfig.cs` file the `Home` default controller (which doesn't exist) with the `Country` controller you created earlier (the `RouteConfig` class, line **19**).

In the `Country` document stored on RavenDB, the `Country Id` value looks like `country/1098`. This will create problems when working with ASP.NET MVC's route rule. For a route `Country/edit/id`, the URI would be `Country/edit/country/1098`. This will fail to connect to the appropriate method in the `CountryController` class.

To solve this problem, you just put `*` (star) in front of the `id` variable to let that work with the default ID separator (slash) of RavenDB (the `RouteConfig` class, line **18**).

 Another alternative is to create an appropriate route without specifying a specific controller.

```
22    routes.MapRoute(
23        "RavenIdWithSlash",            // Route name
24        "{controller}/{action}/{*id}" // URL with parameters
25    );
```

When running the `World` application the counties list is displayed.

Index

Create New

Name	Code	Area	Capital	Province	Flæde	
Antigua and Barbuda	AG	440	Saint Johns	Antigua and Barbuda		Edit | Details
Albania	AL	28750	Tirane	Albania		Edit | Details
Andorra	AND	450	Andorra la Vella	Andorra		Edit | Details
Angola	ANG	1246700	Luanda	Luanda		Edit | Details
Armenia	ARM	29800	Yerevan	Armenia		Edit | Details
Australia	AUS	7686850	Canberra	Australia Capital Territory		Edit | Detail
Azerbaijan	AZ	86600	Baku	Azerbaijan		Edit | Details
Belgium	B	30510	Brussels	Brabant		Edit | Details
Bangladesh	BD	144000	Dhaka	Bangladesh		Edit | Details
Barbados	BDS	430	Bridgetown	Barbados		Edit | Details
Benin	BEN	112620	Porto-Novo	Benin		Edit | Details
Burkina Faso	BF	274200	Ouagadougou	Burkina Faso		Edit | Details

Doing more with the World application

We started the World application with basic features to get connected to RavenDB. In a real-world application, you may need to implement more features. In this section, we will see some new features such as paging a query result and registering indexes automatically and add them to the World application.

Creating the RavenDB Indexes automatically

As you learned in the previous chapters, the RavenDB Indexes allow you to query RavenDB efficiently and this is a powerful feature of RavenDB. Unfortunately, indexes require that you pre-define them before you can use them.

The problem with RavenDB Indexes is essentially when you need to move a RavenDB database from one location to another you may also need to move the entire database indexes to the new location.

This is where creating indexes automatically is helpful. It is also helpful when you modify your indexes definitions and want to ensure that your application uses the latest versions.

To create indexes automatically, you will call the CreateIndexes() method on the IndexCreation object. This method takes an Assembly file as a parameter and uses reflection to get all the index definitions in this assembly, then store them into the database.

The server will automatically compare the index definition sent by the CreateIndexes() method and check to see if it already exists. If one exists with the same name and definition then it is left alone. If one exists with the same name but the definition has changed then the old one is dropped and the new one is created.

Usually, the CreateIndexes() method is called once within the application startup process in the Global.asax file.

Time for action – creating indexes automatically

You will create a new index definition (Countries_Population) which will return the population sum for each Country in the World database. Then you will register this index automatically within the application startup.

1. Open the World project, create a new folder and name it Indexes.
2. Add a new class to the Indexes folder and name it Countries_Population.

3. Modify the `Countries_Population` class as follows:

```
11  class Countries_Population : AbstractIndexCreationTask<City,
12                          Countries_Population.ReduceResult>
13  {
14      public class ReduceResult
15      {
16          public string CountryId { get; set; }
17          public long Population { get; set; }
18      }
19
20      public Countries_Population()
21      {
22          Map = cities => cities
23                      .Select(city => new
24                      {
25                          CountryId = city.CountryId,
26                          Population = city.Population,
27                      });
28
29          Reduce = results => from result in results
30                          group result by result.CountryId
31                              into g
32                              select new
33                              {
34                                  CountryId = g.Key,
35                                  Population = g.Sum(x => x.Population),
36                              };
37
38
39          TransformResults = (database, results) =>
40              from result in results
41              let country = database.Load<Country>(result.CountryId)
42
43              select new
44              {
45                  Population = result.Population,
46              };
47      }
48  }
```

4. Modify the `RavenStore` class to call the `CreateIndexes()` method:

```
25
26          IDocumentStore Store = new DocumentStore
27          {
28              Url = parser.ConnectionStringOptions.Url,
29              DefaultDatabase = DefautlDatabase,
30          };
31
32          Store.Initialize();
33
34          IndexCreation.CreateIndexes(Assembly.GetExecutingAssembly(), Store);
35
36          return Store;
37      }
```

5. Save the `World` application and press *F5* to build it and run it.

What just happened?

You just modified the `World` application in order to automatically create the `Countries_Poupulation` index on the `World` database.

You began by creating the `Countries_Poupulation` index definition. This index defines a `Map/Reduce` function that retrieves the `Population` for each `City Id` and then aggregates them by `Country Id`.

Then within the `RavenStore` class (in `World.DAL`), you call the `CreateIndexes()` method during the RavenDB Document Store initialization process. This method requires an `Assembly` file as a parameter and a valid RavenDB Document Store where the index will be created. The `CreateIndexes()` method uses reflection to retrieve all the index definitions in the given assembly (the `RavenStore` class, line **34**).

> Once the `World` application is launched, you may use the Management Studio to see that the `Countries/Population` index has been created on the database.

Adding a page navigation bar

Paging query results has been discussed in previous chapters. In this section, you will learn how this can be implemented in the `World` application.

Remember that the `Index()` action method of the `Country` controller will only send the first `128` documents to the View. To show the whole result of the query, we will display the query results over a number of pages, each linked to the next, to allow users to browse the content in bite-sized pieces.

In order to implement paging, we need to create a specific View-Model which will handle data that would be displayed by the View. This View-Model will contain information about the total number of pages, the number of documents to display per page, the current page, and the list of the `Country` documents to be displayed within a page.

Time for action – the paging query <Country>() result

To implement the paging query result, you will create a View-Model to handle information about each page to be displayed. Then you will create a specific Controller and View to display the query result.

Optionally, to make pagination elements look better, we will use `Twitter Bootstrap`, which is a CSS and JavaScript framework that is used within HTML pages and provides advanced functionality to a website. You may ignore steps 6 and 7 if you don't want to implement `Twitter Bootstrap`.

1. Open the `World` application, select the `Models` folder and create a new folder and name it `ViewModels`.

2. Right-click on the `ViewModels` folder, add a new class and name it `PagedCountryList`.

3. Modify the `PagedCountryList` class as follows:

```
9    public class PagedCountryList
10   {
11       public IEnumerable<Country> CountriesToDisplay { get; set; }
12       public int Total { get; set; }
13       public int PerPage { get; set; }
14       public int PageNumber { get; set; }
15
16       public PagedCountryList(IEnumerable<Country> countries,
17                   int totalResult, int elementsPerPage, int pageNumber)
18       {
19           this.CountriesToDisplay = countries;
20           this.Total = totalResult;
21           this.PerPage = elementsPerPage;
22           this.PageNumber = pageNumber;
23       }
24   }
```

4. Create a new `Controller` class, select the **Empty MVC Controller** template, and name it `PagedCountryController`.

5. Make sure the `PagedCountryController` class inherits from `RavenBaseController` and modify it as follows:

```
14   public class PagedCountryController : RavenBaseController
15   {
16       private const int elementsPerPage = 10;
17
18       //
19       // GET: /PagedCountry/
20
21       public ActionResult Index(int pageNumber = 1)
22       {
23           RavenQueryStatistics stats;
24
25           IEnumerable<Country> countries = RavenSession.Query<Country>()
26                                   .Statistics(out stats)
27                                   .Skip((pageNumber - 1) * elementsPerPage)
28                                   .Take(elementsPerPage)
29                                   .OrderBy(x => x.Name)
30                                   .ToList();
31
32           PagedCountryList list = new PagedCountryList(countries, stats.TotalResults,
33                                   elementsPerPage, pageNumber);
34
35           return View(list);
36       }
37   }
```

6. Use the `NuGet Package Manager` to add the `Bootstrap` package.

7. Modify the `BundleConfig.cs` file to register the `Bootstrap` bundle package.

```
20
21
22    // Use the development version of Modernizr to develop with and learn from. The
23    // ready for production, use the build tool at http://modernizr.com to pick onl
24    bundles.Add(new ScriptBundle("~/bundles/modernizr").Include(
25                "~/Scripts/modernizr-*"));
26
27    bundles.Add(new StyleBundle("~/Content/css").Include("~/Content/site.css",
28                "~/Content/bootstrap.css"));
29
30    bundles.Add(new StyleBundle("~/Content/themes/base/css").Include(
31
```

 To learn more about `Twitter Bootstrap`, you may browse its official website at `http://twitter.github.io/bootstrap/`.

8. Build the `World` solution.

9. Right-click on the `Index()` action method of the `PagedContryController` class, select **Add View...** to create the `Index` view.

1. In the **Add View** dialog, check the **Create a strongly typed-view option**.

2. Choose the `PagedCountryList (World.Models.ViewModels)` class Model.

3. Select `Empty` as **Scaffold Template** and check **Use a layout or master page**.

4. Select the `~/Views/Shared/_Layout.cshtml` layout.

10. In the `Index` view, add the `foreach` loop in order to display the `Country` document data.

```
1   @model World.Models.ViewModels.PagedCountryList
2
3   @{
4       ViewBag.Title = "Index";
5   }
6
7   <h2>Countries</h2>
8
9   <ol>
10      @foreach (var country in Model.CountriesToDisplay)
11      {
12          <li>
13              @country.Name, @country.Code, @country.Area,
14              @country.Capital, @country.Province, @country.FlagId,
15              @country.ContinentCode
16          </li>
17      }
18  </ol>
```

11. Below the `foreach` loop, add the following code snippet to the View in order to display pagination elements:

```
20  <div class="pagination">
21  <ul>
22      @for (int i = 1; i <= (int) Math.Ceiling((double)Model.Total/Model.PerPage); i++)
23      {
24          if (i == Model.PageNumber)
25          {
26              <li class="active"> @Html.ActionLink(@i.ToString(),
27              "Index", "PagedCountry",
28              new RouteValueDictionary { { "pageNumber", @i.ToString() } }, null)
29              </li>
30          }
31          else
32          {
33              <li> @Html.ActionLink(@i.ToString(),
34              "Index", "PagedCountry",
35              new RouteValueDictionary { {"pageNumber" , @i}}, null)
36              </li>
37          }
38      }
39  </ul>
40  </div>
```

12. In order to open the `PagedCountry` view, modify the `Default MapRoute()` method as follows:

```
routes.MapRoute(
    name: "Default",
    url: "{controller}/{action}/{*id}",
    defaults: new { controller = "PagedCountry",
                    action = "Index",
                    id = UrlParameter.Optional
                  }
);
```

13. Save the `World` application and press *F5* to build it and run it.

What just happened?

You just implemented the paging feature in order to display the `Country` query result using a paging navigation bar.

In order to implement this paging feature, you create a specific View-Model class, `PagedCountryList`, which will handle data that will be displayed by the View. `PagedCountryList` contains four properties:

- `IEnumerable<Country> CountriesToDisplay`: This is a list of `Country` elements that will be displayed when a page number is selected

- `int Total`: This is the total number of documents returned by the query

- `int PerPage`: This is a constant number which indicates how many `Country` elements will be displayed on one single page

- `int PageNumber`: This is returned by the View; it indicates the page number that the user wants to display

Once you create the View-Model class, you create a dedicated Controller, the `PagedCountryController` class, in order to handle browser requests. This Controller implements only one action method, the `Index()` method.

The `Index()` method defines the `PageNumber` parameter with a default value set to 1. Then, in the `Index()` method, you define the query results pagination by setting the `.Skip()` and `.Take()` values. The result of the query and the current page information are encapsulated in a new instance of the `PagedCountryList()` class and then transmitted to the View (the `PagedCountryController` class, lines **21-36**).

After that, you create the `Index` view which is assigned to the `Index()` action method of the `PagedCountryController` class. This view is based on the `PagedCountryList` View-Model and contains two loops. The first one is a `foreach` loop used to display the `Country` list. The second is a `for` loop responsible for displaying the pagination navigation bar.

To get the number of pages to display, you use the `Math.Ceiling()` method which returns the smallest integral value that is greater than or equal to `Model.Total/Model.PerPage`.

When running the application, the paging navigation bar is displayed and only ten `Country` elements are displayed per page (which is the `elementsPerPage` number specified in the `PagedCountryController` class).

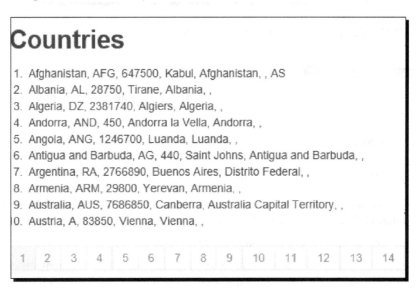

Adding the Country master/details View

One of the most common scenarios in real-world applications is the master/detail data display. Basically in RDBMS, it is a parent/child based relationship between two database tables. One element in the master table may have one or more related element in the child table. But an element in the child table has only one parent element in master table.

RavenDB is schema-less and there is no relationship between documents. Creating a relationship between documents can be done only on the client side by the client application.

Time for action – creating the Country master/details View

To illustrate a master/detail relationship in RavenDB, you will use the `Countries` and the `Cities` collections. Each `Country` in the collection may have one or more related `City`. Then you will create a new controller and two views in order to display a given `Country` with all its related `Cities`.

1. Open the `World` application, create a new `Controller` class, select the **Empty MVC Controller** template, and name it `CitiesPerCountryController`.

2. Make sure the `CitiesPerCountryController` class inherits from `RavenBaseController` and modify it as follows:

```
10    public class CitiesPerCountryController : RavenBaseController
11    {
12        //
13        // GET: /CitiesPerCountry/
14
15        public ActionResult Index()
16        {
17            string countryId = "country/1005";
18
19            var country = RavenSession
20                .Include<City>(x => x.CountryId)
21                .Load<Country>(countryId);
22
23            country.Cities = RavenSession.Query<City>()
24                .Where(x => x.CountryId.Equals(countryId))
25                .ToList();
26            return View(country);
27        }
28    }
```

3. Right-click on the `Shared` folder, select **Add View…**, and create the `PartialCities` view as follows:

    1. In the **Add View** dialog, check the **Create a strongly typed-view option**.

    2. Choose the `City (World.Models)` class model.

    3. Select `List` as **Scaffold Template**.

    4. Make sure to check **Create as a partial view**.

4. Right-click on the `Index()` action method of the `CitiesPerCountryController` class, select **Add View...**
   to create the `Index` view as follows:

   1. In the **Add View** dialog, check the **Create a strongly typed-view option**.

   2. Choose the `Country (World.Models)` class model.

   3. Select `Details` as **Scaffold Template**.

   4. Check **Use a layout or master page**.

   5. Select the `~/Views/Shared/_Layout.cshtml` layout.

5. Modify the `Index()` view (in the `CitiesPerCountry` folder) and add the following code at the end of the file in order to load the partial view:

```
47  <div id="content">
48
49      <h2>Cities</h2>
50
51      @if (Model.Cities.Count > 0)
52      {
53          @Html.Partial("PartialCities", Model.Cities)
54      }
55      else
56      {
57          <p>No city found!</p>
58      }
59
60  </div>
```

6. Modify the `Default MapRoute()` method to point to the `CitiesPerCountry` Controller.

7. Save the `World` application and press *F5* to build it and run it.

What just happened?

You just implemented a master/detail View in order to display a `Country` document with all its related `Cities`.

In order to implement the master/detail view representation, you create a new `Controller`, the `CitiesPerCountryController` class, which inherits from the `RavenBaseController` class to access to the RavenDB store. After that, you implement the controller `Index()` method, its unique action method.

In this master/detail representation, one parent (`Country`) has one or more child (`Cities`). So we load a `Country` document from the RavenDB store by calling the `Load()` method on the `Session` object. The `Load()` method requires the Country ID key to load, which you set explicitly as (`country/1005`) using the `countryId` string variable (the `CitiesPerCountryController` class, line **17**).

As we want to load all related cities, you pre-load all the `Cities` documents that have the same `CountryID` value using the `Include()` method. Then you call the `Query()` method on the `Session` object to load all the pre-loaded `Cities` documents (the `CitiesPerCountryController` class, lines **17-26**).

Once the `CitiesPerCountryController` class is ready, you create a new partial strongly-typed-view, the `PartialCities` view (it will represent the `Details` view in the master/details representation) which is responsible for displaying the `City` collection. Basically, the partial views are created and placed in the `Shared` folder of the solution. `PartialCities` has to render and display the list of all related `Cities` for a given `Country`. So you select the **Scaffold Template** list when creating the view and `City` for the **Model** class.

Then you create the `Index()` view for the `CitiesPerCountryController` class (which will represent the master view in the master/details representation). This view will display a single `Country` document, for which you select the `Details` **Scaffold Template** and `Country` for the **Model** class.

The last thing to do in order to implement the master/details representation is to call the partial view `PartialCities` from the parent view `Country`. For that, you call the `@Html.Partial()` method in the parent view to call the partial view (the `Index()` view, lines **47-60**).

When running the application, you can see that all the `Cities` documents related to the `CountryId` = `country/1005` (France) are displayed.

Country

Name : France
Code : F
Area : 547030
Capital : Paris
Province : Ile de France
FlagId :
ContinentCode :
Edit | Back to List

Cities

Create New

Name	CountryCode	Population	Province	CountryId			
Aix en Provence	F	123842	Provence Cote dAzur	country/1005	Edit	Details	Delete
Ajaccio	F	53500	Corse	country/1005	Edit	Details	Delete
Amiens	F	131872	Picardie	country/1005	Edit	Details	Delete
Angers	F	141404	Pays de la Loire	country/1005	Edit	Details	Delete
Besancon	F	113828	Franche Comte	country/1005	Edit	Details	Delete
Bordeaux	F	210336	Aquitaine	country/1005	Edit	Details	Delete
Boulogne Billancourt	F	101743	Ile de France	country/1005	Edit	Details	Delete
Brest	F	147956	Bretagne	country/1005	Edit	Details	Delete

Adding the search Cities view

It is a very common scenario that an application provides the users several ways to find data in its data store. In a database world, we are often likely to be looking for a row or a document that you know is in a particular table or database. Browsing for the row or document might mean looking through hundreds of rows and collections.

In this section, you will learn how to enhance the World application with a search box feature. The search box is a simple view that contains one textbox and one button. When you click on the submit button, the text you typed is transmitted to the appropriate action method which filters the Cities collection on the Name field, based on the text that you type, and returns the result back to the view.

Time for action – implementing the Search view

To implement the Search view, you will create an index that enables searching on the Name field. Then you will create the SearchingCitiesController class and its dedicated View. To display the search results, you will reuse the PartialCities view created in the previous section.

1. Open the World application, right-click on the Indexes folder, add a new class, and name it Cities_SearchByName.

2. Modify the Cities_SearchByName class as follows:

```
12  public class Cities_SearchByName : AbstractIndexCreationTask<City, City>
13  {
14      public Cities_SearchByName()
15      {
16          Map = cities => from city in cities
17                          select new
18                          {
19                              Name        = city.Name,
20                          };
21
22          // Enable text searching on 'Name' field
23          Indexes.Add(x => x.Name, Raven.Abstractions.Indexing.FieldIndexing.Analyzed);
24      }
25  }
```

3. Create a new Controller class, select the **Empty MVC Controller** template, and name it SearchingCitiesController.

4. Make the SearchingCitiesController class inherit from RavenBaseController, and add a using statement for the Raven.Client namespace.

5. Modify the `SearchingCitiesController` class as follows:

```
12  public class SearchingCitiesController : RavenBaseController
13  {
14      //
15      // GET: /SearchingCities/
16
17      public ActionResult Index()
18      {
19          return View();
20      }
21
22      [HttpPost]
23      public ActionResult SearchResults(string searchText)
24      {
25          //Query the index
26          var cities = RavenSession.Query<City, Cities_SearchByName>()
27
28              .Search(x => x.Name, searchText,
29                      escapeQueryOptions: EscapeQueryOptions.AllowPostfixWildcard)
30              .ToList();
31
32          return View("Index", cities);
33      }
34  }
```

6. Right-click on the `Index()` action method of the `SearchingCitiesController` class, select **Add View...** to create the `Index` view.

1. In the **Add View** dialog, check the **Create a strongly typed-view option**.

2. Choose the `City (World.Models)` class model.

3. Select `Empty` as **Scaffold Template**.

4. Check **Use a layout or master page**.

5. Select the `~/Views/Shared/_Layout.cshtml` layout.

7. Modify the `Index` view to add a `Textbox` control to handle the user input and a **Search** button to submit the user search criteria.

```
1    @model IEnumerable<World.Models.City>
2
3    @{
4        ViewBag.Title = "Index";
5        Layout = "~/Views/Shared/_Layout.cshtml";
6    }
7
8    <h2>Search Cities by Name</h2>
9
10   <div class="search-bar">
11     @using (Html.BeginForm("SearchResults", "SearchingCities"))
12     {
13         @Html.TextBox("SearchText")
14         <input class="btn btn-primary" type="submit" value="Search" />
15     }
16   </div>
```

8. Then add to the `Index` view the code to call to the `PartialCities` view which will display the search result.

```
18   <div id="content">
19
20     <h3>Search Result</h3>
21
22     @if (Model != null)
23     {
24         if(Model.Count() > 0)
25         {
26             @String.Format("{0}, found", Model.Count().ToString());
27             @Html.Partial("PartialCities", Model)
28         }
29         else
30         {
31             <p>No city found!</p>
32         }
33     }
34   </div>
```

9. Modify the `Default MapRoute()` method to point the `SearchingCities` controller.

10. Save the `World` application and press *F5* to build it and run it.

What just happened?

You just implemented the `Search Cities` view in order to allow users to find one or more `City` by their names.

To allow text searching on the `Name` field of the `City` entity, you create the `Cities_SearchByName` index which will add the `Name` field to the `Indexes` collection. This index is created automatically on the RavenDB store when the `World` application is launched.

Then you create the `SearchingCities` controller which contains two action methods: `Index()` and `SearchResults()`. There is nothing to do with the `Index()` method because when the view is first displayed the user has not yet entered the search criteria and there is nothing to send to the view (the `SearchingCitiesController` class, lines **17-20**).

The `SearchResults()` method is called only when the user has submitted the search criteria due to the `[HttpPost]` attribute that decorates the `SearchResults()` method. To search on the `Name` field, you query the `Cities_SearchByName` index and call the `Searching()` method. This method will perform a search for `City` documents with the `Name` field that match the user search criteria. Then the query result is sent back to the `Index` view (the `SearchingCitiesController` class, lines **23-34**).

In the `Index` view, you add an HTML form that contains one textbox and one submit button to post the user search criteria. Once the user has clicked on the submit button, this HTTP POST request is routed to the `SearchResults()` action method of the `SearchingCities` controller (the `Index` view, lines **10-16**).

Also, in the `Index` View, you add an `Html.Partial()` statement to load the partial view `PartialCities`. This partial view is only loaded when the underlying model has some data or is not `null`. If a search result is not empty, the partial view is loaded and the number of elements found is displayed (the `Index` view, lines **18-34**).

Once you launch the `World` application, the `Search Cities` view is displayed. You can enter a search criterion in the textbox which may contain a post wildcard (for example, `los*`). When you submit the search criteria the result is displayed below the search form as follows:

Have a go hero – creating the Search view with paginated result

The `Search Cities` view you just created may return more than `128` documents. To allow user to view all the returned documents, the query result must be paginated. Why not try to create such a Search view?

In previous sections you can find all the necessary information to create this view.

Summary

In this chapter we learned about creating ASP.NET MVC 4 project with RavenDB as a backing store. We created the `World` application which is a basic ASP.NET MVC 4 application that you can use as a base for your future development. Specially, we covered how to get connected to RavenDB and how to create a base controller to access RavenDB and handle sessions and connections.

Then we enhanced the `World` application by adding Models, Controllers, Views and learned how to create RavenDB indexes automatically when the application starts.

After that we learned how to page query results. We extended the application and added a page navigation bar, a Master/Details view to display all Cities related to a given Country, and the Search Cities view which allowed you to search cities by their name.

This concludes our journey of learning RavenDB. I hope you have enjoyed it as much as I did. I would encourage you to keep learning more about the topics covered in this book using the official website and other sources on the Internet, master advanced topics such as the Transaction support, the Faceted search, the Spatial search, and build really cool web applications with .NET and RavenDB!

Pop Quiz Answers

Chapter 3, RavenDB.NET Client API

Q1	3
Q2	3
Q3	4

Chapter 4, RavenDB Indexes and Queries

Q1	2
Q2	1
Q3	4

Chapter 5, Advanced RavenDB Indexes and Queries

Pop quiz – searching the right way

Q1	4
Q2	3
Q3	1
Q4	3

Chapter 7, RavenDB Administration

Pop quiz – RavenDB administration

Q1	3
Q2	1
Q3	1, 2, 3, 4, 5
Q4	2

Chapter 9, Scaling-out RavenDB

Pop quiz – scaling-out RavenDB

Q1	1
Q2	4
Q3	4
Q4	4

Chapter 11, RavenDB HTTP API

Pop quiz – deep into RavenDB

Q1	4
Q2	4
Q3	2
Q4	1

Index

BLOBs 12, 152
built-in authentication, RavenDB
  OAuth authentication 15
  Windows authentication 15
bundles 63

C

Cassandra 9
cls command 23
Codd's rules
  about 8
  URL 8
collection 11
  querying, lambda expression used 87
Collections screen, RavenDB
     Management Studio
  about 42
  document, modifying 42-44
column-oriented databases 9
command line
  used, for restoring databases 186
  used, for restoring World database 186, 187
configuration options, RavenDB 174, 175
configuration, RavenDB server 22
console mode
  RavenDB server, running in 21
console mode, RavenDB server
  launching 23, 24
  RavenDB database, creating 25-28
  RavenDB server, configuring 22
  shutting down 28
  Start.cmd file, exploring 21, 22
Controllers
  about 290
  adding, to World ASP.NET MVC
     application 298-303
CouchDB 10
Country master/details View
  adding, to World ASP.NET MVC application
     316-319
CreateIndexes() method 123, 308
CreateIndex() method 119
CSV file
  database, exporting to 38
  documents, exporting to 39
  used, for importing external data 58

CurrentRequestSessions() method 255
custom analyzer
  used, for searching 142-145
custom metadata key
  adding 40, 41

D

database
  creating 33, 34
  exporting, to CSV file 38
  restoring, command line used 186
database replication
  creating, between RavenDB and Microsoft SQL
     Express 200-204
database settings
  System database settings 62
  viewing 61, 62
database sharding 232
Data Manipulation Language (DML) 8
data replication 195
DeleteAttachment() method 157
DELETE command 196
Delete() method 85
DELETE request
  about 264, 282
  performing 282, 283
denormalization 160, 232
deployment strategies, RavenDB 215
development environment
  requisites 72
  setting up 72
development environment setup
  NuGet Package Manager, installing 73
Dispose() method 78
document field
  adding, PatchRequest used 170-172
document-oriented database 9, 10
document patching 167
documents
  about 11
  anatomy 15, 16
  creating 35, 36
  deleting, in RavenDB database 85
  exporting, from different views 59
  exporting, to CSV file 39
  inserting, into RavenDB database 82

loading 37
loading, from RavenDB database 79-81
modifying 42-44
obtaining, with single request 284, 285
patching, PatchRequest used 169, 170
patching, ScriptedPatchRequest used 167-169
preloading, Include feature used 161
searching for 38
updating, into RavenDB database 83, 84
documents collection
querying 86
documents metadata, RavenDB
about 40
custom metadata key, adding 40, 41
documents relationships
handling 160
Documents screen, RavenDB Management Studio
about 34
database, exporting to CSV file 38
document, creating 35, 36
document, loading 37
documents, exporting to CSV file 39
searching, for document 38
Document Store 234
Don't repeat yourself (DRY) 291
dynamic indexes
about 92, 93
querying 94-96
dynamic queries
creating 51-54

E

embedded mode
RavenDB, running in 225-227
e-tag (entity tag) 40
exact matching searching index class
adding 138
ExportData() method 193
Export feature 32
external data
importing, CSV file used 58

F

FlockDB 10

full-text searching index
about 135
creating 136, 137
functional partitioning approach 232

G

gc command 23
GenerateShardIdFor method 233
GetAttachment() method 156
GET command 157
GetIndexNames() method 116
GET request
about 264, 267
performing 268-270
graphical user interface, RavenDB visual host 256, 257
graph-oriented databases 10
Guid (Globally Unique Identifier) 40

H

HBase 9
HeadAttachment() method 158
horizontal scaling
about 8, 232
Cassandra 9
MongoDB 9
RavenDB 9
host name
setting, to RavenDB 218
Hypertable 9

I

IIS application
RavenDB, running as 222-224
IIS (Internet Information Server) 19, 174, 215
IIS virtual directory
RavenDB, running from 219-222
images
storing, attachments used 152-155
ImportData() method 193
Include feature
used, for preloading documents 161
used, for reducing query calls 161-163

Model-View-Controller. *See* MVC pattern
ModifyDocumentId element 234
MongoDB 9, 10
MSI installer 216
multi-databases feature, RavenDB
        Management Studio
  about 33
  database, creating 33, 34
multi fields searching index
  creating 139-141
multi map indexes
  about 130
  creating 131-133
multiple documents
  loading 81
MVC pattern
  about 290
  Controller 290
  Model 290
  View 290

N

Non-Authoritive-Information 40
non-stale index results
  waiting for 114, 115
NoSQL 8
NoSQL Databases
  about 8
  types 9
  URL 10
NoSQL System 8, 9
NuGet Package Manager
  about 20, 73
  installing 73
  URL 73

O

OAuth 15
OLTP (Online Transaction Processing) 14
OpenSession() method 77, 81
optimization 250
optimizing keys concepts, RavenDB
  hardware improvements 176
  index storage and log paths 176
  initialization delay 176
  querying delay 177

storing delay 176
Orders collection
  patching 57

P

paging
  implementing, in RavenDB 145-147
paging query result
  implementing, in World ASP.NET MVC
        application 311-315
Pascal Casing 278
Patch Document 278
patching 54
PatchingDocument() method 170
Patch() method 167
PatchRequest
  used, for adding field to document 170-172
PATCH request
  about 278
  document properties, removing with 282
  performing 279-281
PatchRequest method
  used, for patching documents 169, 170
Patch screen, RavenDB Management Studio
  about 54, 56
  document, patching 55
  Orders collection, patching 57
Periodic Backup Bundle
  about 63
  enabling 64, 65
POST request
  about 264, 275
  performing 275-277
PotentialShardsFor method 234
profiler information
  using 255, 256
profiling
  about 249
projections
  creating, Linq queries used 101
PutAttachment() method 154, 158
PutIndex() method 119
PUT request
  about 270, 271
  performing 272-274

Q

q command 23
query
  executing, against index 47
query calls
  reducing, Include feature used 161-163
Query Index screen
  about 50
  index, querying 50, 51
Query() method 86, 87
QueryOrders() method 87
query result
  paging 145-147

R

Raven/ActiveBundles 176
Raven/AnonymousAccess 175
Raven/AnonymousAccess setting 22, 23
Raven.Backup.exe tool 182
Raven-Clr-Type 40
Raven/DataDir 175
Raven/DataDir setting 22, 23
RavenDB
  about 7, 9-11
  advantages 13
  ASP.NET MVC 4 project, creating 292
  attachments, retrieving from 156, 157
  authentication functionality 205, 206
  configuration options 174, 175
  connecting to 76, 78
  database, creating 25-28
  deployment strategies 215
  documents metadata 40
  downloading 19-21
  installation package directories 21
  installing 18-21
  interacting with 78, 79
  launching modes 15
  Map/Reduce, implementing 91
  need for 13
  preparing, for sharding 234, 235
  prerequisites 18
  running, as IIS application 222-224
  running, as Windows Service 216, 217
  running, from IIS virtual directory 219-222
  running, in embedded mode 225-227

scaling-out 231, 232
  working 14
RavenDB authorization bundle 205
RavenDB backup tool
  used, for backing up databases 179
RavenDB Client
  adding, to Visual Studio project 74, 75
RavenDB Client .NET API 193
RavenDB client/server application
    architecture 14
RavenDB databases
  backing up 178, 179
  deleting 193
  document, deleting 85
  document, inserting into 82
  document, loading from 79-81
  document, updating 83, 84
  exporting 189
  importing 191
  restoring 185
RavenDB Embedded
  running, in memory mode 227, 228
RavenDB HTTP API 264
RavenDB logging
  enabling 208, 209
RavenDB Management Studio 18
  about 31
  Alerts screen 59
  Collections screen 42
  columns, selecting 65, 67
  database, deleting 68, 69
  document, copying to clipboard 67
  Documents screen 34
  Indexes screen 44
  Logs screen 60
  multi-databases feature 33
  Patch screen 54-56
  Tasks screen 57, 58
  user interface 32
RavenDB performances
  optimizing 177, 178
RavenDB profiler
  about 250
  enabling 251-255
  implementing 251
  launching 251

Thank you for buying
RavenDB 2.x Beginner's Guide

About Packt Publishing

Packt, pronounced 'packed', published its first book "*Mastering phpMyAdmin for Effective MySQL Management*" in April 2004 and subsequently continued to specialize in publishing highly focused books on specific technologies and solutions.

Our books and publications share the experiences of your fellow IT professionals in adapting and customizing today's systems, applications, and frameworks. Our solution based books give you the knowledge and power to customize the software and technologies you're using to get the job done. Packt books are more specific and less general than the IT books you have seen in the past. Our unique business model allows us to bring you more focused information, giving you more of what you need to know, and less of what you don't.

Packt is a modern, yet unique publishing company, which focuses on producing quality, cutting-edge books for communities of developers, administrators, and newbies alike. For more information, please visit our website: www.packtpub.com.

About Packt Open Source

In 2010, Packt launched two new brands, Packt Open Source and Packt Enterprise, in order to continue its focus on specialization. This book is part of the Packt Open Source brand, home to books published on software built around Open Source licences, and offering information to anybody from advanced developers to budding web designers. The Open Source brand also runs Packt's Open Source Royalty Scheme, by which Packt gives a royalty to each Open Source project about whose software a book is sold.

Writing for Packt

We welcome all inquiries from people who are interested in authoring. Book proposals should be sent to author@packtpub.com. If your book idea is still at an early stage and you would like to discuss it first before writing a formal book proposal, contact us; one of our commissioning editors will get in touch with you.

We're not just looking for published authors; if you have strong technical skills but no writing experience, our experienced editors can help you develop a writing career, or simply get some additional reward for your expertise.

Ruby and MongoDB Web Development Beginner's Guide

ISBN: 978-1-84951-502-3   Paperback: 332 pages

Create dynamic web applications by combining the power of Ruby and MongoDB

1. Step-by-step instructions and practical examples to creating web applications with Ruby and MongoDB

2. Learn to design the object model in a NoSQL way

3. Create objects in Ruby and map them to MongoDB

CouchDB and PHP Web Development Beginner's Guide

ISBN: 978-1-84951-358-6   Paperback: 304 pages

Get your PHP application from conception to deployment by leveraging CouchDB's robust features

1. Build and deploy a flexible Social Networking application using PHP and leveraging key features of CouchDB to do the heavy lifting

2. Explore the features and functionality of CouchDB, by taking a deep look into Documents, Views, Replication, and much more

3. Conceptualize a lightweight PHP framework from scratch and write code that can easily port to other frameworks

Please check **www.PacktPub.com** for information on our titles

Cassandra High Performance Cookbook

ISBN: 978-1-84951-512-2   Paperback: 310 pages

Over 150 recipes to design and optimize large-scale
Apache Cassandra deployments

1. Get the best out of Cassandra using this efficient
   recipe bank

2. Configure and tune Cassandra components to
   enhance performance

3. Deploy Cassandra in various environments and
   monitor its performance

4. Well illustrated, step-by-step recipes to make all
   tasks look easy!

Getting Started with NoSQL

ISBN: 978-1-84969-498-8   Paperback: 142 pages

Your guide to the world and technology of NoSQL

1. First hand, detailed information about NoSQL
   technology

2. Learn the differences between NoSQL and RDBMS
   and where each is useful

3. Understand the various data models for NoSQL

4. Compare and contrast some of the popular NoSQL
   databases on the market

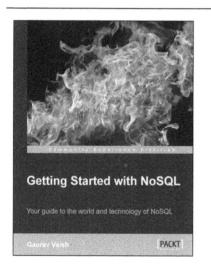

Please check **www.PacktPub.com** for information on our titles